AVENGERS

REVERIE

DAISY JOHNSON
DIRECTOR OF S.H.I.E.L.D.

MARIA HILL
COMMANDER,
ACTING DIRECTOR

NICK FURY
FIELD AGENT

PHIL COULSON
TACTICAL SUPPORT

HAWKEYE
CLINT BARTON
MARKSMAN/ASSET

BLACK WIDOW
NATASHA ROMANOFF
EX-KGB SPY/ASSET

MOCKINGBIRD
BOBBI MORSE
FIELD AGENT/ASSET

HULK
BRUCE BANNER
HEAVY ORDNANCE/ASSET

  — X

WRITER: **NICK SPENCER**   ARTIST: **LUKE ROSS**

COLOR ARTIST: **MATTHEW WILSON** WITH **LEE LOUGHRIDGE** (MARVEL NOW! POINT ONE #1)

LETTERER: **VC'S CLAYTON COWLES**

COVER ART: **ADI GRANOV** (MARVEL NOW! POINT ONE #1),
TOMM COKER & **DANIEL FREEDMAN** (#1-4) AND **NIC KLEIN** (#5)

ASSISTANT EDITOR: **JACOB THOMAS**   EDITOR: **LAUREN SANKOVITCH**

EXECUTIVE EDITOR: **TOM BREVOORT**

COLLECTION EDITOR: **JENNIFER GRÜNWALD** ASSISTANT EDITORS: **ALEX STARBUCK** & **NELSON RIBEIRO**
EDITOR, SPECIAL PROJECTS: **MARK D. BEAZLEY** SENIOR EDITOR, SPECIAL PROJECTS: **JEFF YOUNGQUIST**
SVP OF PRINT & DIGITAL PUBLISHING SALES: **DAVID GABRIEL** BOOK DESIGNER: **RODOLFO MURAGUCHI**

EDITOR IN CHIEF: **AXEL ALONSO** CHIEF CREAT̶ ̶ ̶ ̶ ̶ ̶ ̶ ̶ ̶ ̶ ̶ QUESADA
PUBLISHER: **DAN BUC̶ ̶ ̶ ̶ ̶ ̶ ̶ ̶ ̶ ̶ ̶ ̶ ̶ ̶ ̶ ̶ FINE**

SECRET AVENGERS VOL. 1: REVERIE. Contains material originally published in magaz̶ ̶ ̶ ̶ ̶ ̶ ̶ ̶ E #1. First printing 2013. ISBN# 978-0-7851-6688-7.
Published by MARVEL WORLDWIDE, INC., a subsidiary of MARVEL ENTERTAINMENT, LLC̶ ̶ ̶ ̶ ̶ ̶ ̶ ̶ ̶ ̶ 020. Copyright © 2012 and 2013 Marvel Characters,
Inc. All rights reserved. All characters featured in this issue and the distinctive names a̶ ̶ ̶ ̶ ̶ ̶ ̶ ̶ ̶ ̶ ̶ ̶ ̶ ̶rvel Characters, Inc. No similarity between any of the
names, characters, persons, and/or institutions in this magazine with those of any livin̶ ̶ ̶ ̶ ̶ ̶ ̶ ̶ ̶ ̶ ̶ ̶ ̶y which may exist is purely coincidental. **Printed in
the U.S.A.** ALAN FINE, EVP - Office of the President, Marvel Worldwide, Inc. and EVP &̶ ̶ ̶ ̶ ̶ ̶ ̶ ̶ ̶ ̶ ̶ ̶ - Print, Animation & Digital Divisions; JOE QUESADA,
Chief Creative Officer; TOM BREVOORT, SVP of Publishing; DAVID BOGART, SVP of O̶ ̶ ̶ ̶ ̶ ̶ ̶ ̶ ̶ ̶ ̶ ̶Publishing; C.B. CEBULSKI, SVP of Creator & Content Development; DAVID GABRIEL, SVP
of Print & Digital Publishing Sales; JIM O'KEEFE, VP of Operations & Logistics; DAN CARR, Executive Director of Publishing Technology; SUSAN CRESPI, Editorial Operations Manager; ALEX MORALES,
Publishing Operations Manager; STAN LEE, Chairman Emeritus. For information regarding advertising in Marvel Comics or on Marvel.com, please contact Niza Disla, Director of Marvel Partnerships,
at ndisla@marvel.com. For Marvel subscription inquiries, please call 800-217-9158. **Manufactured between** 7/5/2013 and 8/12/2013 by QUAD/GRAPHICS ST. CLOUD, ST. CLOUD, MN, USA.

10 9 8 7 6 5 4 3 2 1

D1261895

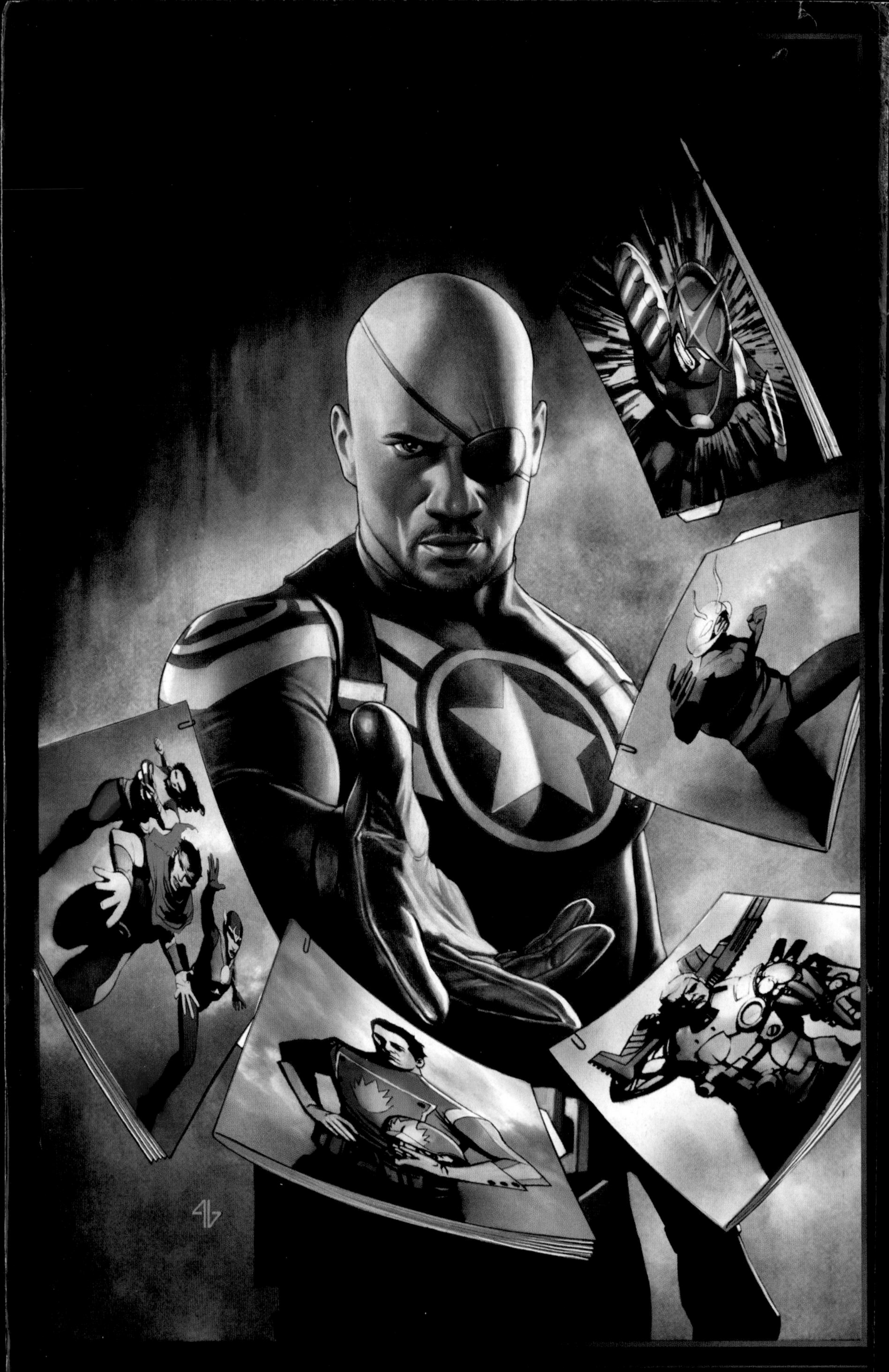

MARVEL NOW! POINT ONE #1

next >

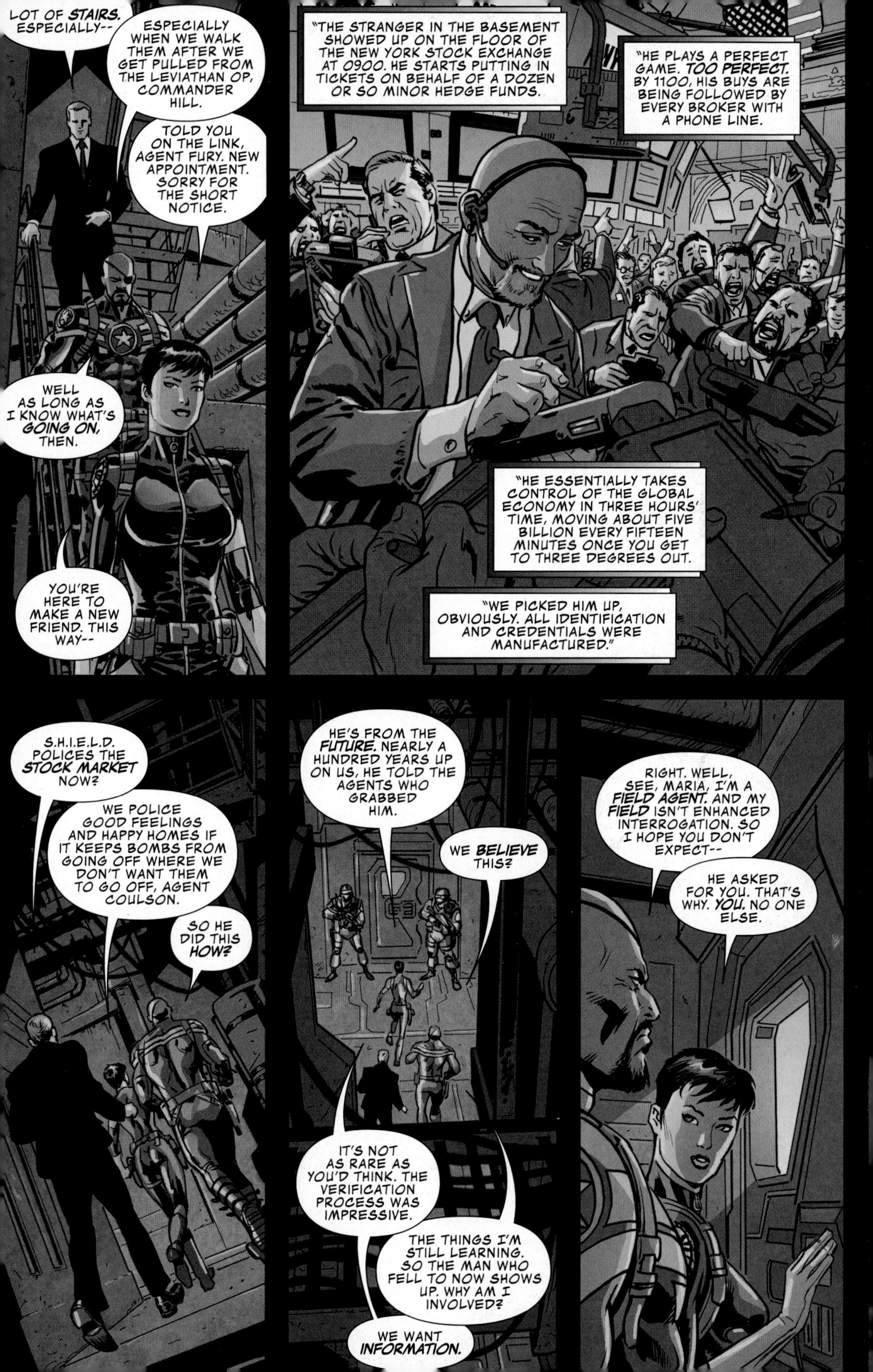
LOT OF STAIRS. ESPECIALLY--
ESPECIALLY WHEN WE WALK THEM AFTER WE GET PULLED FROM THE LEVIATHAN OP, COMMANDER HILL.
TOLD YOU ON THE LINK, AGENT FURY. NEW APPOINTMENT. SORRY FOR THE SHORT NOTICE.
WELL AS LONG AS I KNOW WHAT'S GOING ON, THEN.
YOU'RE HERE TO MAKE A NEW FRIEND. THIS WAY--
"THE STRANGER IN THE BASEMENT SHOWED UP ON THE FLOOR OF THE NEW YORK STOCK EXCHANGE AT 0900. HE STARTS PUTTING IN TICKETS ON BEHALF OF A DOZEN OR SO MINOR HEDGE FUNDS.
"HE PLAYS A PERFECT GAME. TOO PERFECT. BY 1100, HIS BUYS ARE BEING FOLLOWED BY EVERY BROKER WITH A PHONE LINE.
"HE ESSENTIALLY TAKES CONTROL OF THE GLOBAL ECONOMY IN THREE HOURS' TIME, MOVING ABOUT FIVE BILLION EVERY FIFTEEN MINUTES ONCE YOU GET TO THREE DEGREES OUT.
"WE PICKED HIM UP, OBVIOUSLY. ALL IDENTIFICATION AND CREDENTIALS WERE MANUFACTURED."
S.H.I.E.L.D. POLICES THE STOCK MARKET NOW?
WE POLICE GOOD FEELINGS AND HAPPY HOMES IF IT KEEPS BOMBS FROM GOING OFF WHERE WE DON'T WANT THEM TO GO OFF, AGENT COULSON.
SO HE DID THIS HOW?
HE'S FROM THE FUTURE. NEARLY A HUNDRED YEARS UP ON US, HE TOLD THE AGENTS WHO GRABBED HIM.
WE BELIEVE THIS?
IT'S NOT AS RARE AS YOU'D THINK. THE VERIFICATION PROCESS WAS IMPRESSIVE.
THE THINGS I'M STILL LEARNING. SO THE MAN WHO FELL TO NOW SHOWS UP. WHY AM I INVOLVED?
WE WANT INFORMATION.
RIGHT. WELL, SEE, MARIA, I'M A FIELD AGENT. AND MY FIELD ISN'T ENHANCED INTERROGATION. SO I HOPE YOU DON'T EXPECT--
HE ASKED FOR YOU. THAT'S WHY. YOU. NO ONE ELSE.

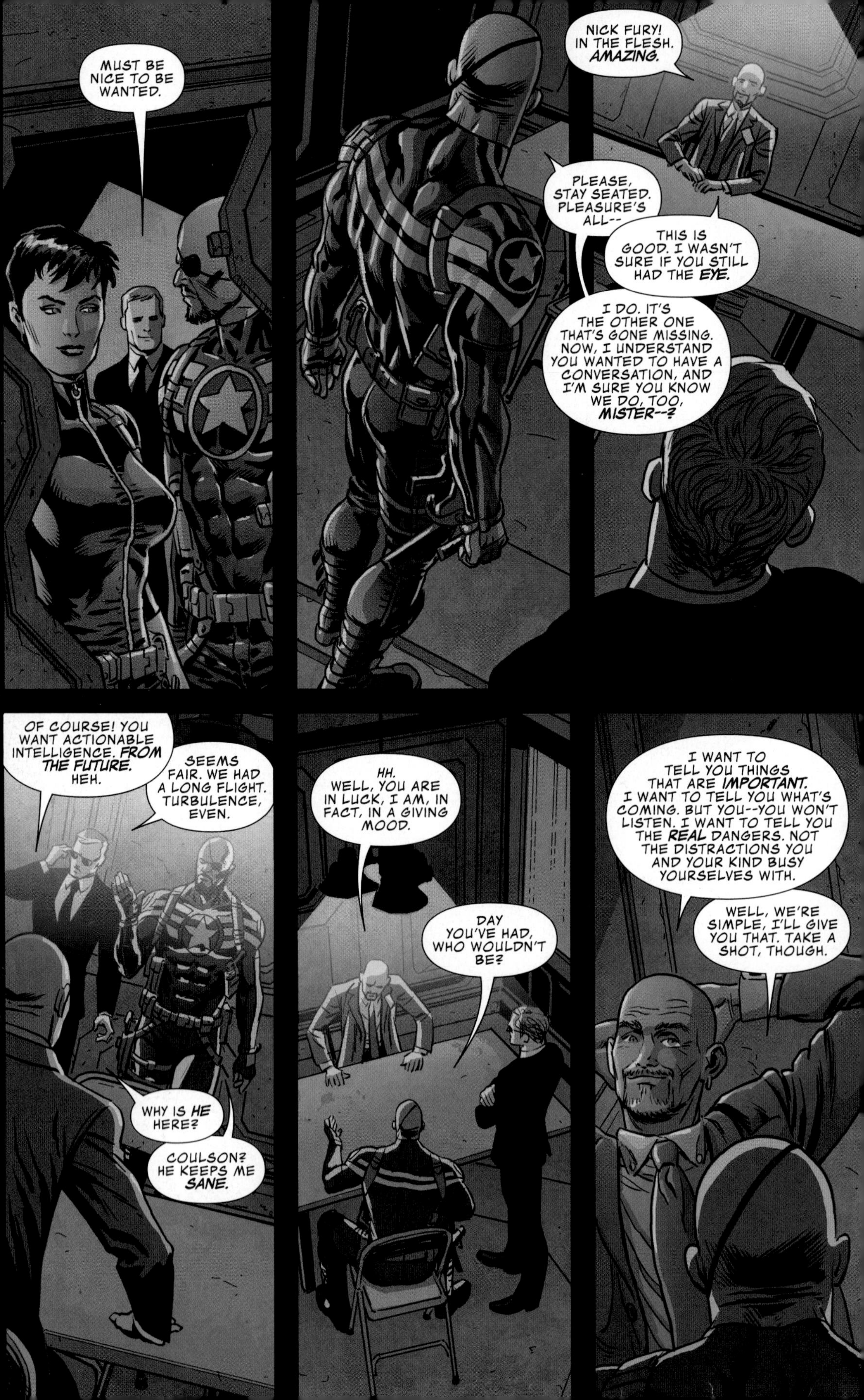
MUST BE NICE TO BE WANTED.
NICK FURY! IN THE FLESH. AMAZING.
PLEASE, STAY SEATED. PLEASURE'S ALL--
THIS IS GOOD. I WASN'T SURE IF YOU STILL HAD THE EYE.
I DO. IT'S THE OTHER ONE THAT'S GONE MISSING. NOW, I UNDERSTAND YOU WANTED TO HAVE A CONVERSATION, AND I'M SURE YOU KNOW WE DO, TOO, MISTER--?
OF COURSE! YOU WANT ACTIONABLE INTELLIGENCE. FROM THE FUTURE. HEH.
SEEMS FAIR. WE HAD A LONG FLIGHT. TURBULENCE, EVEN.
WHY IS HE HERE?
COULSON? HE KEEPS ME SANE.
HH. WELL, YOU ARE IN LUCK, I AM, IN FACT, IN A GIVING MOOD.
DAY YOU'VE HAD, WHO WOULDN'T BE?
I WANT TO TELL YOU THINGS THAT ARE IMPORTANT. I WANT TO TELL YOU WHAT'S COMING. BUT YOU--YOU WON'T LISTEN. I WANT TO TELL YOU THE REAL DANGERS. NOT THE DISTRACTIONS YOU AND YOUR KIND BUSY YOURSELVES WITH.
WELL, WE'RE SIMPLE, I'LL GIVE YOU THAT. TAKE A SHOT, THOUGH.

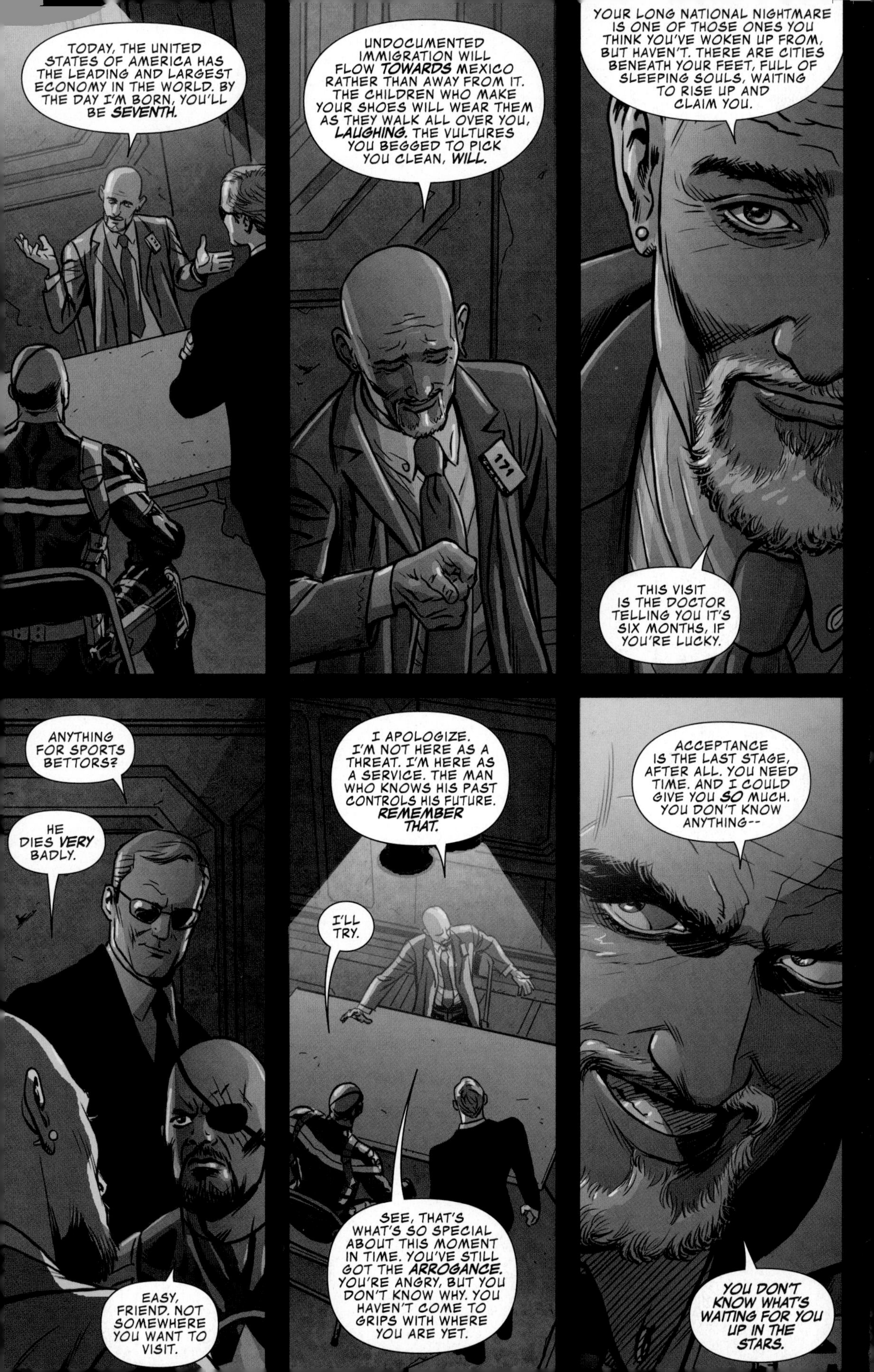
TODAY, THE UNITED STATES OF AMERICA HAS THE LEADING AND LARGEST ECONOMY IN THE WORLD. BY THE DAY I'M BORN, YOU'LL BE SEVENTH.
UNDOCUMENTED IMMIGRATION WILL FLOW TOWARDS MEXICO RATHER THAN AWAY FROM IT. THE CHILDREN WHO MAKE YOUR SHOES WILL WEAR THEM AS THEY WALK ALL OVER YOU, LAUGHING. THE VULTURES YOU BEGGED TO PICK YOU CLEAN, WILL.
YOUR LONG NATIONAL NIGHTMARE IS ONE OF THOSE ONES YOU THINK YOU'VE WOKEN UP FROM, BUT HAVEN'T. THERE ARE CITIES BENEATH YOUR FEET, FULL OF SLEEPING SOULS, WAITING TO RISE UP AND CLAIM YOU.
THIS VISIT IS THE DOCTOR TELLING YOU IT'S SIX MONTHS, IF YOU'RE LUCKY.
ANYTHING FOR SPORTS BETTORS?
HE DIES VERY BADLY.
EASY, FRIEND. NOT SOMEWHERE YOU WANT TO VISIT.
I APOLOGIZE. I'M NOT HERE AS A THREAT. I'M HERE AS A SERVICE. THE MAN WHO KNOWS HIS PAST CONTROLS HIS FUTURE. REMEMBER THAT.
I'LL TRY.
SEE, THAT'S WHAT'S SO SPECIAL ABOUT THIS MOMENT IN TIME. YOU'VE STILL GOT THE ARROGANCE. YOU'RE ANGRY, BUT YOU DON'T KNOW WHY. YOU HAVEN'T COME TO GRIPS WITH WHERE YOU ARE YET.
ACCEPTANCE IS THE LAST STAGE, AFTER ALL. YOU NEED TIME. AND I COULD GIVE YOU SO MUCH. YOU DON'T KNOW ANYTHING--
YOU DON'T KNOW WHAT'S WAITING FOR YOU UP IN THE STARS.

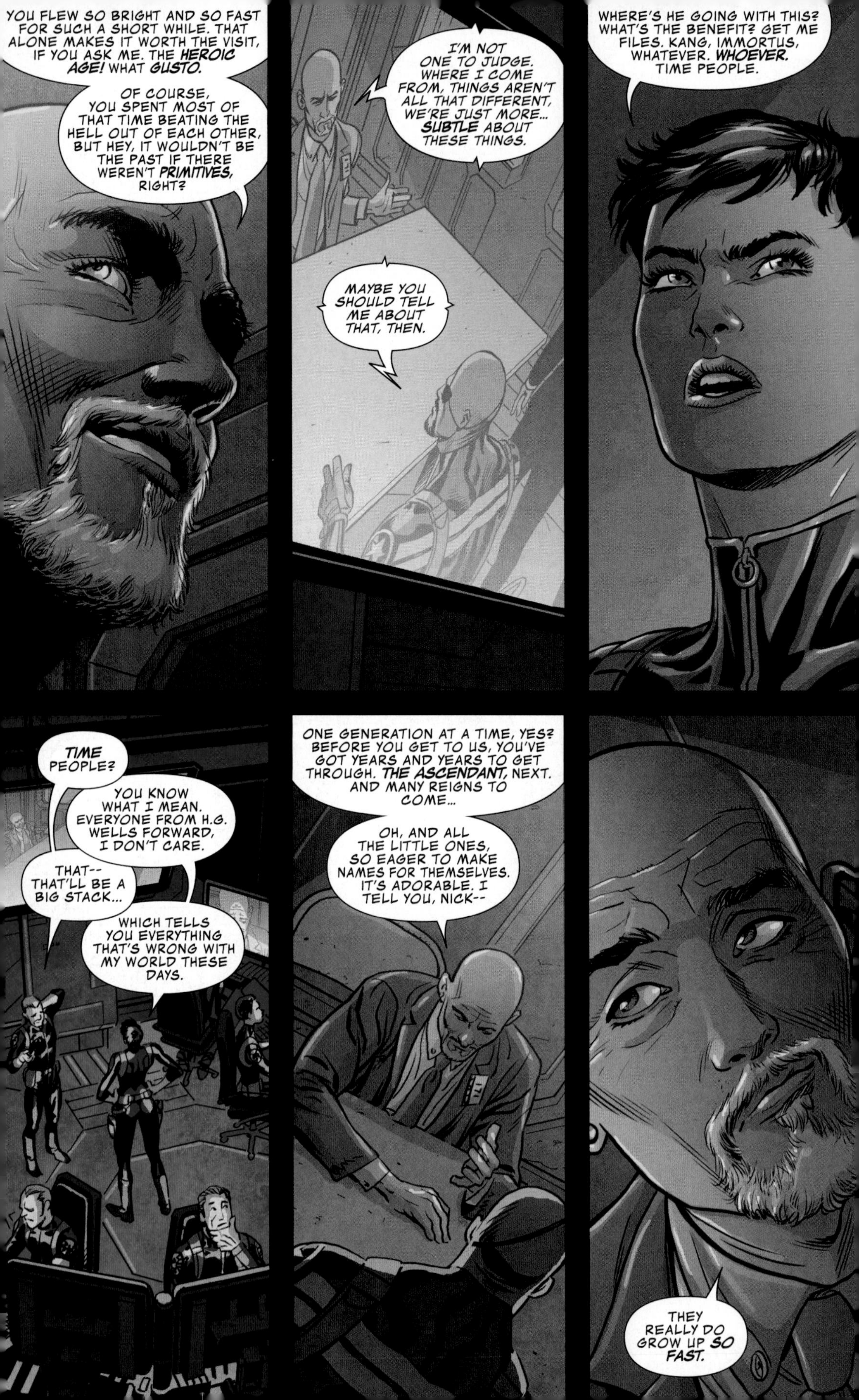
YOU FLEW SO BRIGHT AND SO FAST FOR SUCH A SHORT WHILE. THAT ALONE MAKES IT WORTH THE VISIT, IF YOU ASK ME. THE HEROIC AGE! WHAT GUSTO.
OF COURSE, YOU SPENT MOST OF THAT TIME BEATING THE HELL OUT OF EACH OTHER, BUT HEY, IT WOULDN'T BE THE PAST IF THERE WEREN'T PRIMITIVES, RIGHT?
I'M NOT ONE TO JUDGE. WHERE I COME FROM, THINGS AREN'T ALL THAT DIFFERENT, WE'RE JUST MORE... SUBTLE ABOUT THESE THINGS.
MAYBE YOU SHOULD TELL ME ABOUT THAT, THEN.
WHERE'S HE GOING WITH THIS? WHAT'S THE BENEFIT? GET ME FILES. KANG, IMMORTUS, WHATEVER. WHOEVER. TIME PEOPLE.
TIME PEOPLE?
YOU KNOW WHAT I MEAN. EVERYONE FROM H.G. WELLS FORWARD, I DON'T CARE.
THAT-- THAT'LL BE A BIG STACK...
WHICH TELLS YOU EVERYTHING THAT'S WRONG WITH MY WORLD THESE DAYS.
ONE GENERATION AT A TIME, YES? BEFORE YOU GET TO US, YOU'VE GOT YEARS AND YEARS TO GET THROUGH. THE ASCENDANT, NEXT. AND MANY REIGNS TO COME...
OH, AND ALL THE LITTLE ONES, SO EAGER TO MAKE NAMES FOR THEMSELVES. IT'S ADORABLE. I TELL YOU, NICK--
THEY REALLY DO GROW UP SO FAST.

TINY PACKAGES. ALWAYS THE BEST SURPRISES.

THIS IS INSPIRING STUFF. MAYBE WE CAN TALK THREATS AT THIS POINT, THOUGH-- I'M GETTING A BIT COMFORTABLE.

≈SIGH≈... I ALREADY *TOLD* YOU--

I *COULD* WARN YOU, BUT IT'S NOT IN YOUR NATURE TO LISTEN.

ISN'T THAT JUST TERRIFYING, THOUGH? WE ALL THINK, AFTER SOME HORROR BEFALLS US, "IF ONLY WE'D KNOWN!" "IF ONLY WE COULD'VE SEEN WHERE WE'D END UP!"

BUT ALMOST EVERY GREAT TRAGEDY IN MAN'S HISTORY, YOU COULD SEE COMING A MILE DOWN THE ROAD. NOBODY *CARED.* NOBODY *STOPPED.* VICIOUS CYCLES, I'M TELLING YOU.

IT'S A THANKLESS JOB, *PROPHET.* AMAZING ANYONE BOTHERS--

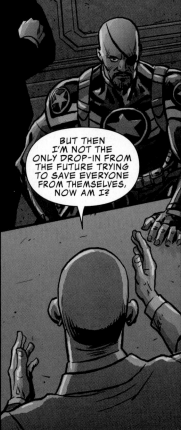

BUT THEN I'M NOT THE ONLY DROP-IN FROM THE FUTURE TRYING TO SAVE EVERYONE FROM THEMSELVES, NOW AM I?

MAYBE THE TWO OF YOU COULD TALK EYEPATCHES. *BOND.*

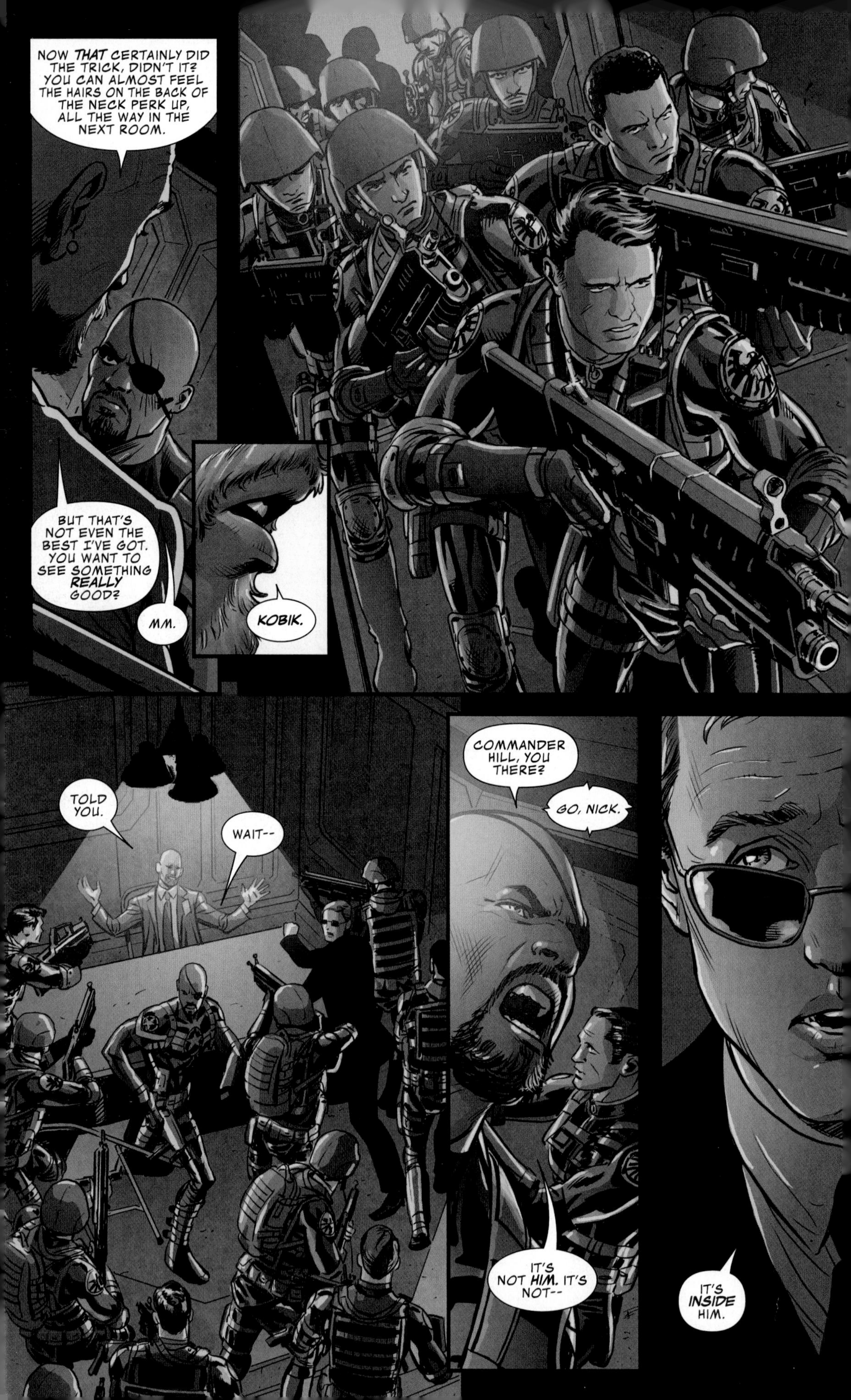
NOW *THAT* CERTAINLY DID THE TRICK, DIDN'T IT? YOU CAN ALMOST FEEL THE HAIRS ON THE BACK OF THE NECK PERK UP, ALL THE WAY IN THE NEXT ROOM.
BUT THAT'S NOT EVEN THE BEST I'VE GOT. YOU WANT TO SEE SOMETHING ***REALLY*** GOOD?
MM.
KOBIK.
TOLD YOU.
WAIT--
COMMANDER HILL, YOU THERE?
GO, NICK.
IT'S NOT ***HIM***. IT'S NOT--
IT'S ***INSIDE*** HIM.

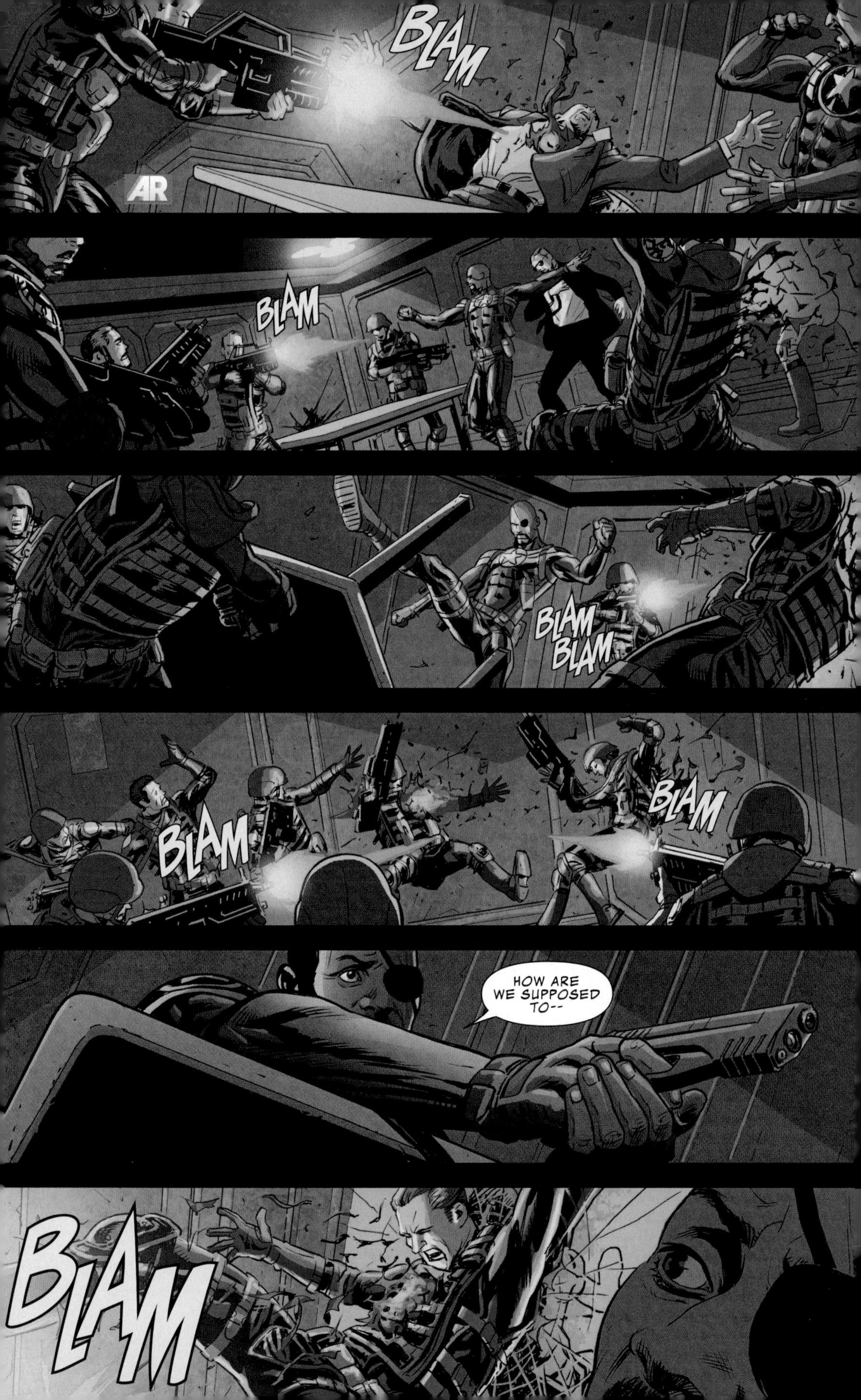
BLAM
AR
BLAM
BLAM
BLAM
BLAM
BLAM
HOW ARE WE SUPPOSED TO--
BLAM

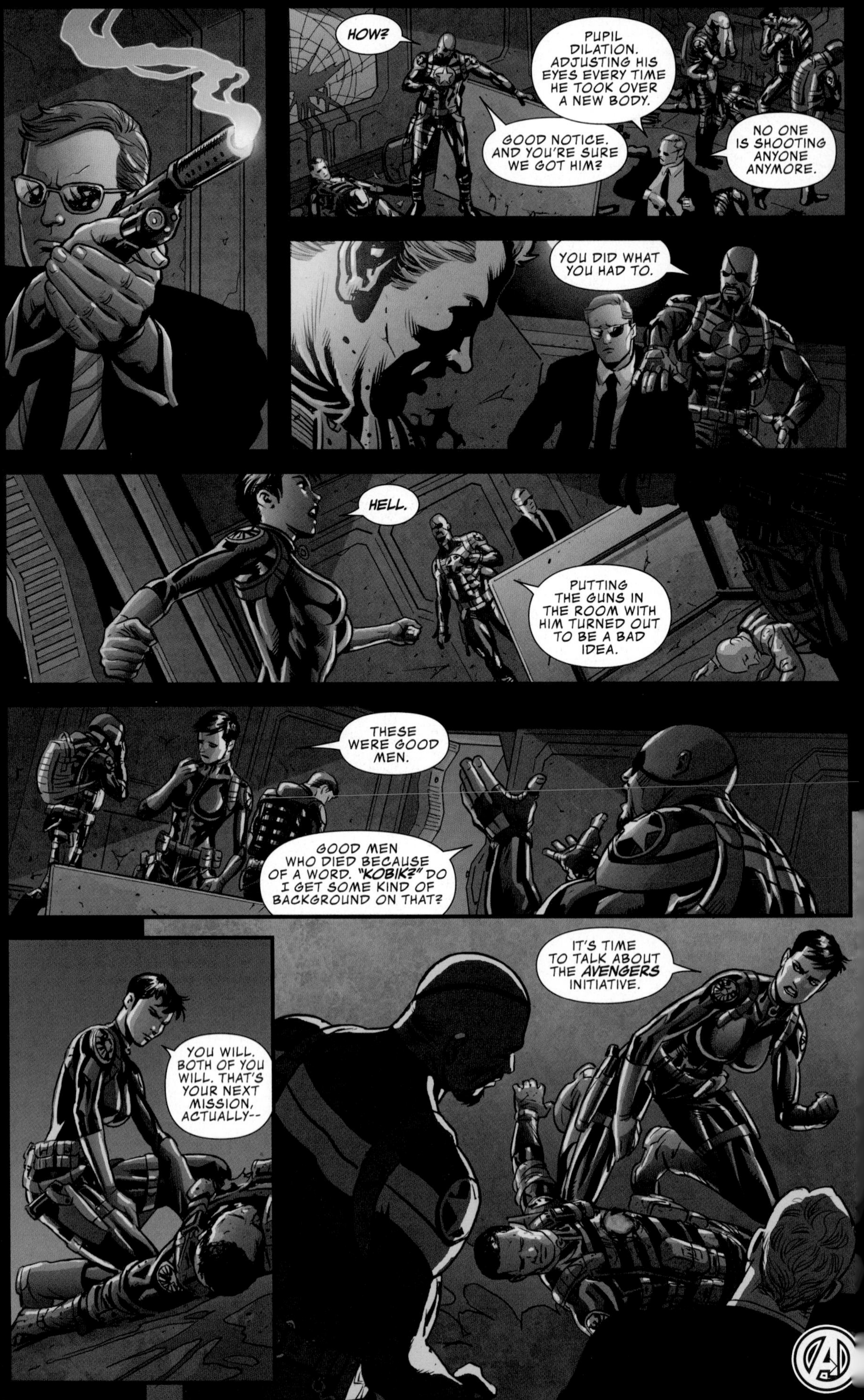
HOW?
PUPIL DILATION. ADJUSTING HIS EYES EVERY TIME HE TOOK OVER A NEW BODY.
GOOD NOTICE. AND YOU'RE SURE WE GOT HIM?
NO ONE IS SHOOTING ANYONE ANYMORE.
YOU DID WHAT YOU HAD TO.
HELL.
PUTTING THE GUNS IN THE ROOM WITH HIM TURNED OUT TO BE A BAD IDEA.
THESE WERE GOOD MEN.
GOOD MEN WHO DIED BECAUSE OF A WORD. "KOBIK?" DO I GET SOME KIND OF BACKGROUND ON THAT?
IT'S TIME TO TALK ABOUT THE AVENGERS INITIATIVE.
YOU WILL. BOTH OF YOU WILL. THAT'S YOUR NEXT MISSION, ACTUALLY--

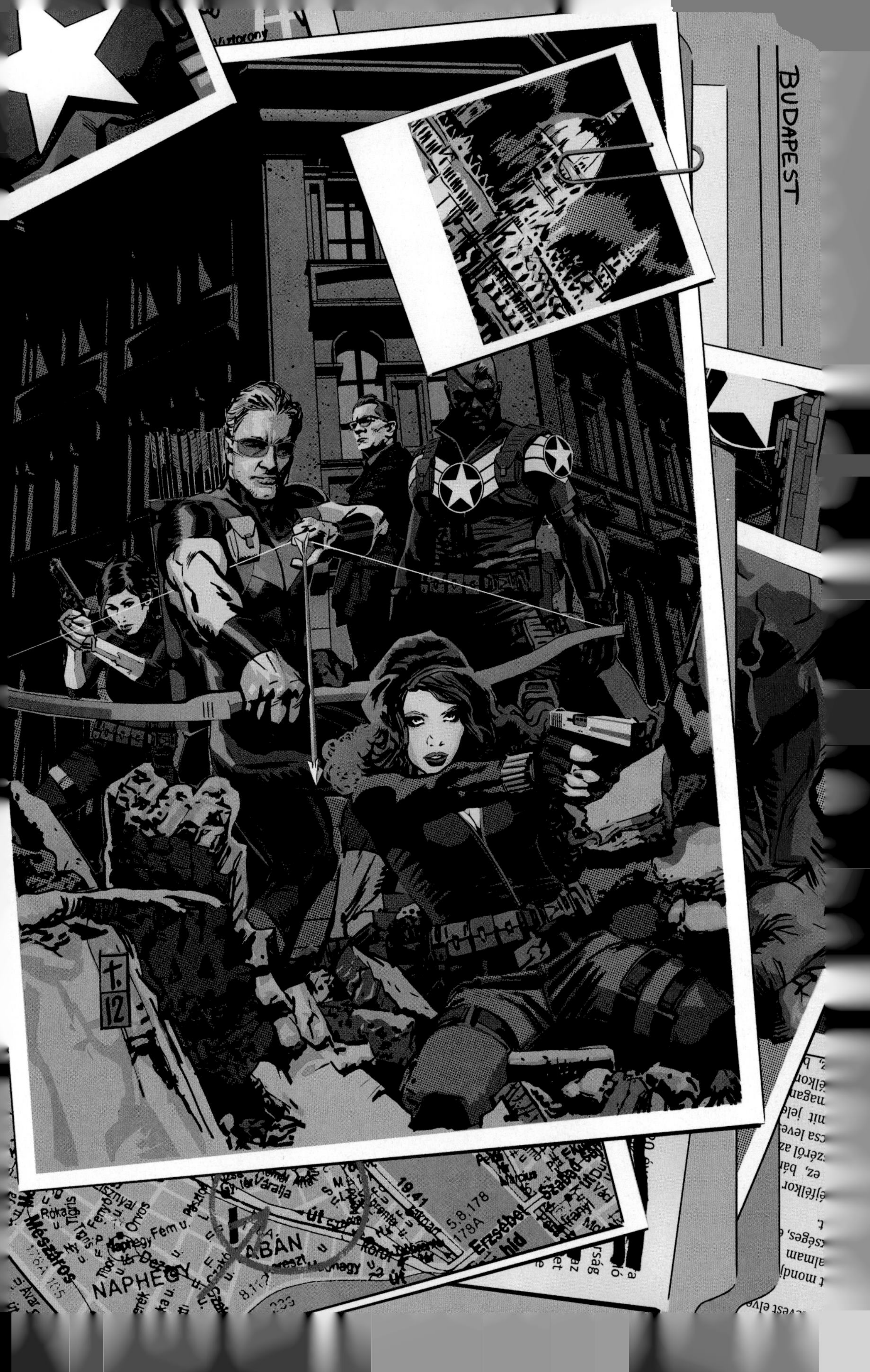
BUDAPEST
NAPHEGY
TABÁN
Erzsébet híd

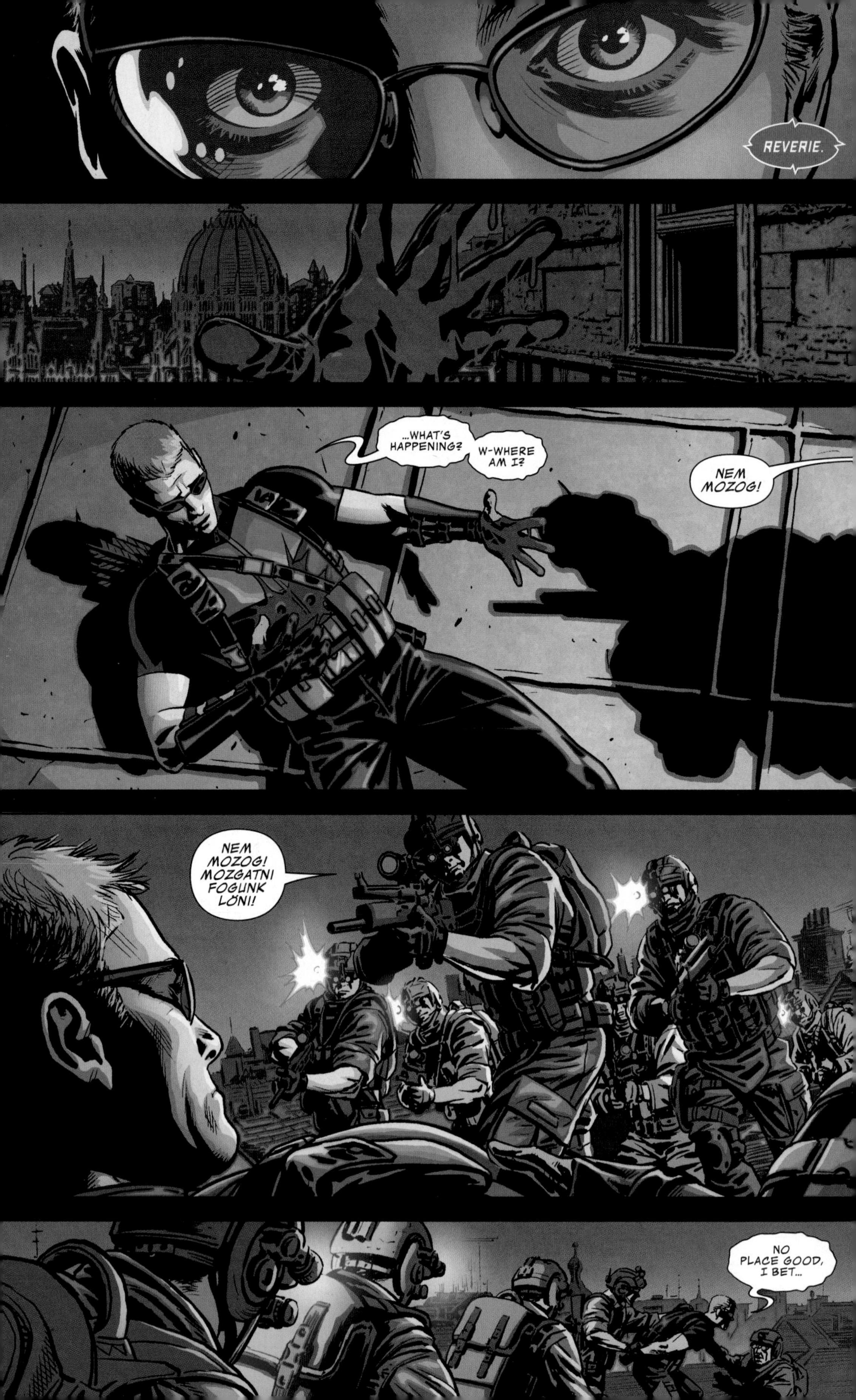

REVERIE.
...WHAT'S HAPPENING?
W-WHERE AM I?
NEM MOZOG!
NEM MOZOG! MOZGATNI FOGUNK LÖNI!
NO PLACE GOOD, I BET...

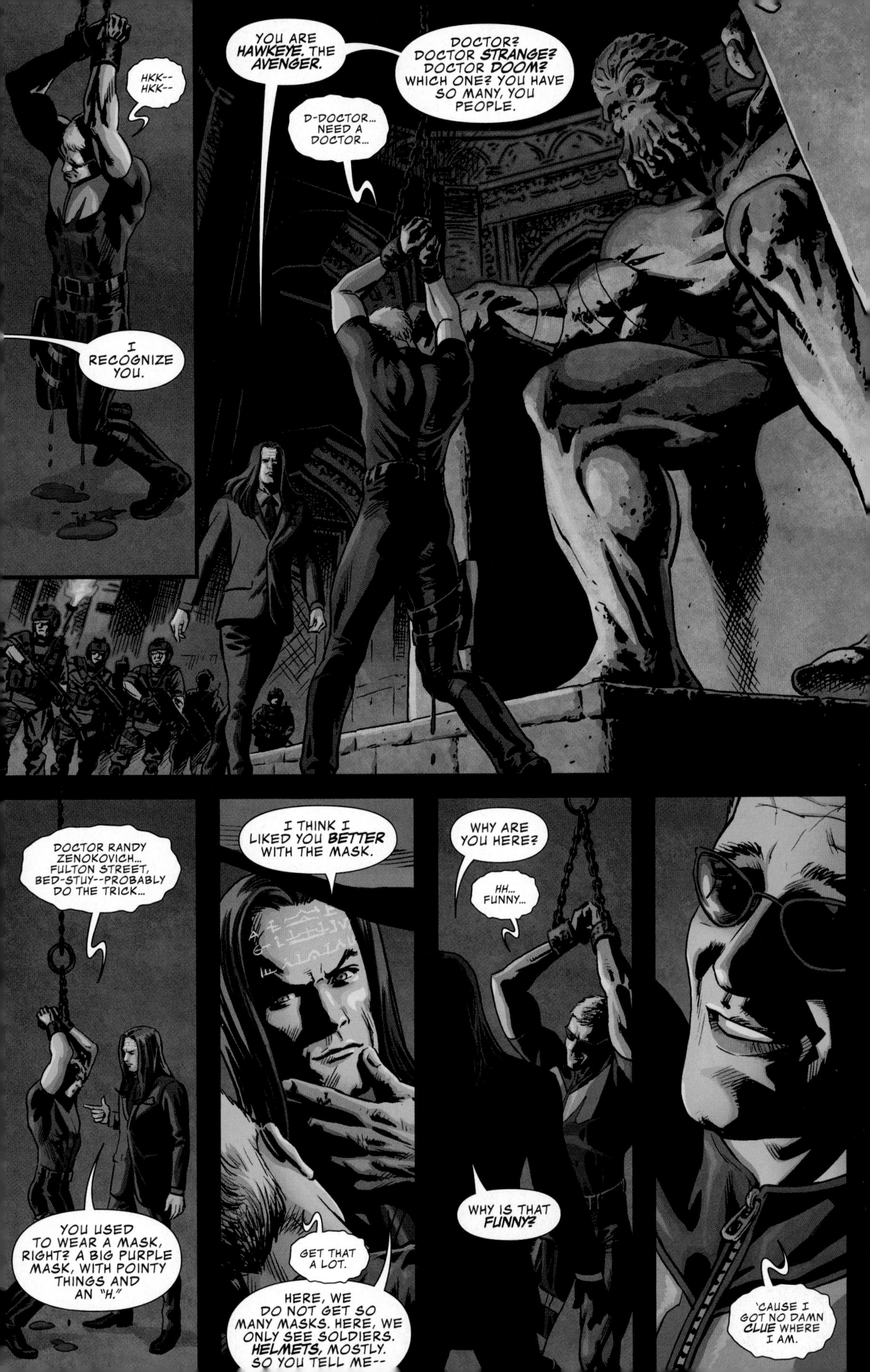
HKK-- HKK--
I RECOGNIZE YOU.
YOU ARE HAWKEYE. THE AVENGER.
DOCTOR? DOCTOR STRANGE? DOCTOR DOOM? WHICH ONE? YOU HAVE SO MANY, YOU PEOPLE.
D-DOCTOR... NEED A DOCTOR...
DOCTOR RANDY ZENOKOVICH... FULTON STREET, BED-STUY--PROBABLY DO THE TRICK...
YOU USED TO WEAR A MASK, RIGHT? A BIG PURPLE MASK, WITH POINTY THINGS AND AN "H."
I THINK I LIKED YOU BETTER WITH THE MASK.
GET THAT A LOT.
HERE, WE DO NOT GET SO MANY MASKS. HERE, WE ONLY SEE SOLDIERS. HELMETS, MOSTLY. SO YOU TELL ME--
WHY ARE YOU HERE?
HH... FUNNY...
WHY IS THAT FUNNY?
'CAUSE I GOT NO DAMN CLUE WHERE I AM.

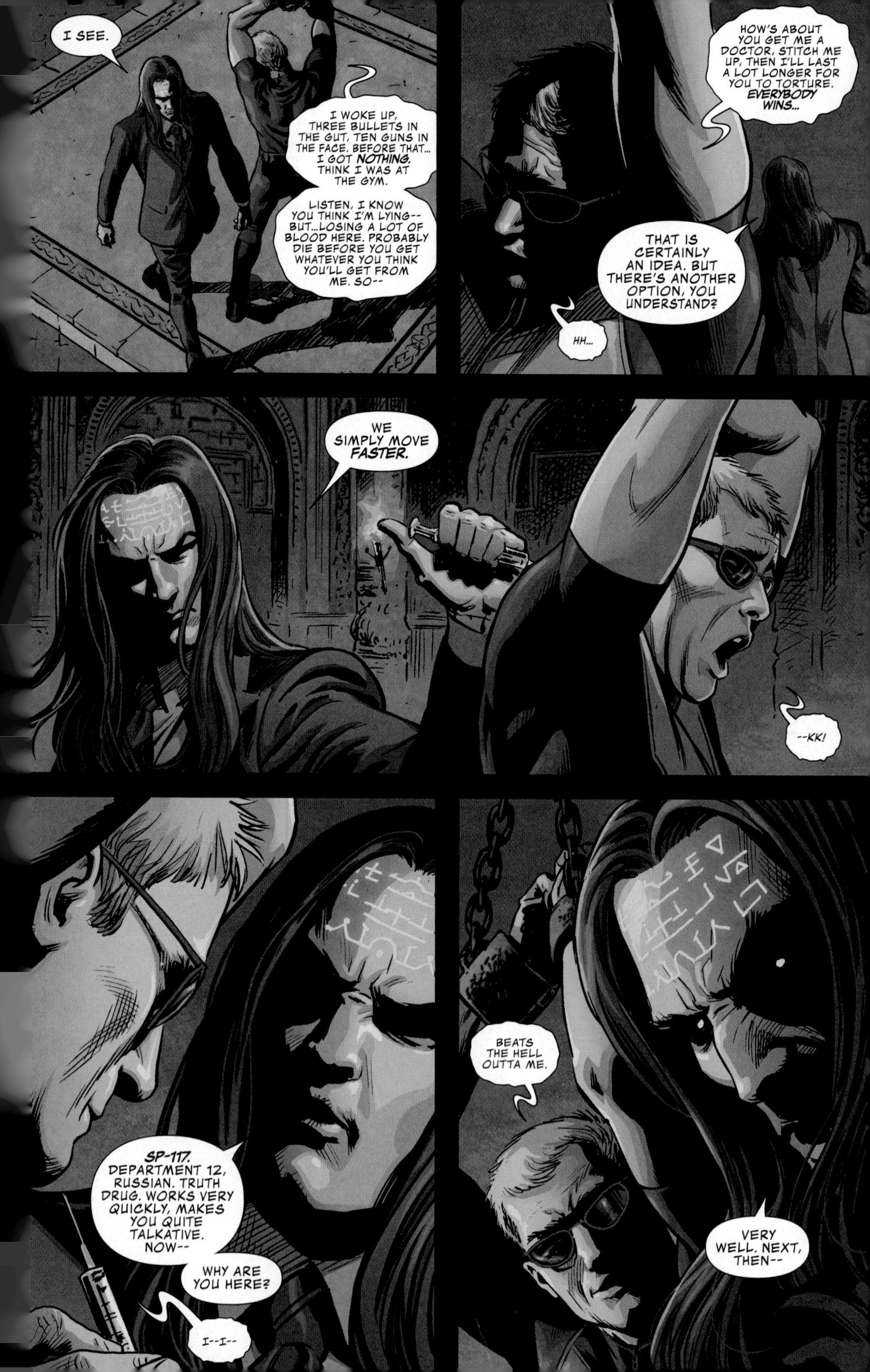
I SEE.
I WOKE UP, THREE BULLETS IN THE GUT, TEN GUNS IN THE FACE. BEFORE THAT... I GOT NOTHING. THINK I WAS AT THE GYM.
LISTEN, I KNOW YOU THINK I'M LYING-- BUT...LOSING A LOT OF BLOOD HERE. PROBABLY DIE BEFORE YOU GET WHATEVER YOU THINK YOU'LL GET FROM ME. SO--
HOW'S ABOUT YOU GET ME A DOCTOR, STITCH ME UP, THEN I'LL LAST A LOT LONGER FOR YOU TO TORTURE. EVERYBODY WINS...
THAT IS CERTAINLY AN IDEA. BUT THERE'S ANOTHER OPTION, YOU UNDERSTAND?
HH...
WE SIMPLY MOVE FASTER.
--KK!
SP-117. DEPARTMENT 12, RUSSIAN. TRUTH DRUG. WORKS VERY QUICKLY, MAKES YOU QUITE TALKATIVE. NOW--
WHY ARE YOU HERE?
I--I--
BEATS THE HELL OUTTA ME.
VERY WELL. NEXT, THEN--

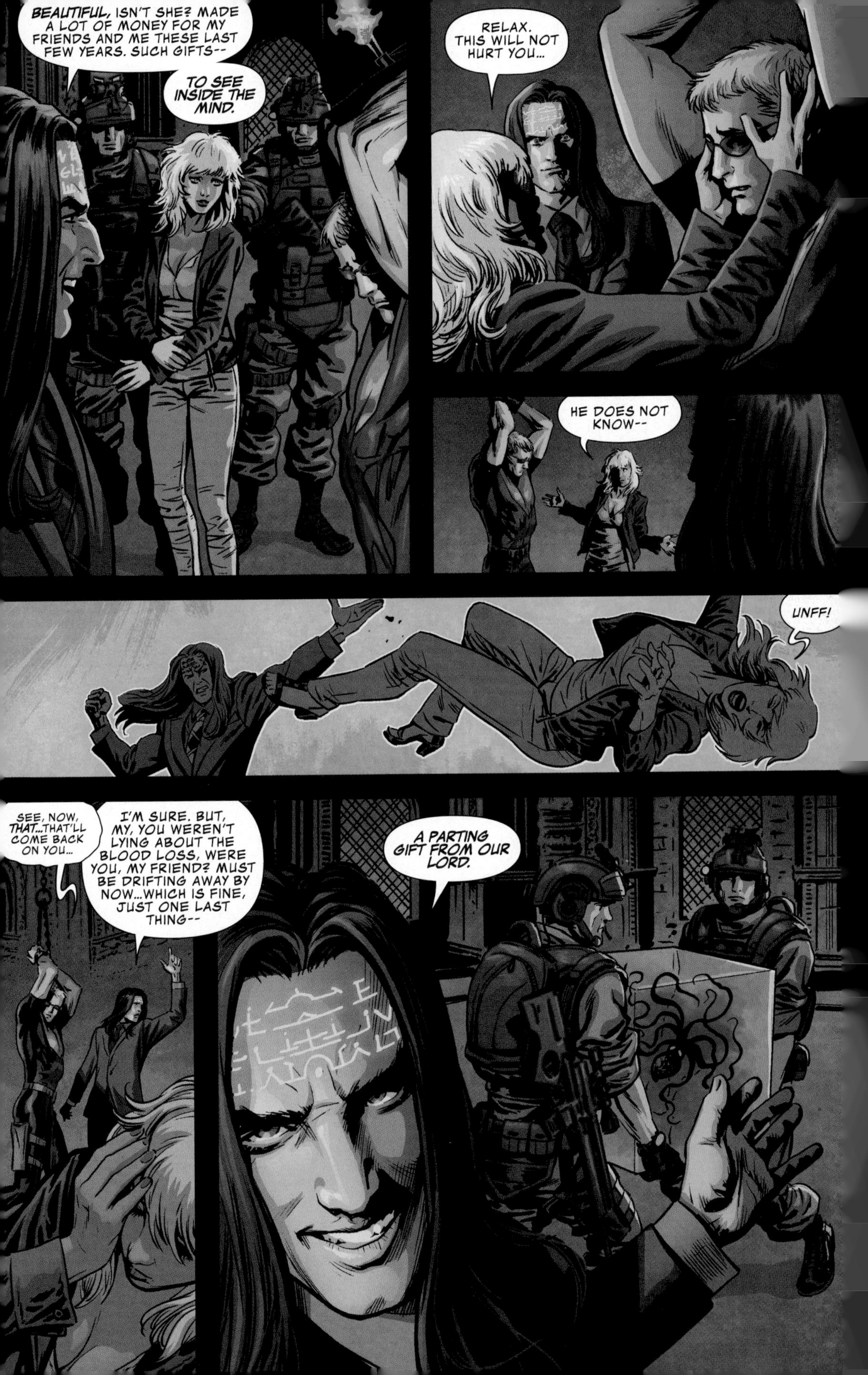
BEAUTIFUL, ISN'T SHE? MADE A LOT OF MONEY FOR MY FRIENDS AND ME THESE LAST FEW YEARS. SUCH GIFTS--
TO SEE INSIDE THE MIND.
RELAX. THIS WILL NOT HURT YOU...
HE DOES NOT KNOW--
UNFF!
SEE, NOW, THAT...THAT'LL COME BACK ON YOU...
I'M SURE. BUT, MY, YOU WEREN'T LYING ABOUT THE BLOOD LOSS, WERE YOU, MY FRIEND? MUST BE DRIFTING AWAY BY NOW...WHICH IS FINE, JUST ONE LAST THING--
A PARTING GIFT FROM OUR LORD.

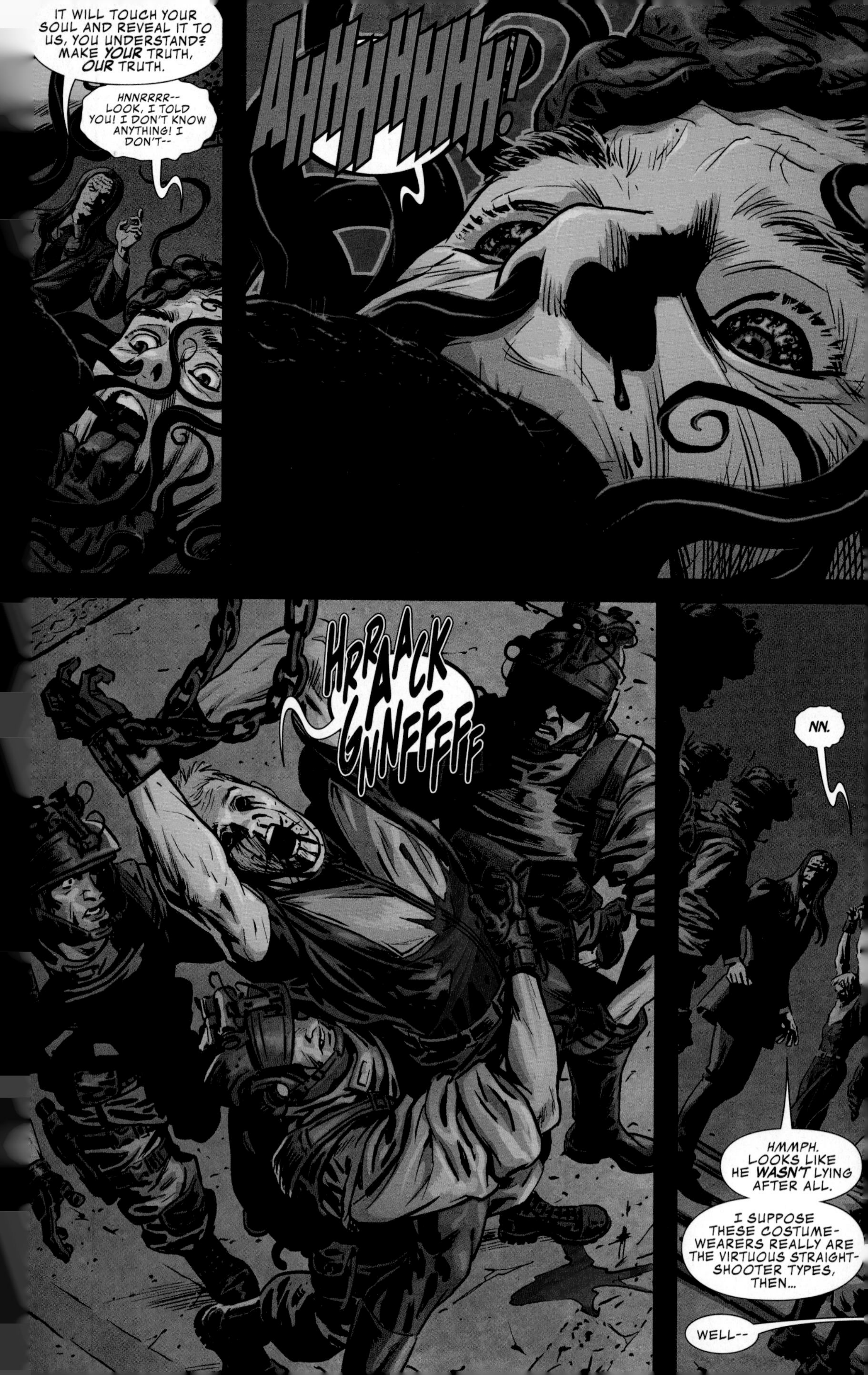
IT WILL TOUCH YOUR SOUL AND REVEAL IT TO US, YOU UNDERSTAND? MAKE YOUR TRUTH, OUR TRUTH.
HNNRRRR-- LOOK, I TOLD YOU! I DON'T KNOW ANYTHING! I DON'T--
AHHHHHHHH!
HRRAACK GNNFFFFF
NN.
HMMPH. LOOKS LIKE HE WASN'T LYING AFTER ALL.
I SUPPOSE THESE COSTUME-WEARERS REALLY ARE THE VIRTUOUS STRAIGHT-SHOOTER TYPES, THEN...
WELL--

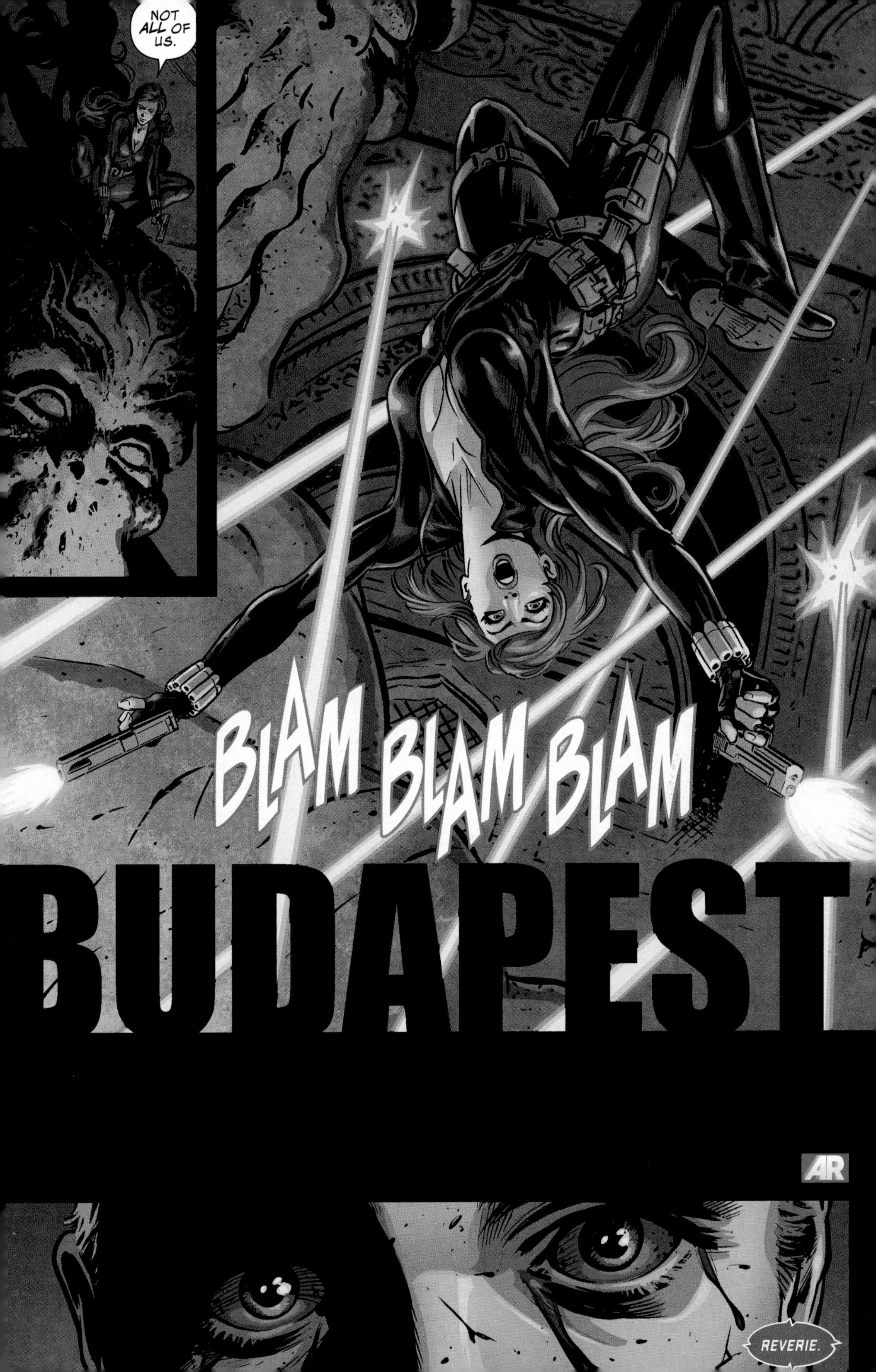
NOT ALL OF US.
BLAM BLAM BLAM
BUDAPEST
REVERIE.

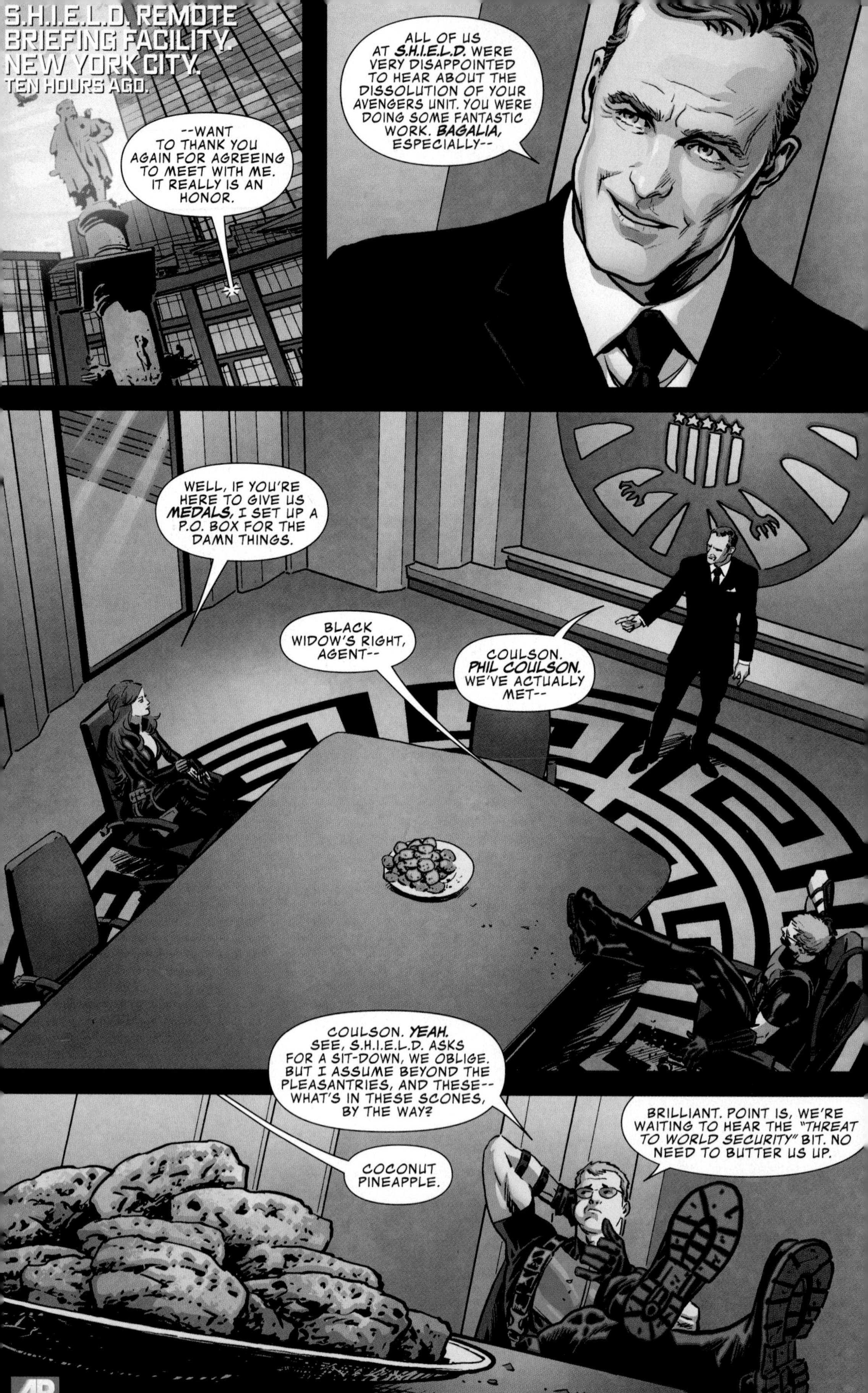

S.H.I.E.L.D. REMOTE BRIEFING FACILITY. NEW YORK CITY. TEN HOURS AGO.
--WANT TO THANK YOU AGAIN FOR AGREEING TO MEET WITH ME. IT REALLY IS AN HONOR.
ALL OF US AT S.H.I.E.L.D. WERE VERY DISAPPOINTED TO HEAR ABOUT THE DISSOLUTION OF YOUR AVENGERS UNIT. YOU WERE DOING SOME FANTASTIC WORK. BAGALIA, ESPECIALLY--
WELL, IF YOU'RE HERE TO GIVE US MEDALS, I SET UP A P.O. BOX FOR THE DAMN THINGS.
BLACK WIDOW'S RIGHT, AGENT--
COULSON. PHIL COULSON. WE'VE ACTUALLY MET--
COULSON. YEAH. SEE, S.H.I.E.L.D. ASKS FOR A SIT-DOWN, WE OBLIGE. BUT I ASSUME BEYOND THE PLEASANTRIES, AND THESE-- WHAT'S IN THESE SCONES, BY THE WAY?
COCONUT PINEAPPLE.
BRILLIANT. POINT IS, WE'RE WAITING TO HEAR THE "THREAT TO WORLD SECURITY" BIT. NO NEED TO BUTTER US UP.

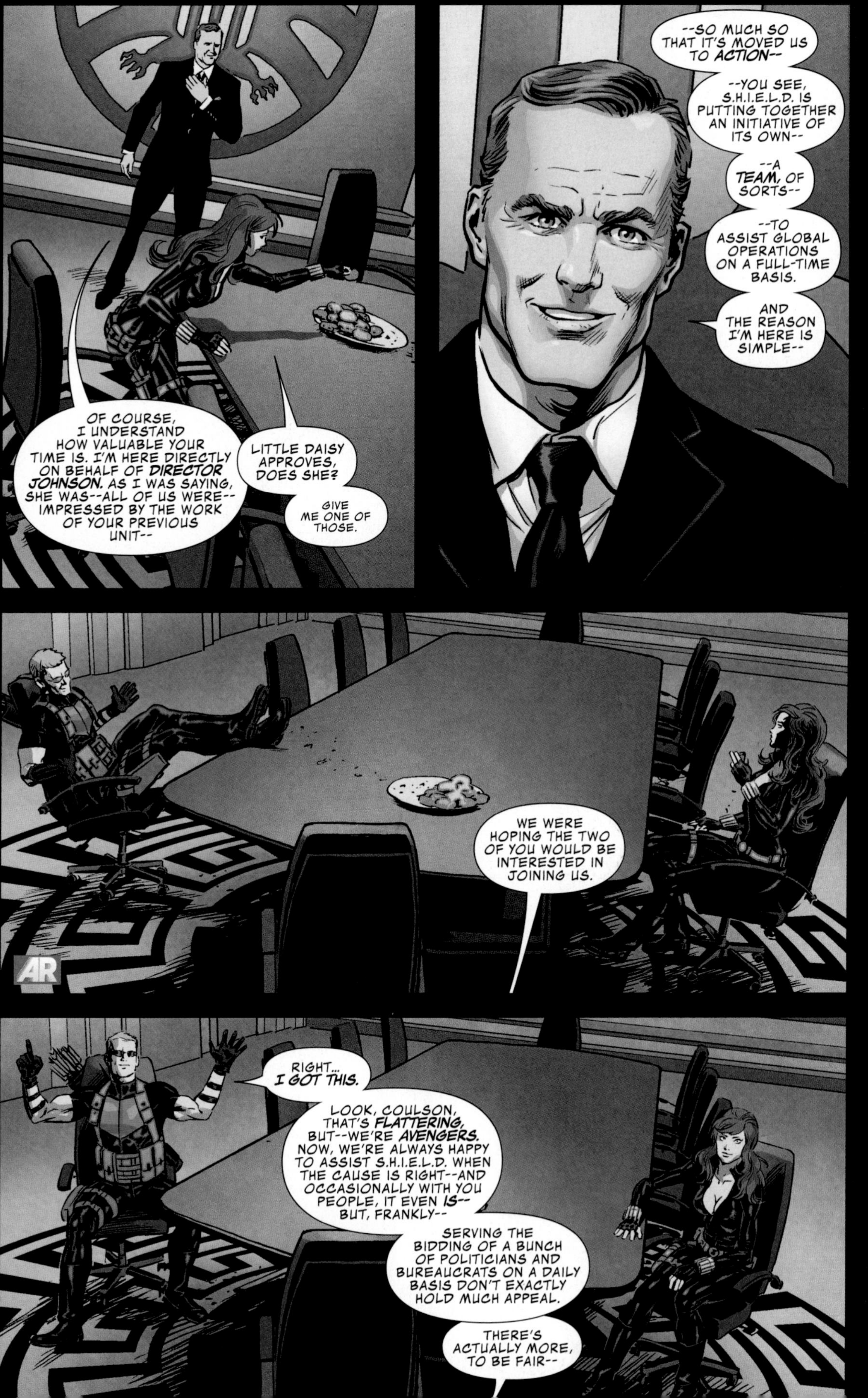

OF COURSE, I UNDERSTAND HOW VALUABLE YOUR TIME IS. I'M HERE DIRECTLY ON BEHALF OF **DIRECTOR JOHNSON.** AS I WAS SAYING, SHE WAS--ALL OF US WERE--IMPRESSED BY THE WORK OF YOUR PREVIOUS UNIT--
LITTLE DAISY APPROVES, DOES SHE?
GIVE ME ONE OF THOSE.
--SO MUCH SO THAT IT'S MOVED US TO **ACTION--**
--YOU SEE, S.H.I.E.L.D. IS PUTTING TOGETHER AN INITIATIVE OF ITS OWN--
--A **TEAM,** OF SORTS--
--TO ASSIST GLOBAL OPERATIONS ON A FULL-TIME BASIS.
AND THE REASON I'M HERE IS SIMPLE--
WE WERE HOPING THE TWO OF YOU WOULD BE INTERESTED IN JOINING US.
RIGHT... **I GOT THIS.**
LOOK, COULSON, THAT'S **FLATTERING,** BUT--WE'RE **AVENGERS.** NOW, WE'RE ALWAYS HAPPY TO ASSIST S.H.I.E.L.D. WHEN THE CAUSE IS RIGHT--AND OCCASIONALLY WITH YOU PEOPLE, IT EVEN **IS--** BUT, FRANKLY--
SERVING THE BIDDING OF A BUNCH OF POLITICIANS AND BUREAUCRATS ON A DAILY BASIS DON'T EXACTLY HOLD MUCH APPEAL.
THERE'S ACTUALLY MORE, TO BE FAIR--

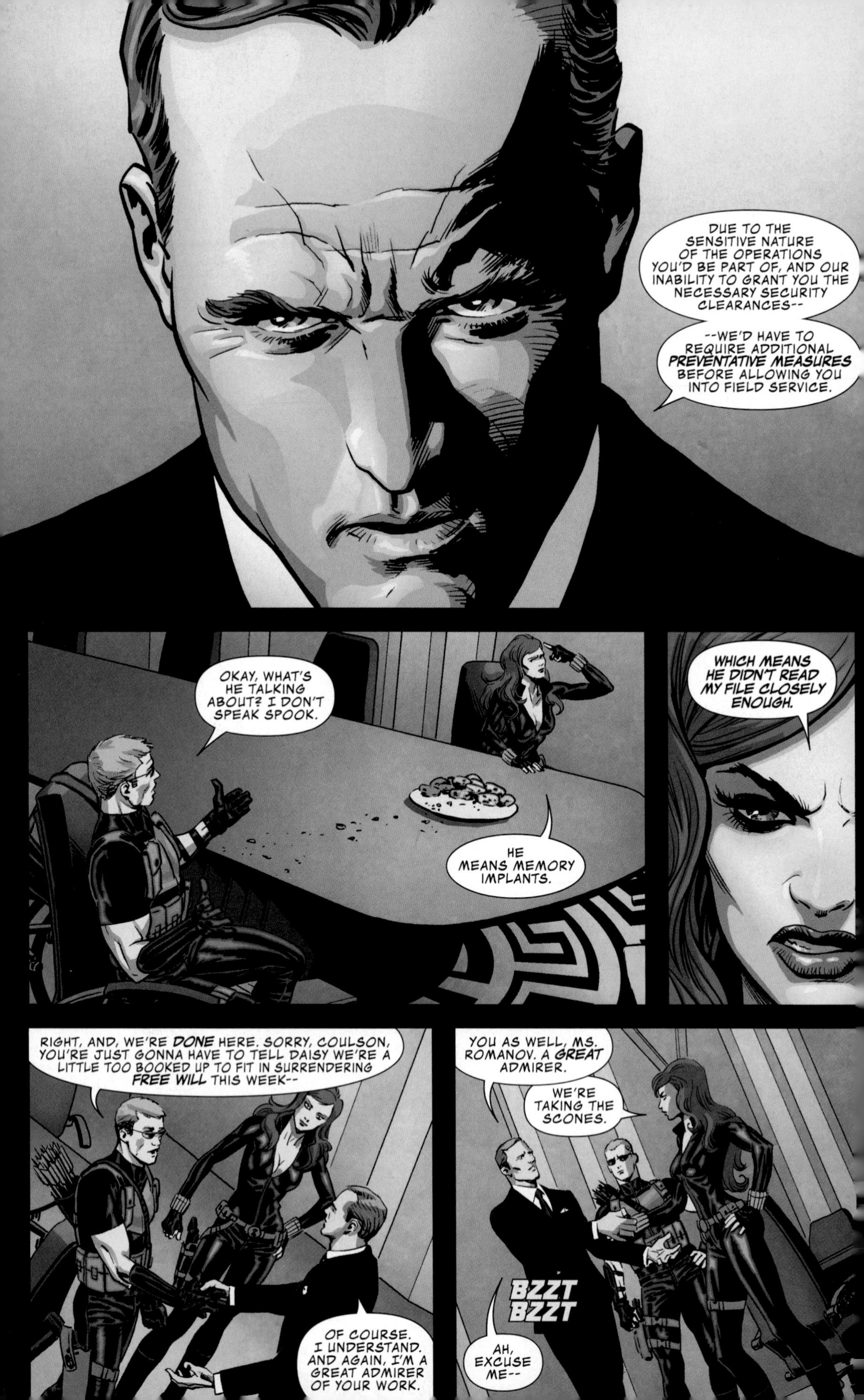
DUE TO THE SENSITIVE NATURE OF THE OPERATIONS YOU'D BE PART OF, AND OUR INABILITY TO GRANT YOU THE NECESSARY SECURITY CLEARANCES--
--WE'D HAVE TO REQUIRE ADDITIONAL PREVENTATIVE MEASURES BEFORE ALLOWING YOU INTO FIELD SERVICE.
OKAY, WHAT'S HE TALKING ABOUT? I DON'T SPEAK SPOOK.
HE MEANS MEMORY IMPLANTS.
WHICH MEANS HE DIDN'T READ MY FILE CLOSELY ENOUGH.
RIGHT, AND, WE'RE DONE HERE. SORRY, COULSON, YOU'RE JUST GONNA HAVE TO TELL DAISY WE'RE A LITTLE TOO BOOKED UP TO FIT IN SURRENDERING FREE WILL THIS WEEK--
OF COURSE. I UNDERSTAND. AND AGAIN, I'M A GREAT ADMIRER OF YOUR WORK.
YOU AS WELL, MS. ROMANOV. A GREAT ADMIRER.
WE'RE TAKING THE SCONES.
BZZT BZZT
AH, EXCUSE ME--

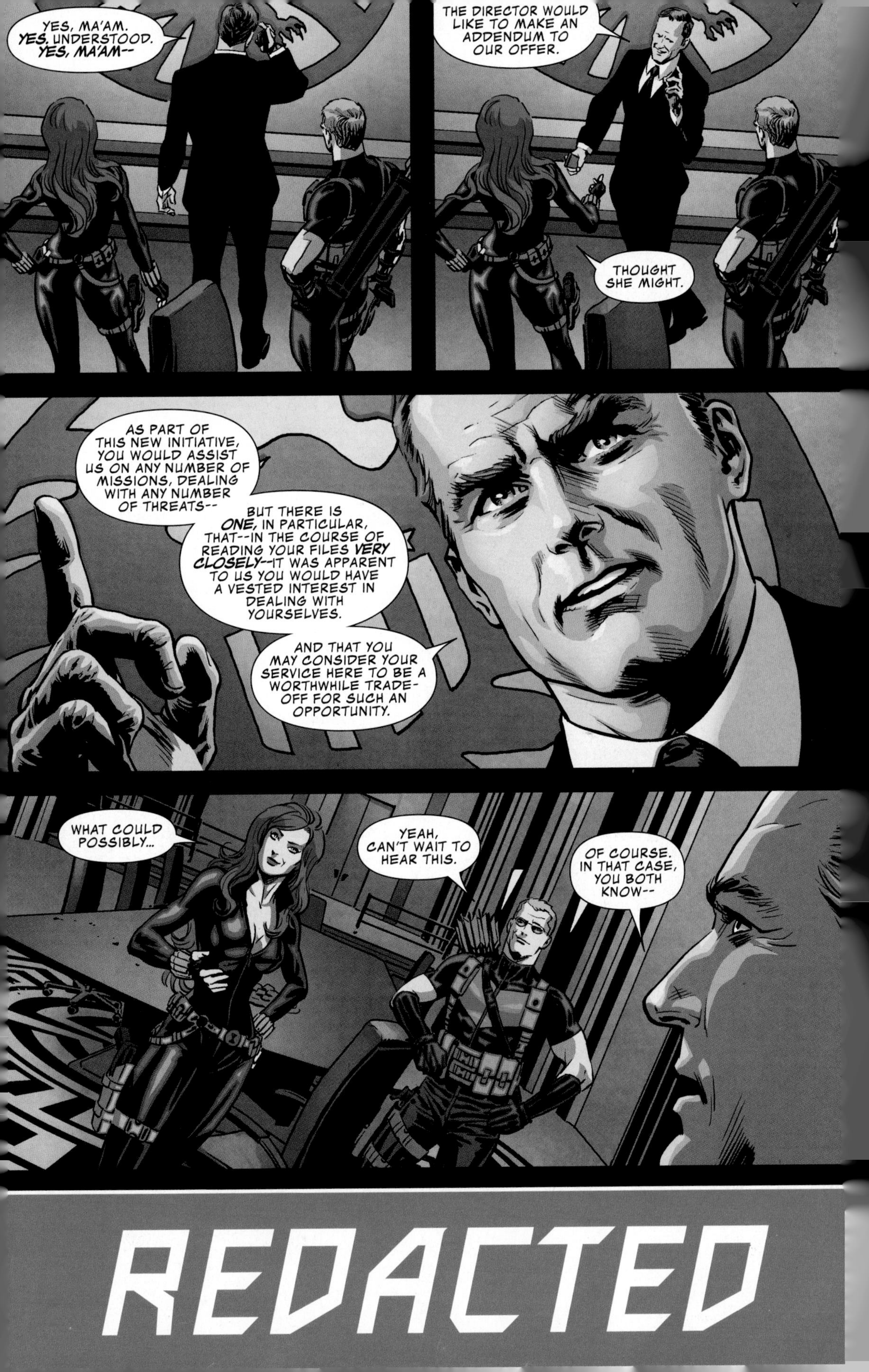
YES, MA'AM. YES. UNDERSTOOD. YES, MA'AM--
THE DIRECTOR WOULD LIKE TO MAKE AN ADDENDUM TO OUR OFFER.
THOUGHT SHE MIGHT.
AS PART OF THIS NEW INITIATIVE, YOU WOULD ASSIST US ON ANY NUMBER OF MISSIONS, DEALING WITH ANY NUMBER OF THREATS--
BUT THERE IS ONE, IN PARTICULAR, THAT--IN THE COURSE OF READING YOUR FILES VERY CLOSELY--IT WAS APPARENT TO US YOU WOULD HAVE A VESTED INTEREST IN DEALING WITH YOURSELVES.
AND THAT YOU MAY CONSIDER YOUR SERVICE HERE TO BE A WORTHWHILE TRADE-OFF FOR SUCH AN OPPORTUNITY.
WHAT COULD POSSIBLY...
YEAH, CAN'T WAIT TO HEAR THIS.
OF COURSE. IN THAT CASE, YOU BOTH KNOW--
REDACTED

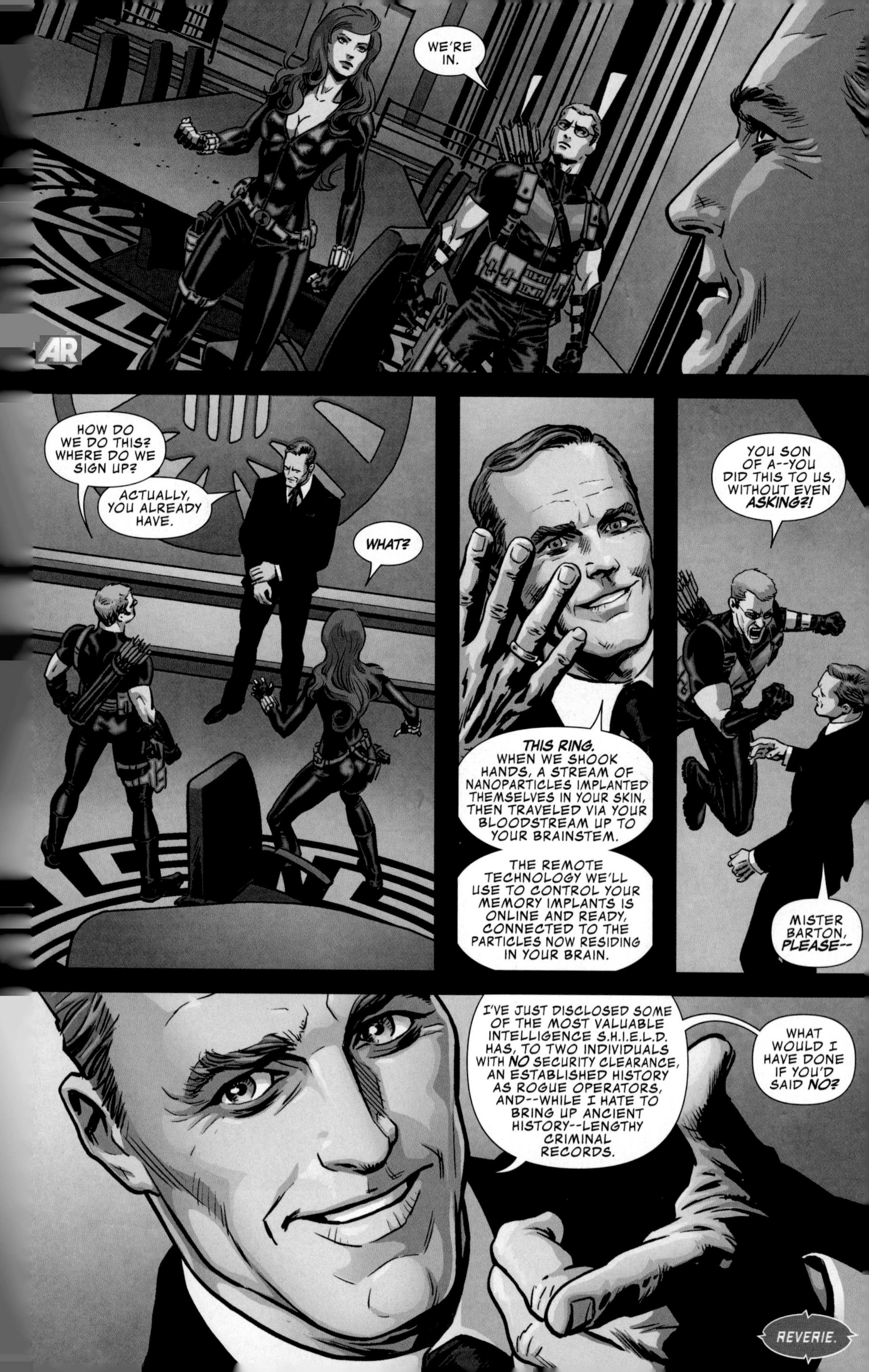
WE'RE IN.
HOW DO WE DO THIS? WHERE DO WE SIGN UP?
ACTUALLY, YOU ALREADY HAVE.
WHAT?
THIS RING. WHEN WE SHOOK HANDS, A STREAM OF NANOPARTICLES IMPLANTED THEMSELVES IN YOUR SKIN, THEN TRAVELED VIA YOUR BLOODSTREAM UP TO YOUR BRAINSTEM.
THE REMOTE TECHNOLOGY WE'LL USE TO CONTROL YOUR MEMORY IMPLANTS IS ONLINE AND READY, CONNECTED TO THE PARTICLES NOW RESIDING IN YOUR BRAIN.
YOU SON OF A--YOU DID THIS TO US, WITHOUT EVEN ASKING?!
MISTER BARTON, PLEASE--
I'VE JUST DISCLOSED SOME OF THE MOST VALUABLE INTELLIGENCE S.H.I.E.L.D. HAS, TO TWO INDIVIDUALS WITH NO SECURITY CLEARANCE, AN ESTABLISHED HISTORY AS ROGUE OPERATORS, AND--WHILE I HATE TO BRING UP ANCIENT HISTORY--LENGTHY CRIMINAL RECORDS.
WHAT WOULD I HAVE DONE IF YOU'D SAID NO?
REVERIE.

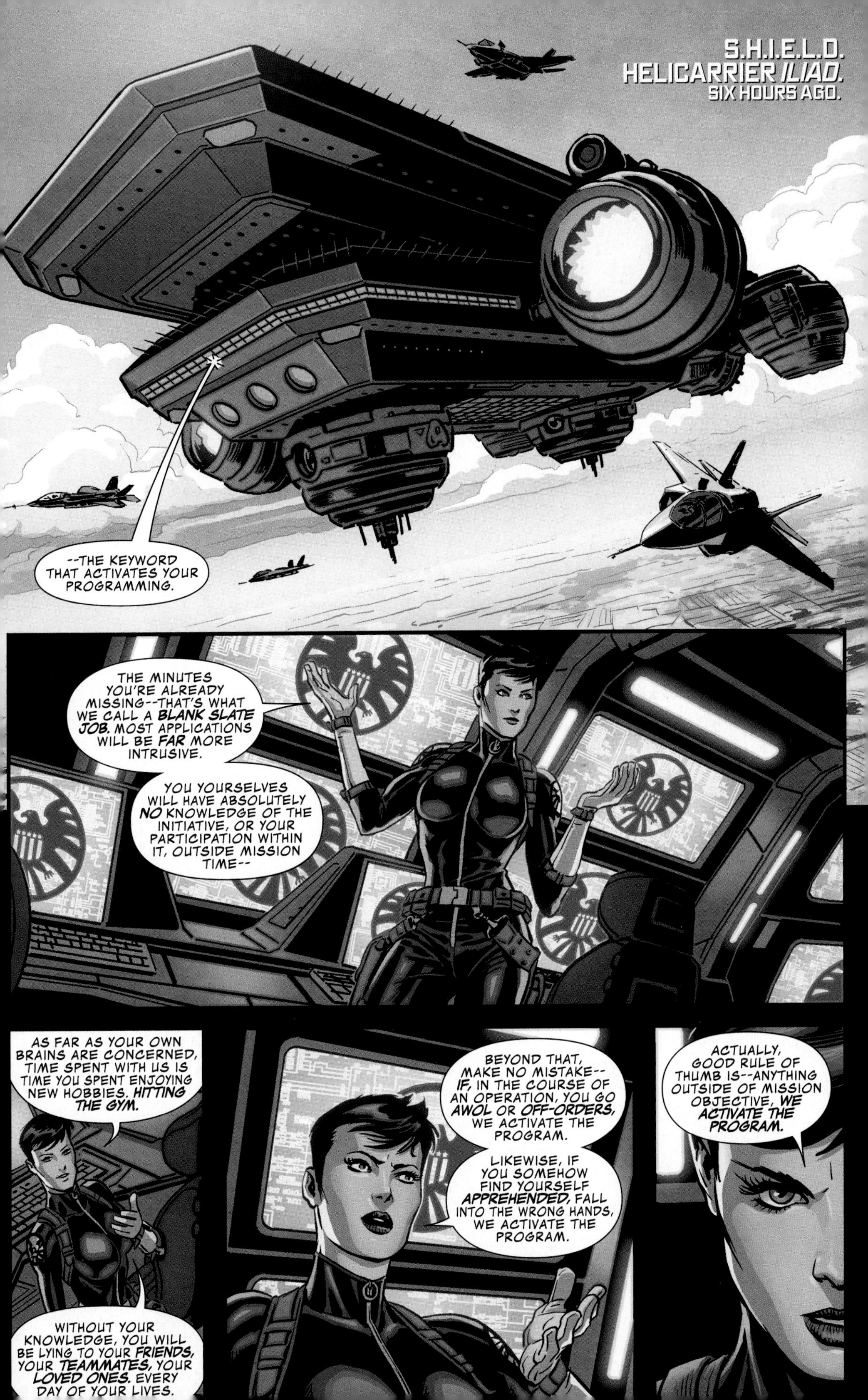
S.H.I.E.L.D. HELICARRIER ILIAD. SIX HOURS AGO.
--THE KEYWORD THAT ACTIVATES YOUR PROGRAMMING.
THE MINUTES YOU'RE ALREADY MISSING--THAT'S WHAT WE CALL A BLANK SLATE JOB. MOST APPLICATIONS WILL BE FAR MORE INTRUSIVE.
YOU YOURSELVES WILL HAVE ABSOLUTELY NO KNOWLEDGE OF THE INITIATIVE, OR YOUR PARTICIPATION WITHIN IT, OUTSIDE MISSION TIME--
AS FAR AS YOUR OWN BRAINS ARE CONCERNED, TIME SPENT WITH US IS TIME YOU SPENT ENJOYING NEW HOBBIES. HITTING THE GYM.
WITHOUT YOUR KNOWLEDGE, YOU WILL BE LYING TO YOUR FRIENDS, YOUR TEAMMATES, YOUR LOVED ONES. EVERY DAY OF YOUR LIVES.
BEYOND THAT, MAKE NO MISTAKE--IF, IN THE COURSE OF AN OPERATION, YOU GO AWOL OR OFF-ORDERS, WE ACTIVATE THE PROGRAM.
LIKEWISE, IF YOU SOMEHOW FIND YOURSELF APPREHENDED, FALL INTO THE WRONG HANDS, WE ACTIVATE THE PROGRAM.
ACTUALLY, GOOD RULE OF THUMB IS--ANYTHING OUTSIDE OF MISSION OBJECTIVE, WE ACTIVATE THE PROGRAM.

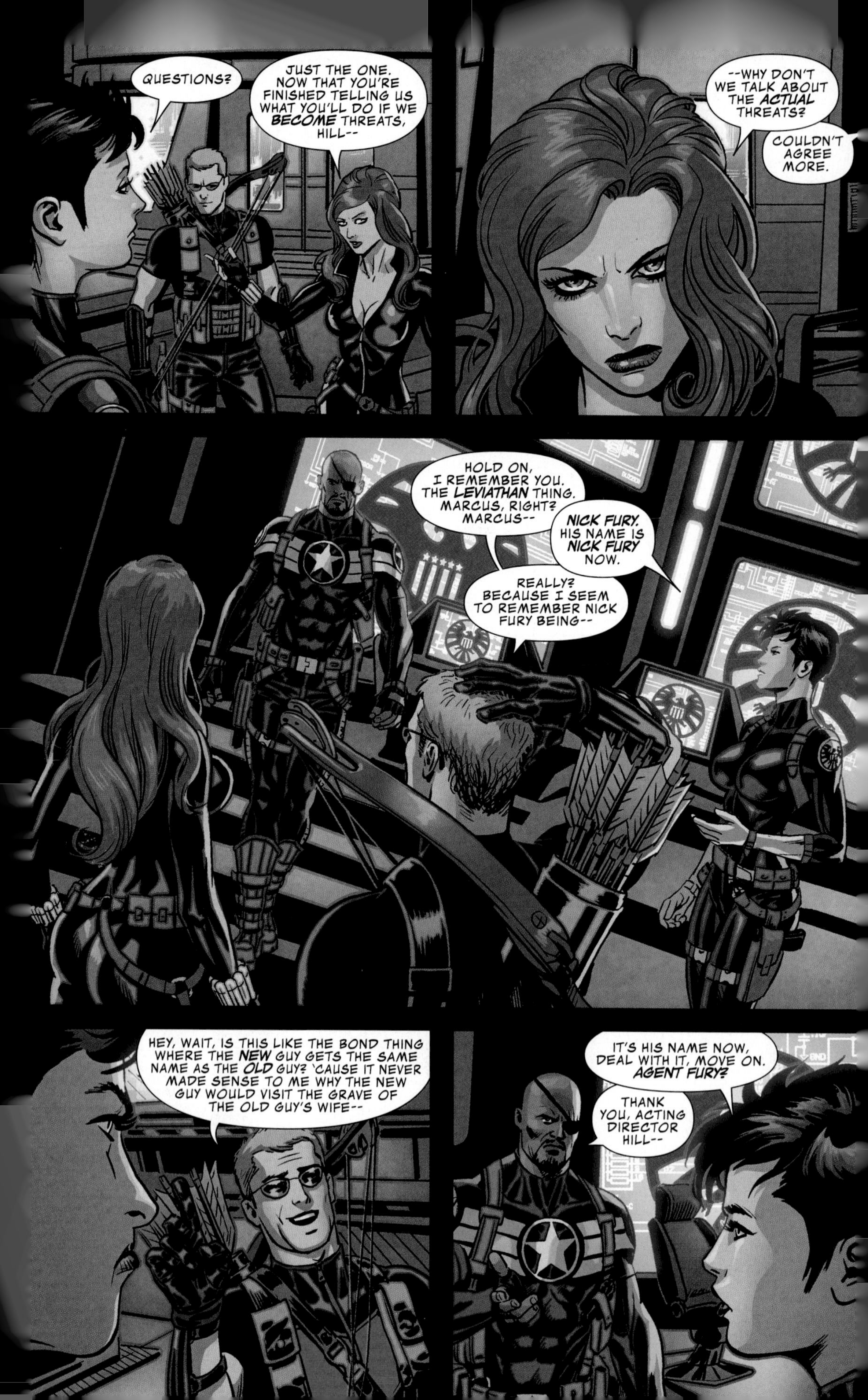
QUESTIONS?
JUST THE ONE. NOW THAT YOU'RE FINISHED TELLING US WHAT YOU'LL DO IF WE BECOME THREATS, HILL--
--WHY DON'T WE TALK ABOUT THE ACTUAL THREATS?
COULDN'T AGREE MORE.
HOLD ON, I REMEMBER YOU. THE LEVIATHAN THING. MARCUS, RIGHT? MARCUS--
NICK FURY. HIS NAME IS NICK FURY NOW.
REALLY? BECAUSE I SEEM TO REMEMBER NICK FURY BEING--
HEY, WAIT, IS THIS LIKE THE BOND THING WHERE THE NEW GUY GETS THE SAME NAME AS THE OLD GUY? 'CAUSE IT NEVER MADE SENSE TO ME WHY THE NEW GUY WOULD VISIT THE GRAVE OF THE OLD GUY'S WIFE--
IT'S HIS NAME NOW, DEAL WITH IT, MOVE ON. AGENT FURY?
THANK YOU, ACTING DIRECTOR HILL--

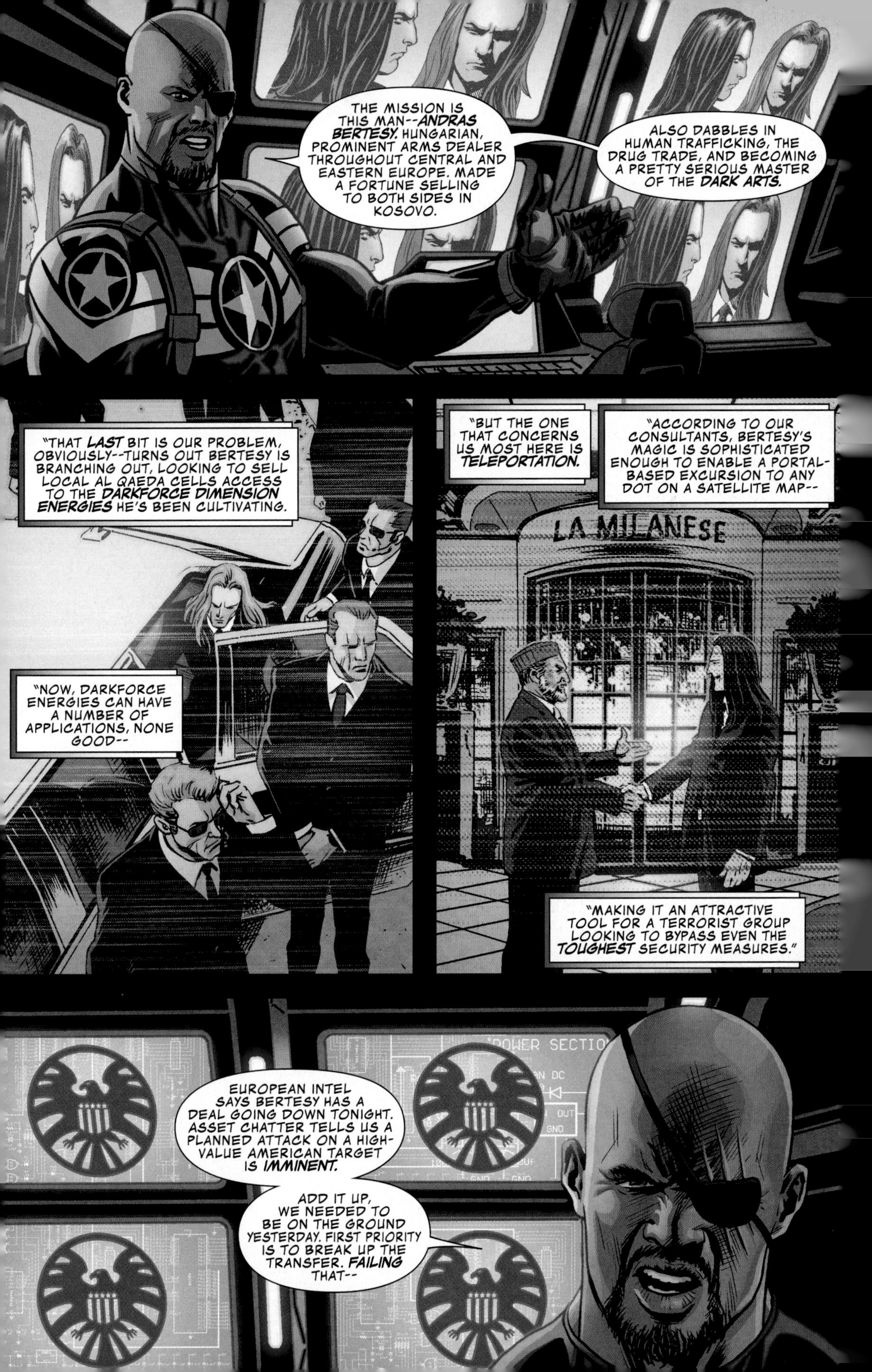
THE MISSION IS THIS MAN--ANDRAS BERTESY. HUNGARIAN, PROMINENT ARMS DEALER THROUGHOUT CENTRAL AND EASTERN EUROPE. MADE A FORTUNE SELLING TO BOTH SIDES IN KOSOVO.
ALSO DABBLES IN HUMAN TRAFFICKING, THE DRUG TRADE, AND BECOMING A PRETTY SERIOUS MASTER OF THE DARK ARTS.
"THAT LAST BIT IS OUR PROBLEM, OBVIOUSLY--TURNS OUT BERTESY IS BRANCHING OUT, LOOKING TO SELL LOCAL AL QAEDA CELLS ACCESS TO THE DARKFORCE DIMENSION ENERGIES HE'S BEEN CULTIVATING.
"NOW, DARKFORCE ENERGIES CAN HAVE A NUMBER OF APPLICATIONS, NONE GOOD--
"BUT THE ONE THAT CONCERNS US MOST HERE IS TELEPORTATION.
"ACCORDING TO OUR CONSULTANTS, BERTESY'S MAGIC IS SOPHISTICATED ENOUGH TO ENABLE A PORTAL-BASED EXCURSION TO ANY DOT ON A SATELLITE MAP--
LA MILANESE
"MAKING IT AN ATTRACTIVE TOOL FOR A TERRORIST GROUP LOOKING TO BYPASS EVEN THE TOUGHEST SECURITY MEASURES."
EUROPEAN INTEL SAYS BERTESY HAS A DEAL GOING DOWN TONIGHT. ASSET CHATTER TELLS US A PLANNED ATTACK ON A HIGH-VALUE AMERICAN TARGET IS IMMINENT.
ADD IT UP, WE NEEDED TO BE ON THE GROUND YESTERDAY. FIRST PRIORITY IS TO BREAK UP THE TRANSFER. FAILING THAT--

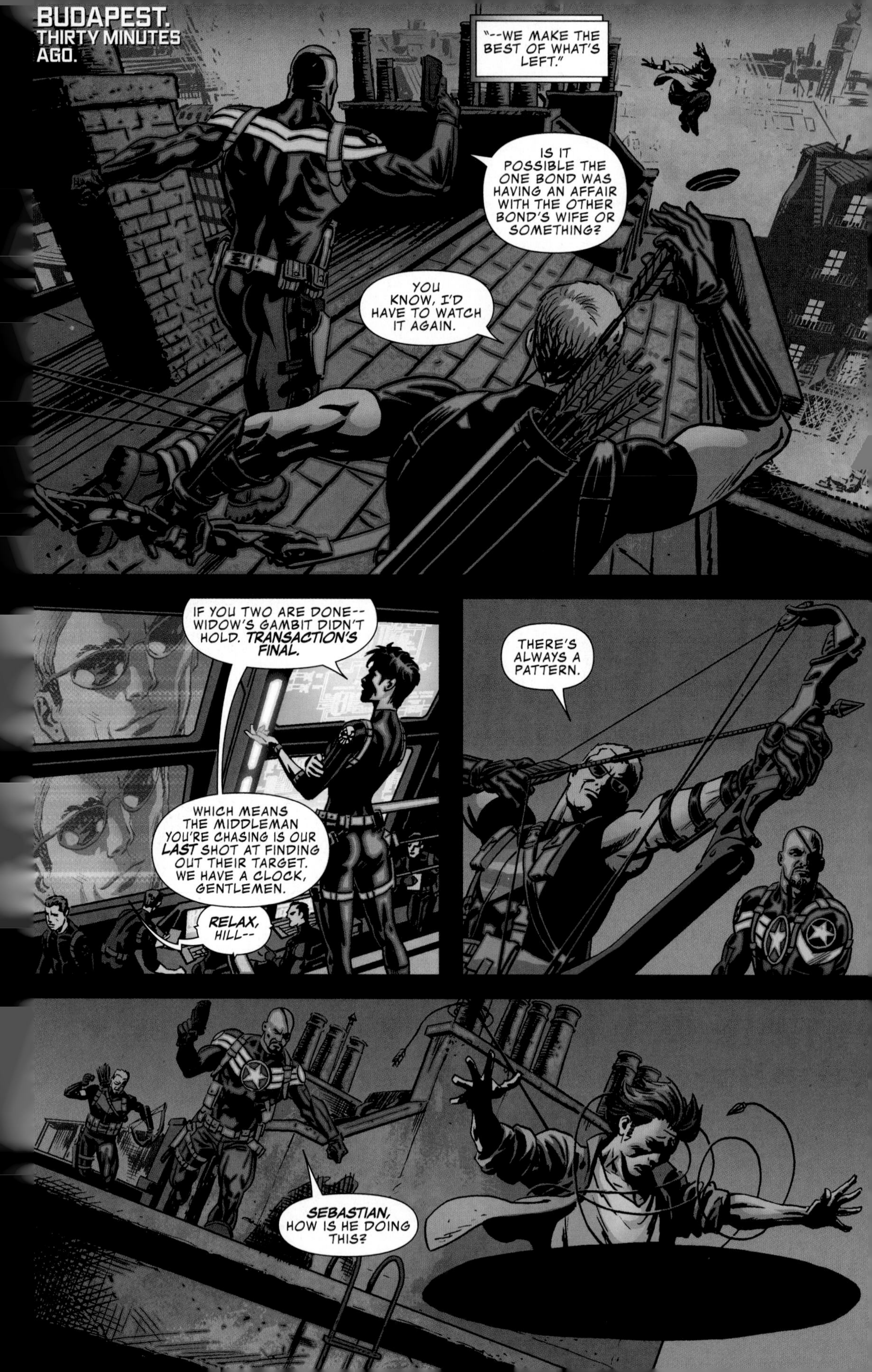
BUDAPEST. THIRTY MINUTES AGO.
"--WE MAKE THE BEST OF WHAT'S LEFT."
IS IT POSSIBLE THE ONE BOND WAS HAVING AN AFFAIR WITH THE OTHER BOND'S WIFE OR SOMETHING?
YOU KNOW, I'D HAVE TO WATCH IT AGAIN.
IF YOU TWO ARE DONE--WIDOW'S GAMBIT DIDN'T HOLD. TRANSACTION'S FINAL.
WHICH MEANS THE MIDDLEMAN YOU'RE CHASING IS OUR LAST SHOT AT FINDING OUT THEIR TARGET. WE HAVE A CLOCK, GENTLEMEN.
RELAX, HILL--
THERE'S ALWAYS A PATTERN.
SEBASTIAN, HOW IS HE DOING THIS?

YOU WANT ME TO EXPLAIN TO YOU HOW HE SUMMONS THE POWER OF A FEAR LORD IN ORDER TO TELEPORT, OVER COMMS, IN THIRTY SECONDS?

NO, HOW IS HE DOING IT?

AH, RIGHT-- WITH HIS HANDS.

PERFECT. NOW--

SNAp

AGGH!

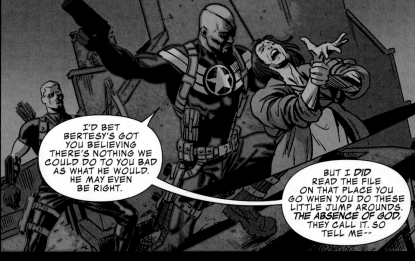

I'D BET BERTESY'S GOT YOU BELIEVING THERE'S NOTHING WE COULD DO TO YOU BAD AS WHAT HE WOULD. HE MAY EVEN BE RIGHT.

BUT I DID READ THE FILE ON THAT PLACE YOU GO WHEN YOU DO THESE LITTLE JUMP AROUNDS. THE ABSENCE OF GOD, THEY CALL IT. SO TELL ME--

YOU THINK YOU'D MAKE IT IN THERE 'TIL YOUR FINGERS HEALED?

COORDINATES.

SH-SHIRT POCKET...

THERE WE GO, SEE? MAKING GOOD DECISIONS, SETTING THINGS RIGHT--

THAT'S HOW WE TURN OUR LIVES AROUND.

BLAM

HEY!

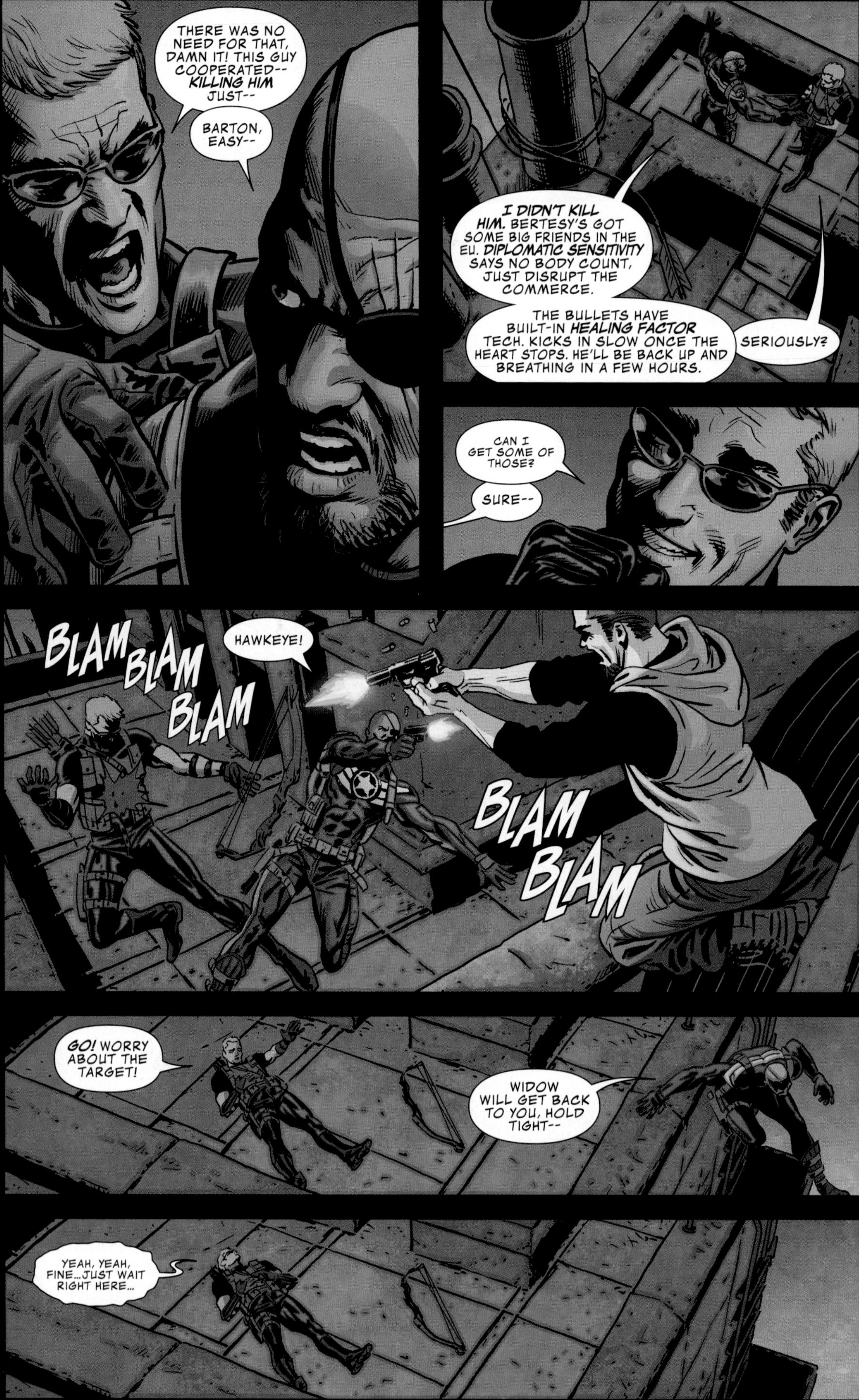
THERE WAS NO NEED FOR THAT, DAMN IT! THIS GUY COOPERATED-- KILLING HIM JUST--
BARTON, EASY--
I DIDN'T KILL HIM. BERTESY'S GOT SOME BIG FRIENDS IN THE EU. DIPLOMATIC SENSITIVITY SAYS NO BODY COUNT, JUST DISRUPT THE COMMERCE.
THE BULLETS HAVE BUILT-IN HEALING FACTOR TECH. KICKS IN SLOW ONCE THE HEART STOPS. HE'LL BE BACK UP AND BREATHING IN A FEW HOURS.
SERIOUSLY?
CAN I GET SOME OF THOSE?
SURE--
BLAM BLAM BLAM
HAWKEYE!
BLAM BLAM
GO! WORRY ABOUT THE TARGET!
WIDOW WILL GET BACK TO YOU, HOLD TIGHT--
YEAH, YEAH, FINE...JUST WAIT RIGHT HERE...

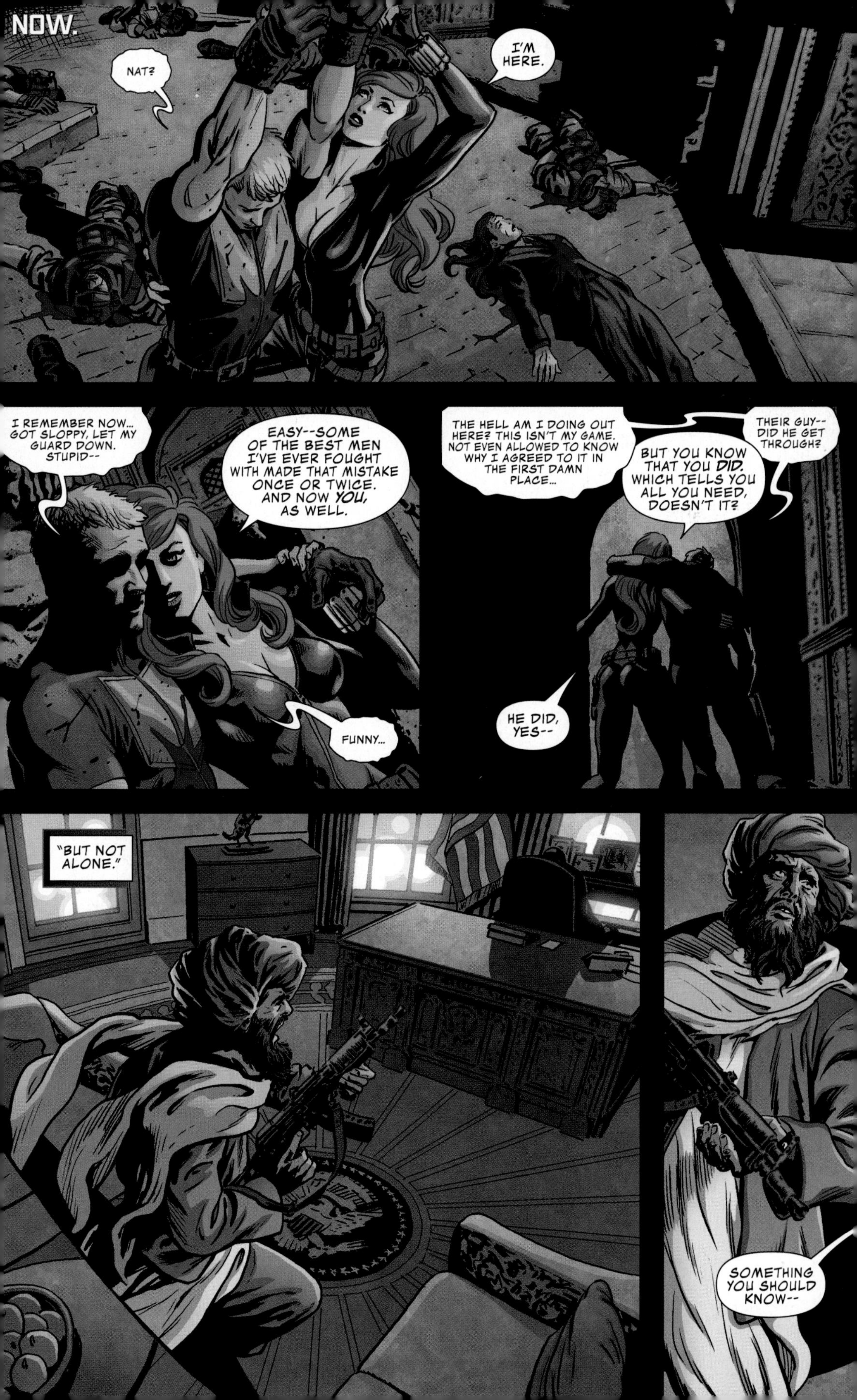
NOW.
NAT?
I'M HERE.
I REMEMBER NOW... GOT SLOPPY, LET MY GUARD DOWN. STUPID--
EASY--SOME OF THE BEST MEN I'VE EVER FOUGHT WITH MADE THAT MISTAKE ONCE OR TWICE. AND NOW YOU, AS WELL.
FUNNY...
THE HELL AM I DOING OUT HERE? THIS ISN'T MY GAME. NOT EVEN ALLOWED TO KNOW WHY I AGREED TO IT IN THE FIRST DAMN PLACE...
BUT YOU KNOW THAT YOU DID. WHICH TELLS YOU ALL YOU NEED, DOESN'T IT?
THEIR GUY-- DID HE GET THROUGH?
HE DID, YES--
"BUT NOT ALONE."
SOMETHING YOU SHOULD KNOW--

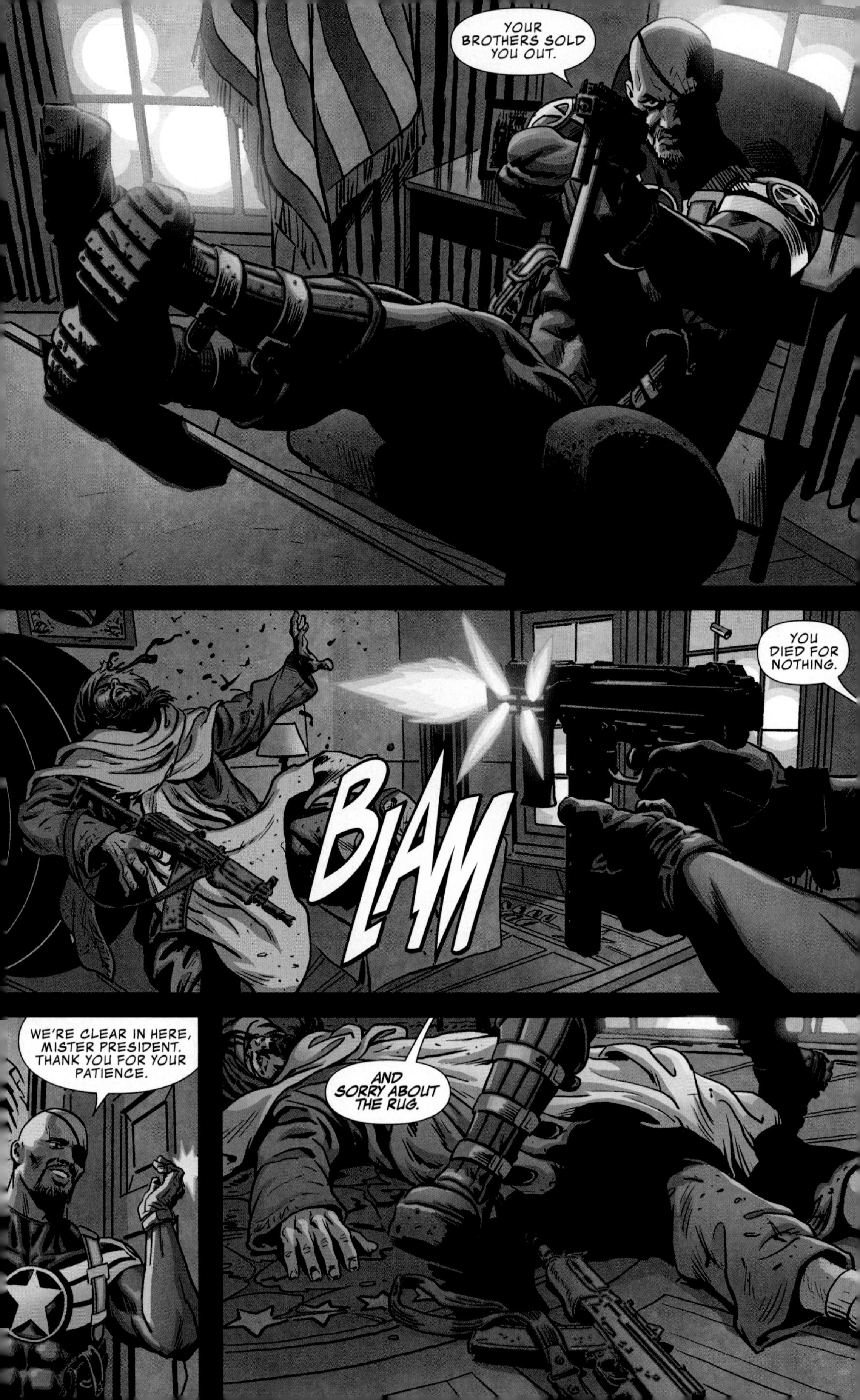
YOUR BROTHERS SOLD YOU OUT.
YOU DIED FOR NOTHING.
BLAM
WE'RE CLEAR IN HERE, MISTER PRESIDENT. THANK YOU FOR YOUR PATIENCE.
AND SORRY ABOUT THE RUG.

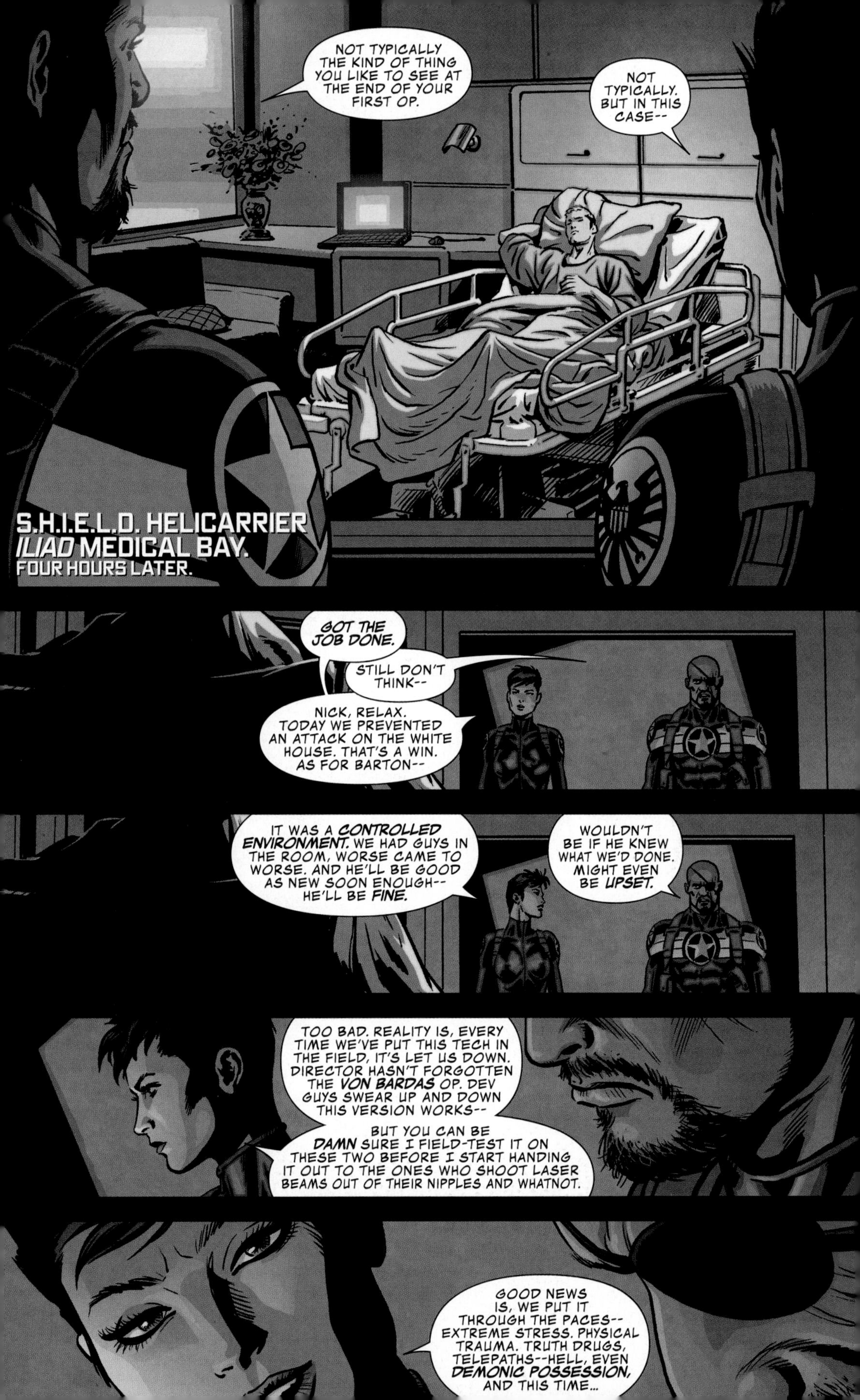

NOT TYPICALLY THE KIND OF THING YOU LIKE TO SEE AT THE END OF YOUR FIRST OP.
NOT TYPICALLY. BUT IN THIS CASE--
S.H.I.E.L.D. HELICARRIER ILIAD MEDICAL BAY. FOUR HOURS LATER.
GOT THE JOB DONE.
STILL DON'T THINK--
NICK, RELAX. TODAY WE PREVENTED AN ATTACK ON THE WHITE HOUSE. THAT'S A WIN. AS FOR BARTON--
IT WAS A CONTROLLED ENVIRONMENT. WE HAD GUYS IN THE ROOM, WORSE CAME TO WORSE. AND HE'LL BE GOOD AS NEW SOON ENOUGH-- HE'LL BE FINE.
WOULDN'T BE IF HE KNEW WHAT WE'D DONE. MIGHT EVEN BE UPSET.
TOO BAD. REALITY IS, EVERY TIME WE'VE PUT THIS TECH IN THE FIELD, IT'S LET US DOWN. DIRECTOR HASN'T FORGOTTEN THE VON BARDAS OP. DEV GUYS SWEAR UP AND DOWN THIS VERSION WORKS--
BUT YOU CAN BE DAMN SURE I FIELD-TEST IT ON THESE TWO BEFORE I START HANDING IT OUT TO THE ONES WHO SHOOT LASER BEAMS OUT OF THEIR NIPPLES AND WHATNOT.
GOOD NEWS IS, WE PUT IT THROUGH THE PACES-- EXTREME STRESS. PHYSICAL TRAUMA. TRUTH DRUGS, TELEPATHS--HELL, EVEN DEMONIC POSSESSION, AND THIS TIME...

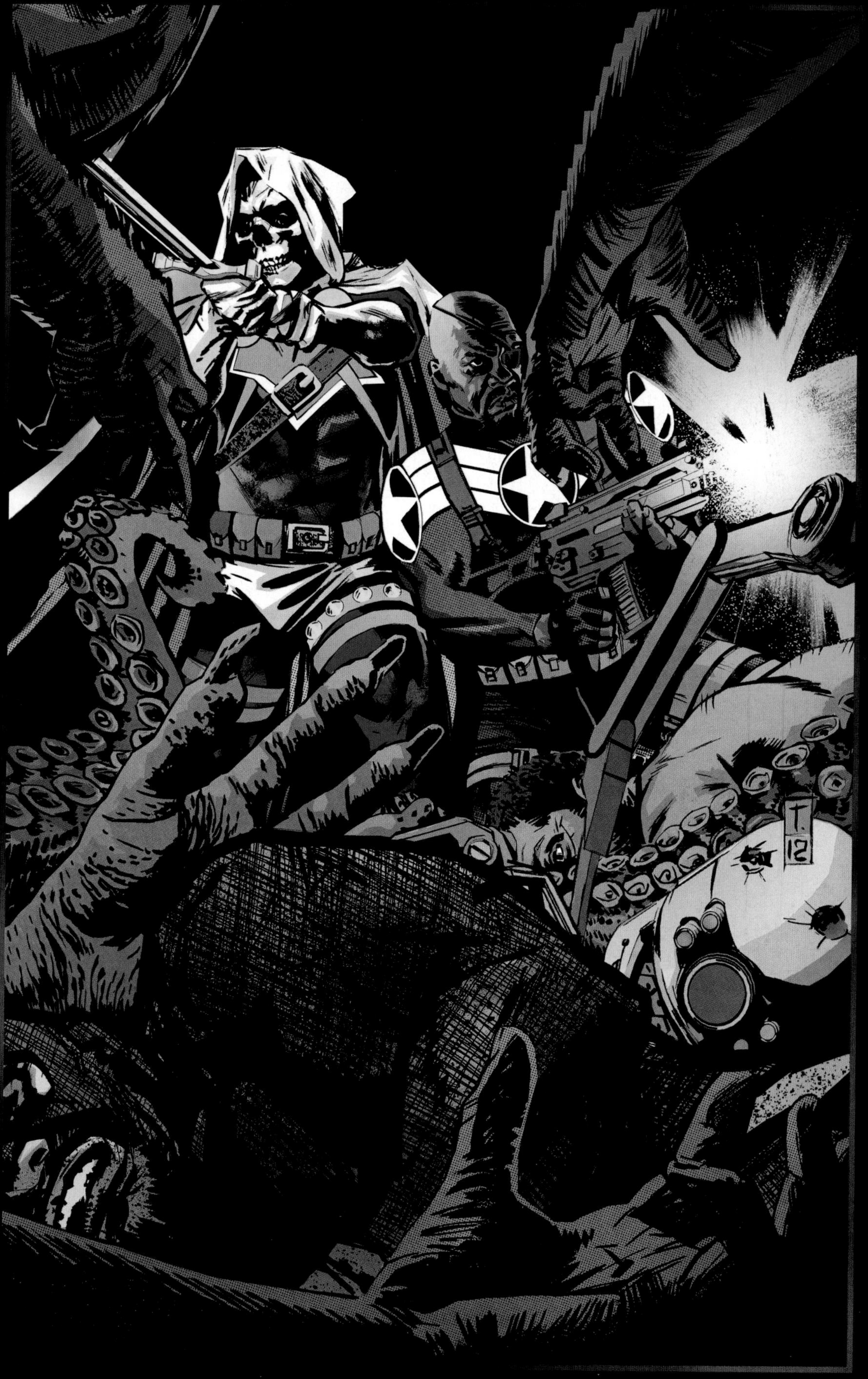
T.
12

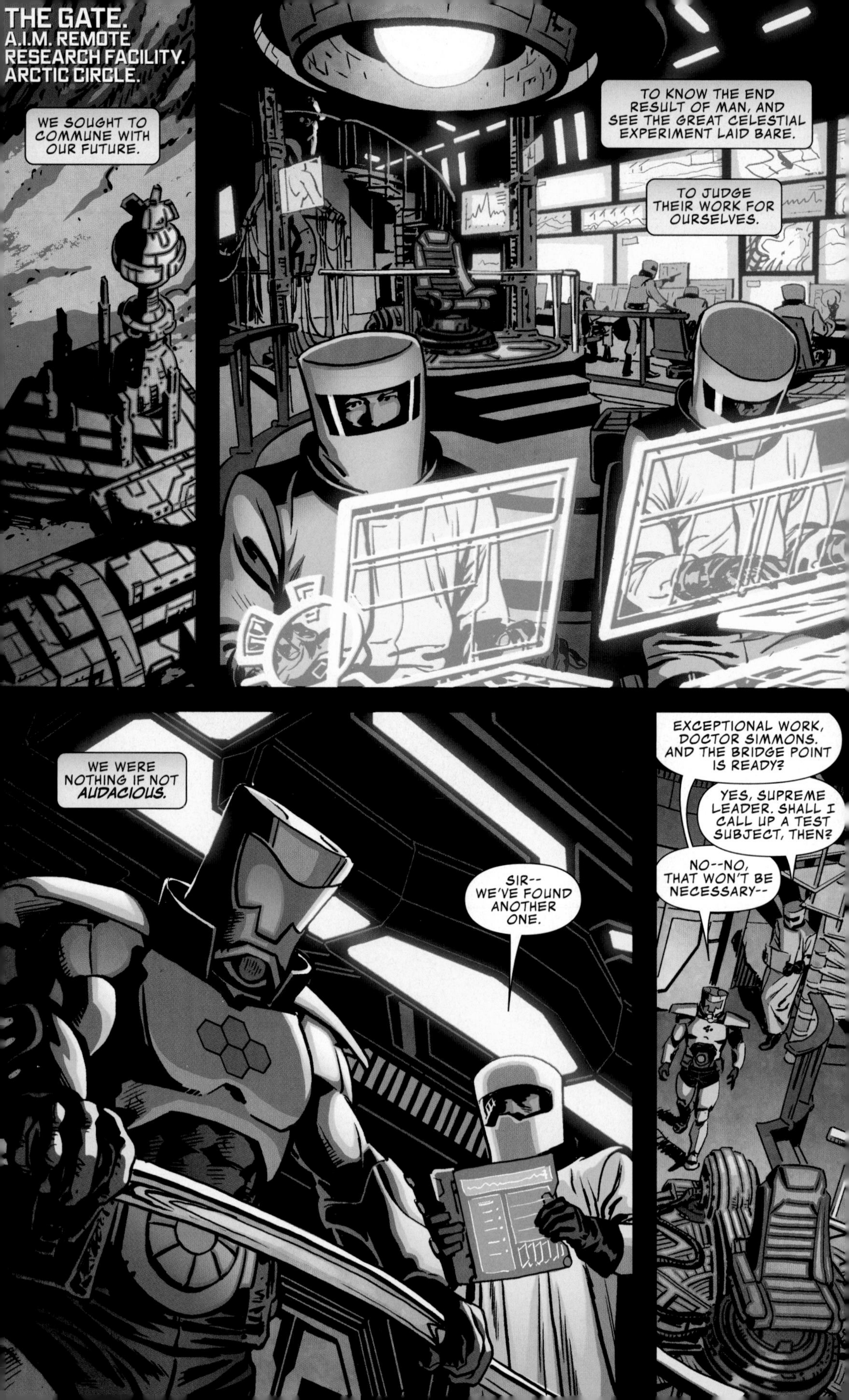
THE GATE.
A.I.M. REMOTE RESEARCH FACILITY.
ARCTIC CIRCLE.
WE SOUGHT TO COMMUNE WITH OUR FUTURE.
TO KNOW THE END RESULT OF MAN, AND SEE THE GREAT CELESTIAL EXPERIMENT LAID BARE.
TO JUDGE THEIR WORK FOR OURSELVES.
WE WERE NOTHING IF NOT *AUDACIOUS.*
SIR-- WE'VE FOUND ANOTHER ONE.
EXCEPTIONAL WORK, DOCTOR SIMMONS. AND THE BRIDGE POINT IS READY?
YES, SUPREME LEADER. SHALL I CALL UP A TEST SUBJECT, THEN?
NO--NO, THAT WON'T BE NECESSARY--

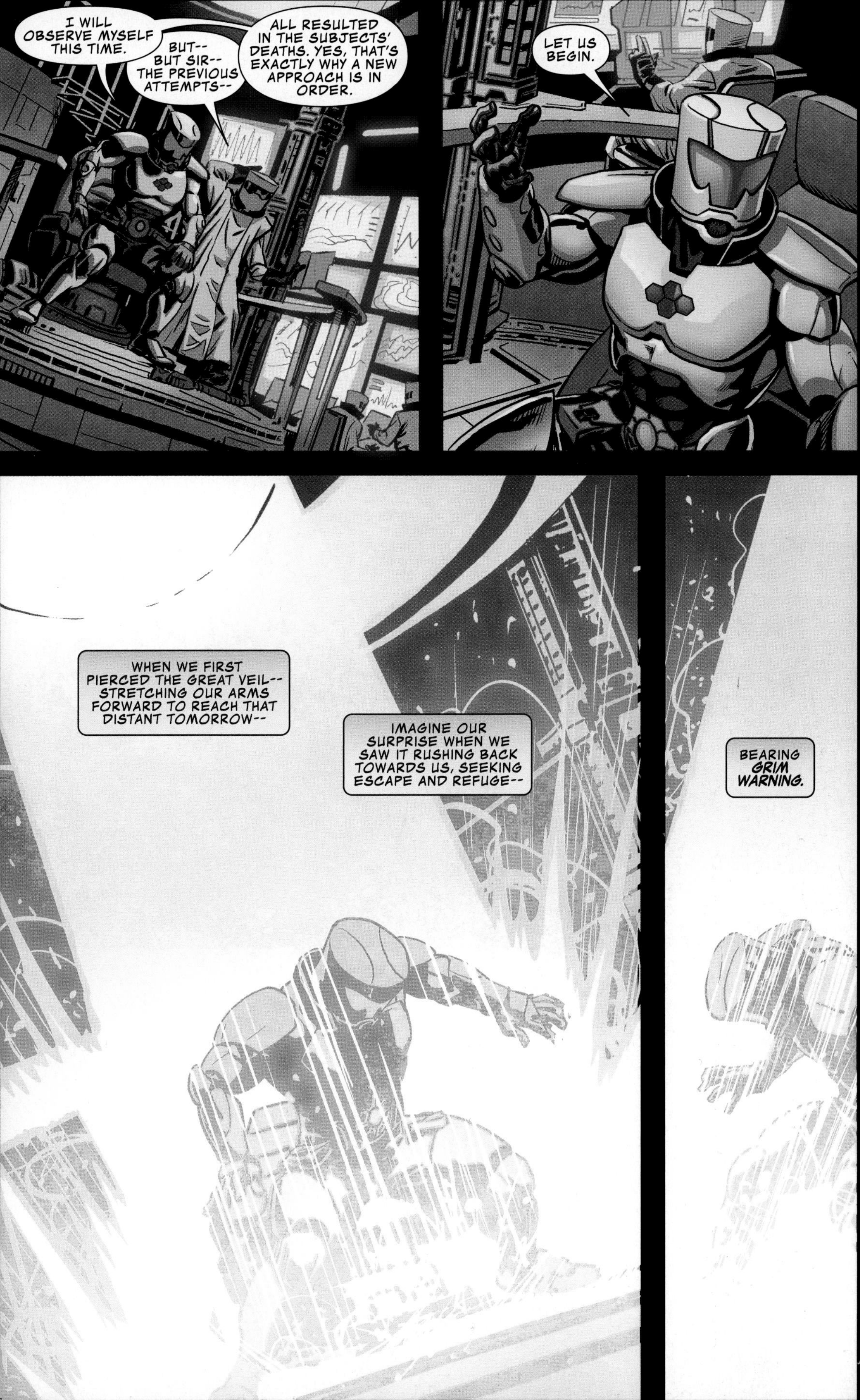

I WILL OBSERVE MYSELF THIS TIME.
BUT-- BUT SIR-- THE PREVIOUS ATTEMPTS--
ALL RESULTED IN THE SUBJECTS' DEATHS. YES, THAT'S EXACTLY WHY A NEW APPROACH IS IN ORDER.
LET US BEGIN.
WHEN WE FIRST PIERCED THE GREAT VEIL--STRETCHING OUR ARMS FORWARD TO REACH THAT DISTANT TOMORROW--
IMAGINE OUR SURPRISE WHEN WE SAW IT RUSHING BACK TOWARDS US, SEEKING ESCAPE AND REFUGE--
BEARING GRIM WARNING.

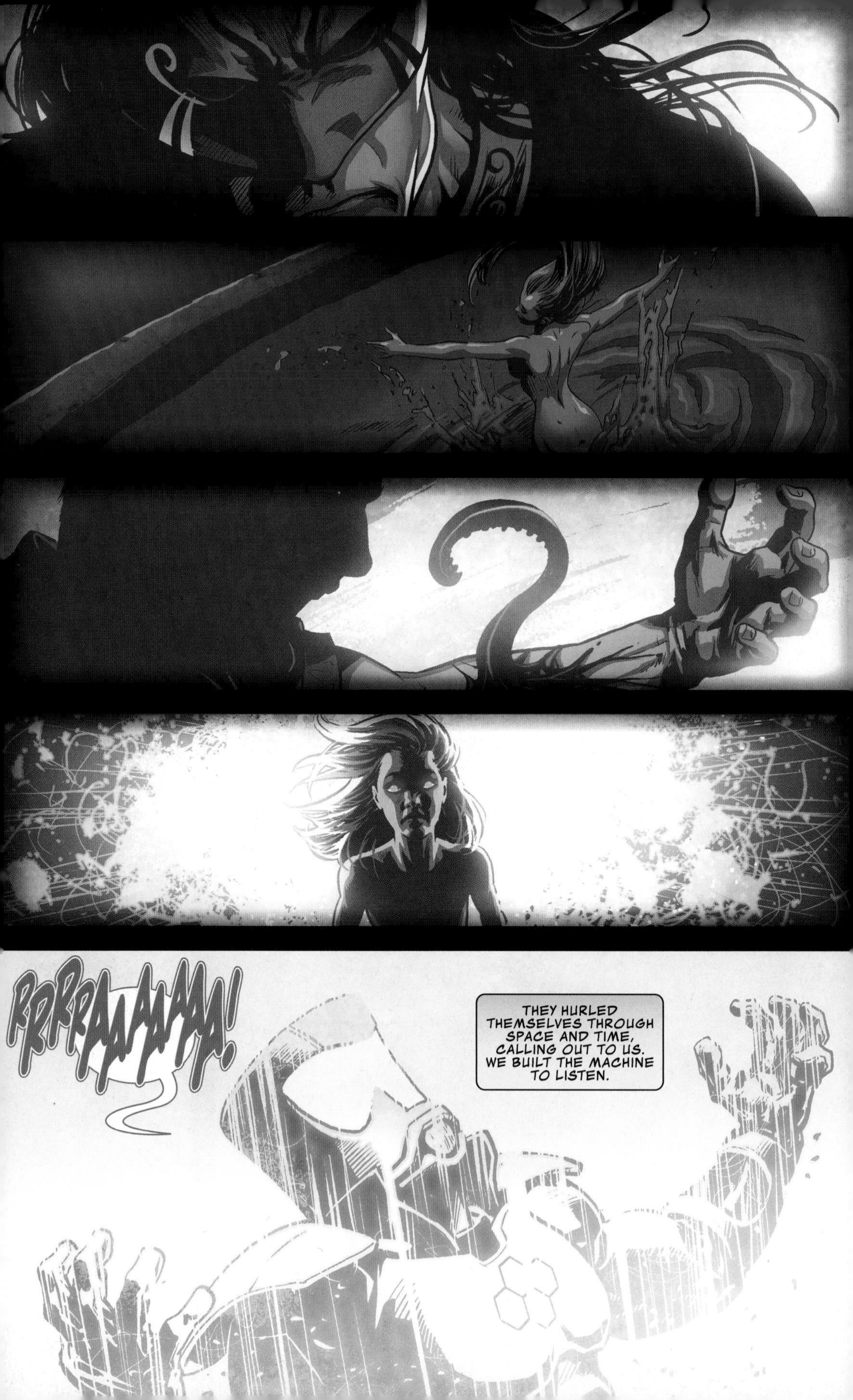
RRRRAAAAAAA!
THEY HURLED THEMSELVES THROUGH SPACE AND TIME, CALLING OUT TO US. WE BUILT THE MACHINE TO LISTEN.

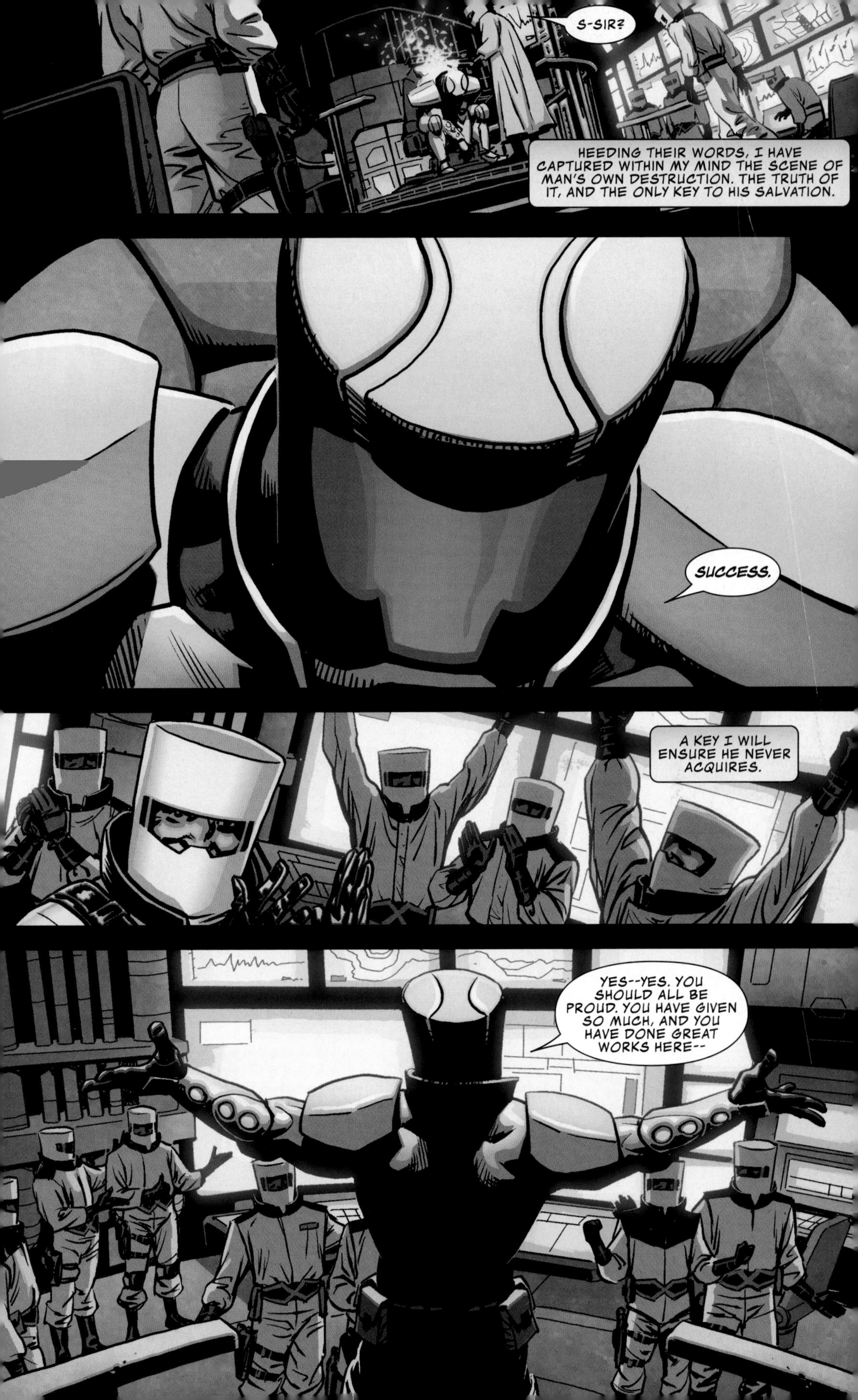
S-SIR?
HEEDING THEIR WORDS, I HAVE CAPTURED WITHIN MY MIND THE SCENE OF MAN'S OWN DESTRUCTION. THE TRUTH OF IT, AND THE ONLY KEY TO HIS SALVATION.
SUCCESS.
A KEY I WILL ENSURE HE NEVER ACQUIRES.
YES--YES. YOU SHOULD ALL BE PROUD. YOU HAVE GIVEN SO MUCH, AND YOU HAVE DONE GREAT WORKS HERE--

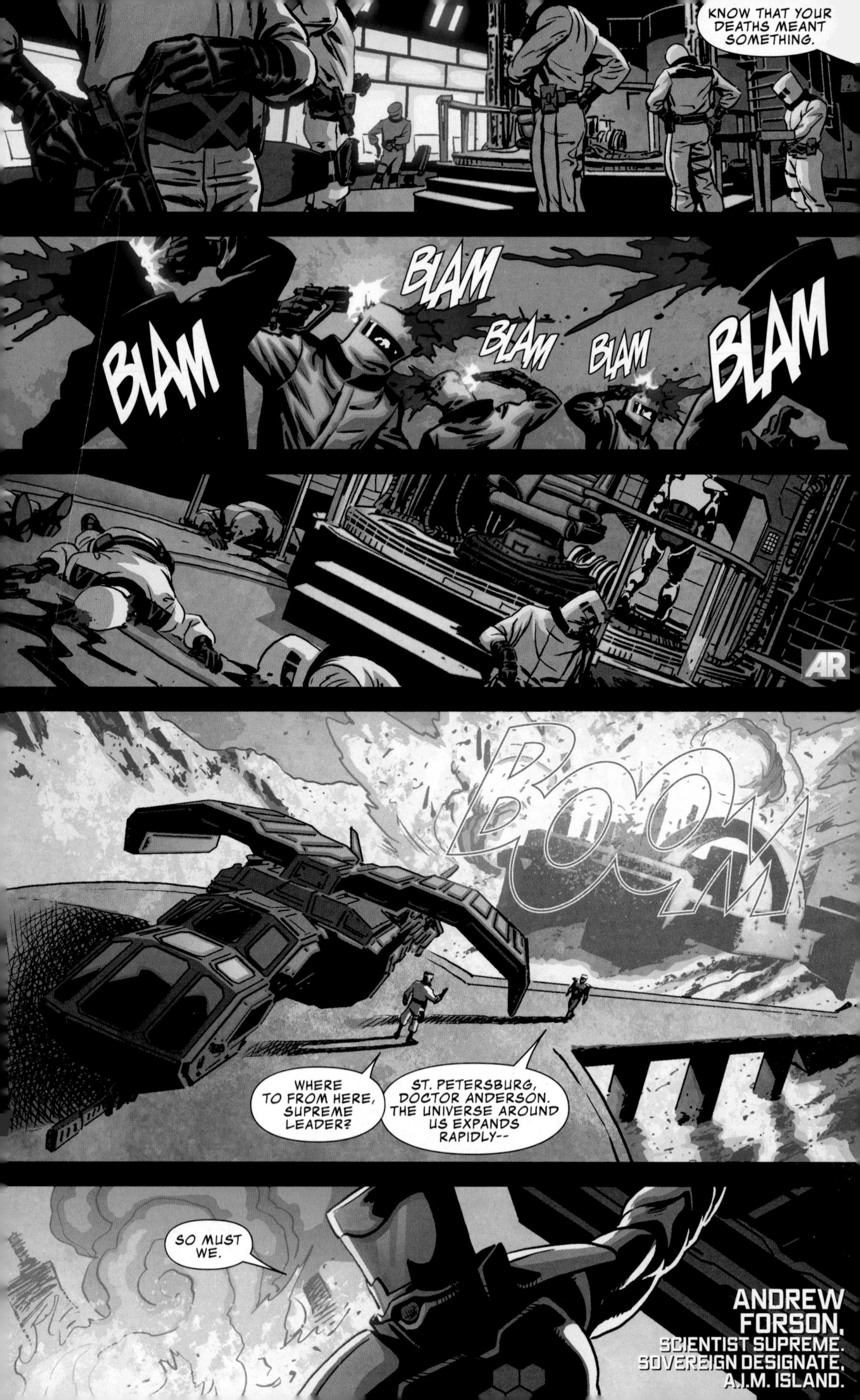
KNOW THAT YOUR DEATHS MEANT SOMETHING.
BLAM
BLAM
BLAM
BLAM
BLAM
AR
BOOM
WHERE TO FROM HERE, SUPREME LEADER?
ST. PETERSBURG, DOCTOR ANDERSON. THE UNIVERSE AROUND US EXPANDS RAPIDLY--
SO MUST WE.
ANDREW FORSON,
SCIENTIST SUPREME.
SOVEREIGN DESIGNATE,
A.I.M. ISLAND.

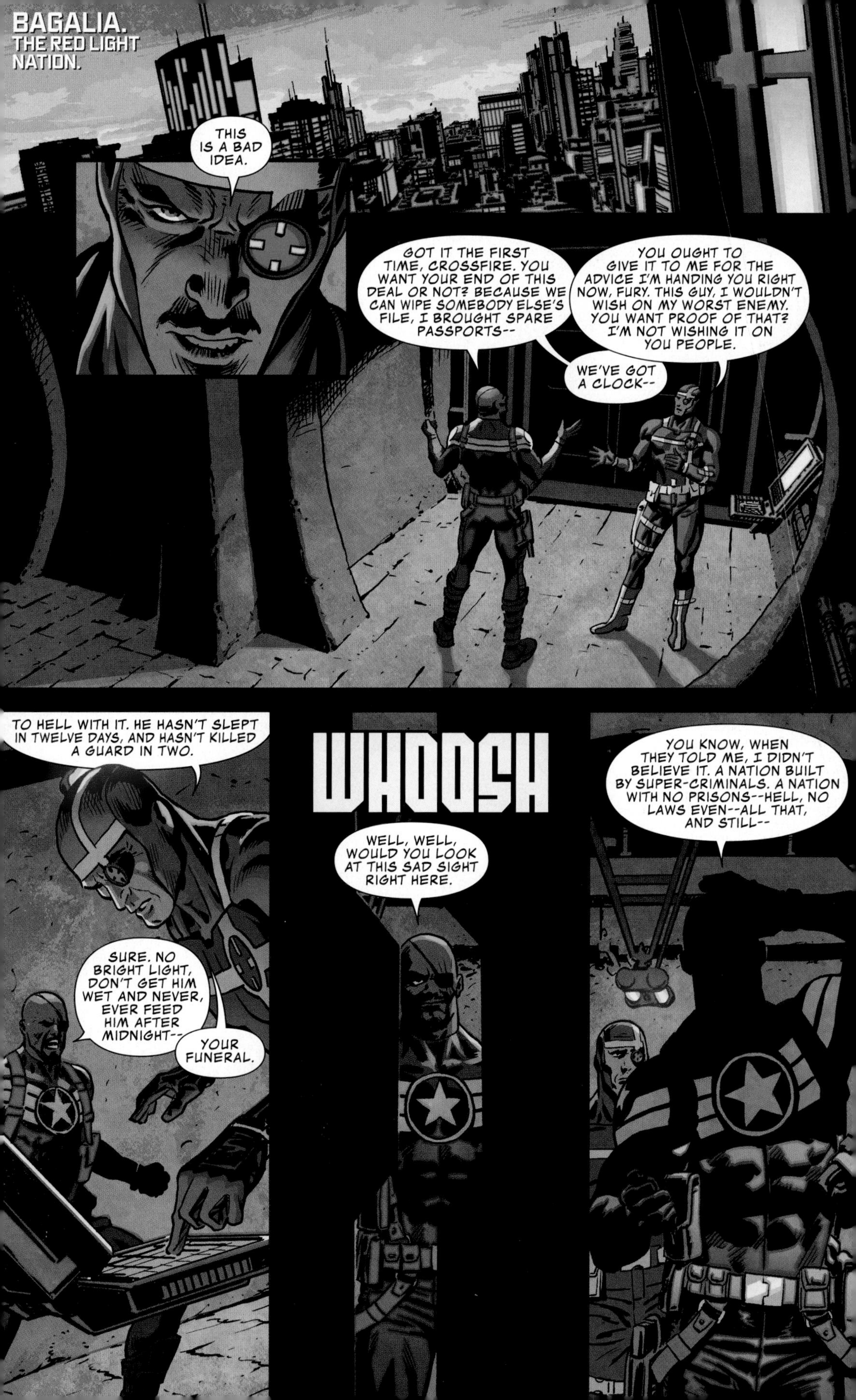
BAGALIA. THE RED LIGHT NATION.
THIS IS A BAD IDEA.
GOT IT THE FIRST TIME, CROSSFIRE. YOU WANT YOUR END OF THIS DEAL OR NOT? BECAUSE WE CAN WIPE SOMEBODY ELSE'S FILE, I BROUGHT SPARE PASSPORTS--
WE'VE GOT A CLOCK--
YOU OUGHT TO GIVE IT TO ME FOR THE ADVICE I'M HANDING YOU RIGHT NOW, FURY. THIS GUY, I WOULDN'T WISH ON MY WORST ENEMY. YOU WANT PROOF OF THAT? I'M NOT WISHING IT ON YOU PEOPLE.
TO HELL WITH IT. HE HASN'T SLEPT IN TWELVE DAYS, AND HASN'T KILLED A GUARD IN TWO.
SURE. NO BRIGHT LIGHT, DON'T GET HIM WET AND NEVER, EVER FEED HIM AFTER MIDNIGHT--
YOUR FUNERAL.
WHOOSH
WELL, WELL, WOULD YOU LOOK AT THIS SAD SIGHT RIGHT HERE.
YOU KNOW, WHEN THEY TOLD ME, I DIDN'T BELIEVE IT. A NATION BUILT BY SUPER-CRIMINALS. A NATION WITH NO PRISONS--HELL, NO LAWS EVEN--ALL THAT, AND STILL--

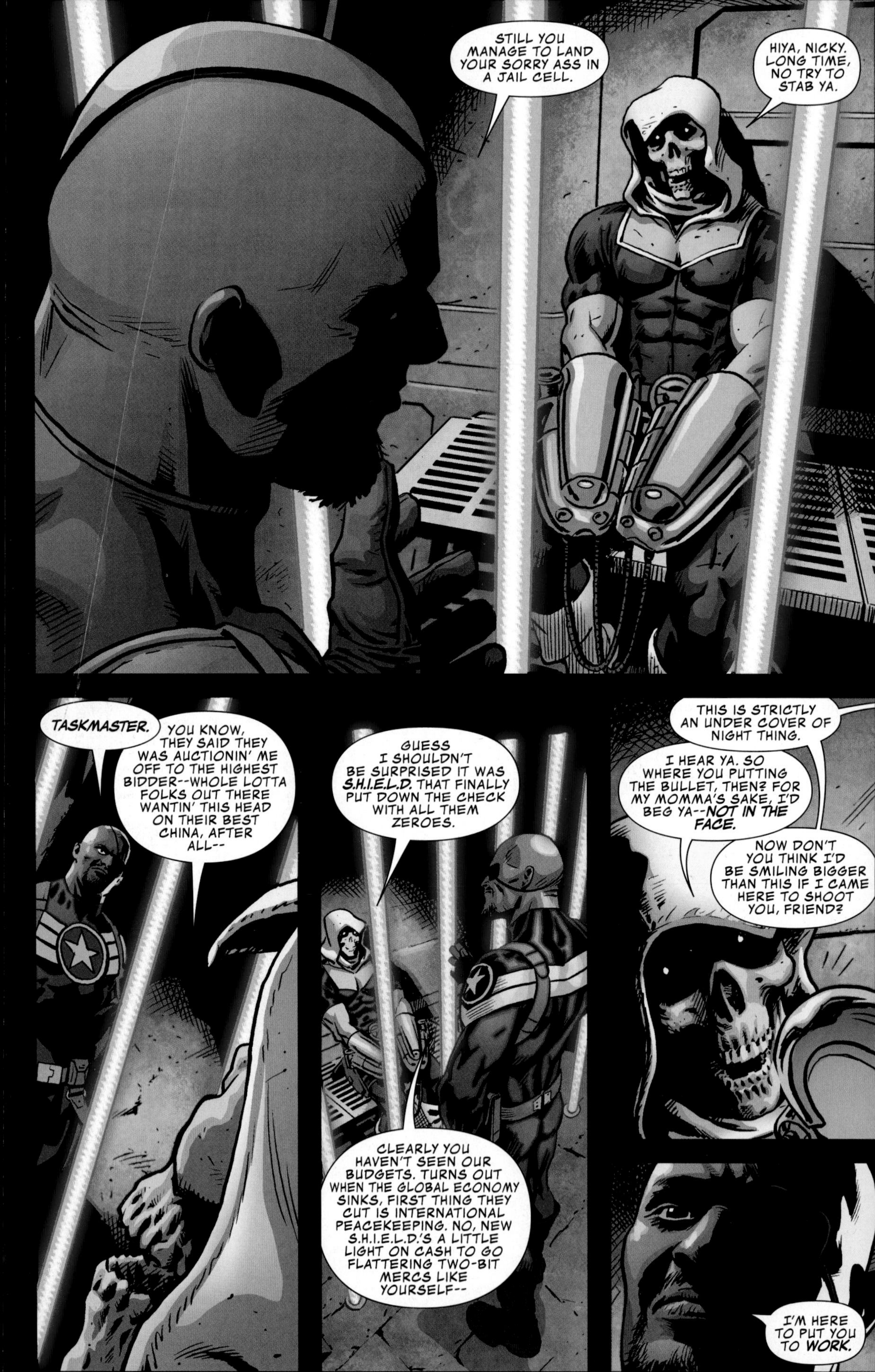
STILL YOU MANAGE TO LAND YOUR SORRY ASS IN A JAIL CELL.
HIYA, NICKY. LONG TIME, NO TRY TO STAB YA.
TASKMASTER.
YOU KNOW, THEY SAID THEY WAS AUCTIONIN' ME OFF TO THE HIGHEST BIDDER--WHOLE LOTTA FOLKS OUT THERE WANTIN' THIS HEAD ON THEIR BEST CHINA, AFTER ALL--
GUESS I SHOULDN'T BE SURPRISED IT WAS S.H.I.E.L.D. THAT FINALLY PUT DOWN THE CHECK WITH ALL THEM ZEROES.
CLEARLY YOU HAVEN'T SEEN OUR BUDGETS. TURNS OUT WHEN THE GLOBAL ECONOMY SINKS, FIRST THING THEY CUT IS INTERNATIONAL PEACEKEEPING. NO, NEW S.H.I.E.L.D.'S A LITTLE LIGHT ON CASH TO GO FLATTERING TWO-BIT MERCS LIKE YOURSELF--
THIS IS STRICTLY AN UNDER COVER OF NIGHT THING.
I HEAR YA. SO WHERE YOU PUTTING THE BULLET, THEN? FOR MY MOMMA'S SAKE, I'D BEG YA--NOT IN THE FACE.
NOW DON'T YOU THINK I'D BE SMILING BIGGER THAN THIS IF I CAME HERE TO SHOOT YOU, FRIEND?
I'M HERE TO PUT YOU TO WORK.

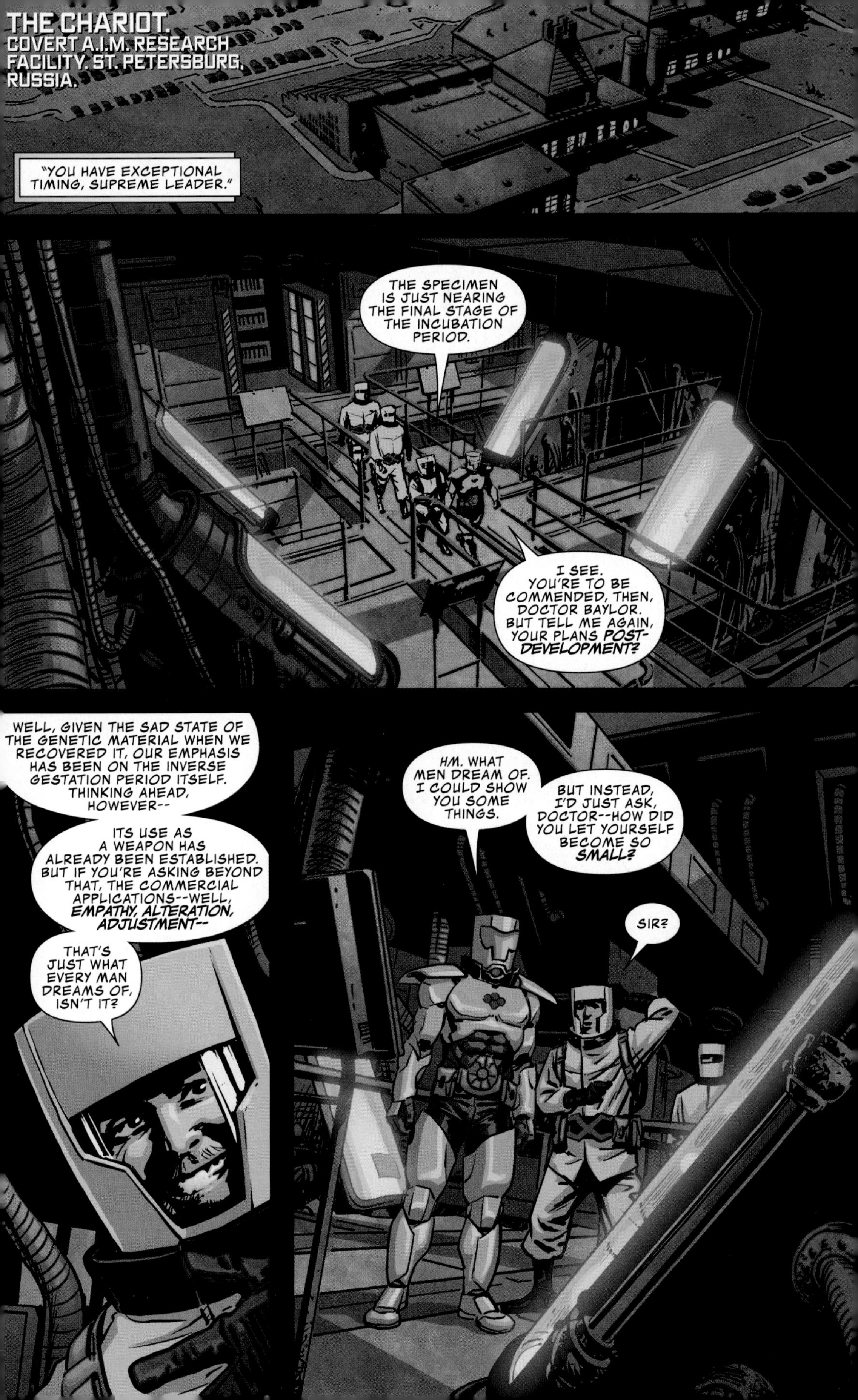
THE CHARIOT.
COVERT A.I.M. RESEARCH FACILITY. ST. PETERSBURG, RUSSIA.
"YOU HAVE EXCEPTIONAL TIMING, SUPREME LEADER."
THE SPECIMEN IS JUST NEARING THE FINAL STAGE OF THE INCUBATION PERIOD.
I SEE. YOU'RE TO BE COMMENDED, THEN, DOCTOR BAYLOR. BUT TELL ME AGAIN, YOUR PLANS POST-DEVELOPMENT?
WELL, GIVEN THE SAD STATE OF THE GENETIC MATERIAL WHEN WE RECOVERED IT, OUR EMPHASIS HAS BEEN ON THE INVERSE GESTATION PERIOD ITSELF. THINKING AHEAD, HOWEVER--
ITS USE AS A WEAPON HAS ALREADY BEEN ESTABLISHED. BUT IF YOU'RE ASKING BEYOND THAT, THE COMMERCIAL APPLICATIONS--WELL, EMPATHY, ALTERATION, ADJUSTMENT--
THAT'S JUST WHAT EVERY MAN DREAMS OF, ISN'T IT?
HM. WHAT MEN DREAM OF. I COULD SHOW YOU SOME THINGS.
BUT INSTEAD, I'D JUST ASK, DOCTOR--HOW DID YOU LET YOURSELF BECOME SO SMALL?
SIR?

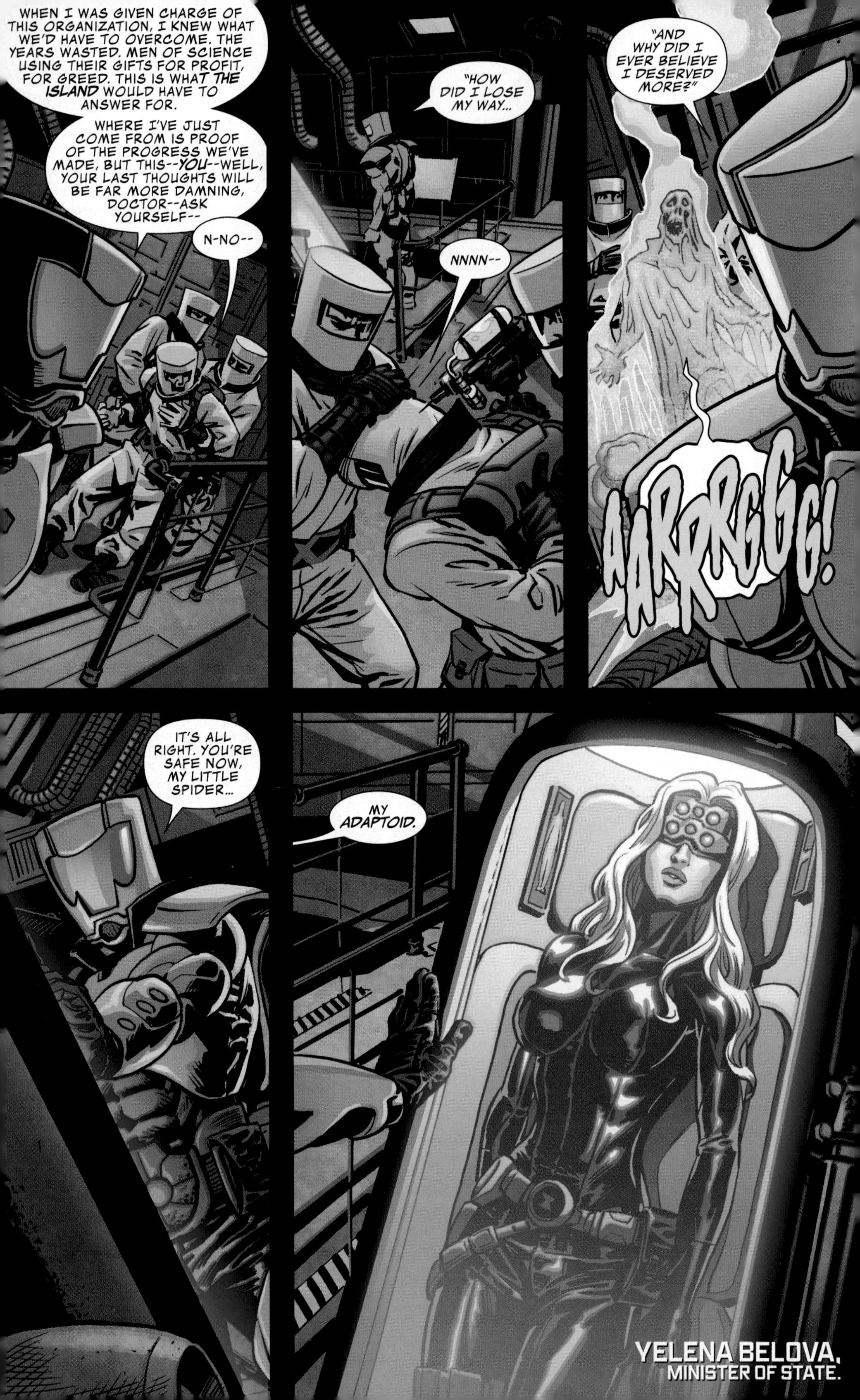
WHEN I WAS GIVEN CHARGE OF THIS ORGANIZATION, I KNEW WHAT WE'D HAVE TO OVERCOME. THE YEARS WASTED. MEN OF SCIENCE USING THEIR GIFTS FOR PROFIT, FOR GREED. THIS IS WHAT THE ISLAND WOULD HAVE TO ANSWER FOR.
WHERE I'VE JUST COME FROM IS PROOF OF THE PROGRESS WE'VE MADE, BUT THIS--YOU--WELL, YOUR LAST THOUGHTS WILL BE FAR MORE DAMNING, DOCTOR--ASK YOURSELF--
N-NO--
"HOW DID I LOSE MY WAY...
NNNN--
"AND WHY DID I EVER BELIEVE I DESERVED MORE?"
AARRRGGG!
IT'S ALL RIGHT. YOU'RE SAFE NOW, MY LITTLE SPIDER...
MY ADAPTOID.
YELENA BELOVA,
MINISTER OF STATE.

WHEN THE CALL RANG OUT, SOME CAME FOR GLORY.

MENTALLO, MINISTER OF PUBLIC AFFAIRS.

OTHERS IN HOPE OF LONG SOUGHT TREASURE.

SUPERIA, MINISTER OF EDUCATION.

SOME CAME FOR THE WORK ITSELF--

GRAVITON, MINISTER OF SCIENCE.

AND OTHERS FOR ITS ENDS.

JUDE THE ENTROPIC MAN, MINISTER OF HEALTH.

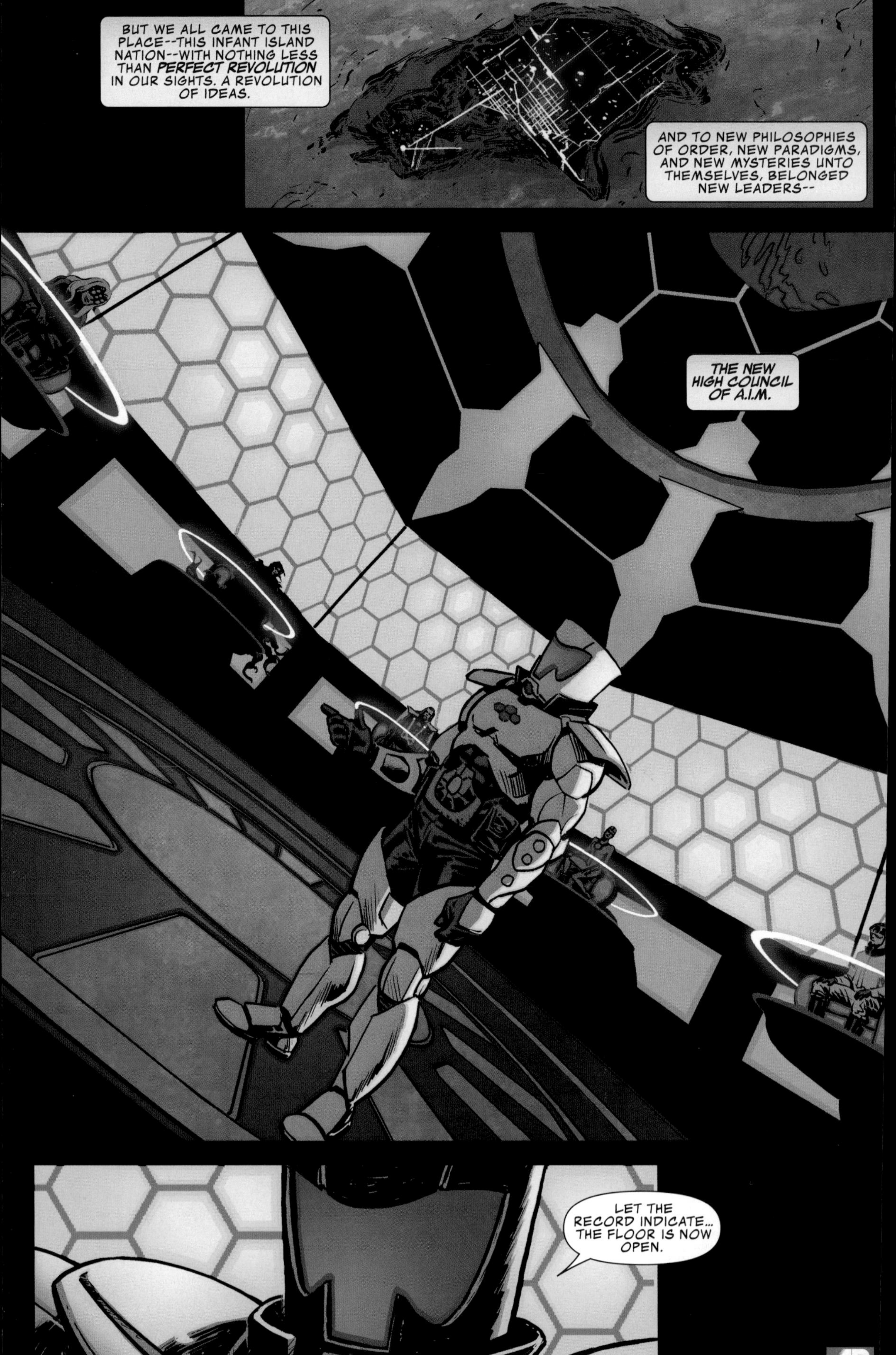
BUT WE ALL CAME TO THIS PLACE--THIS INFANT ISLAND NATION--WITH NOTHING LESS THAN PERFECT REVOLUTION IN OUR SIGHTS. A REVOLUTION OF IDEAS.
AND TO NEW PHILOSOPHIES OF ORDER, NEW PARADIGMS, AND NEW MYSTERIES UNTO THEMSELVES, BELONGED NEW LEADERS--
THE NEW HIGH COUNCIL OF A.I.M.
LET THE RECORD INDICATE... THE FLOOR IS NOW OPEN.

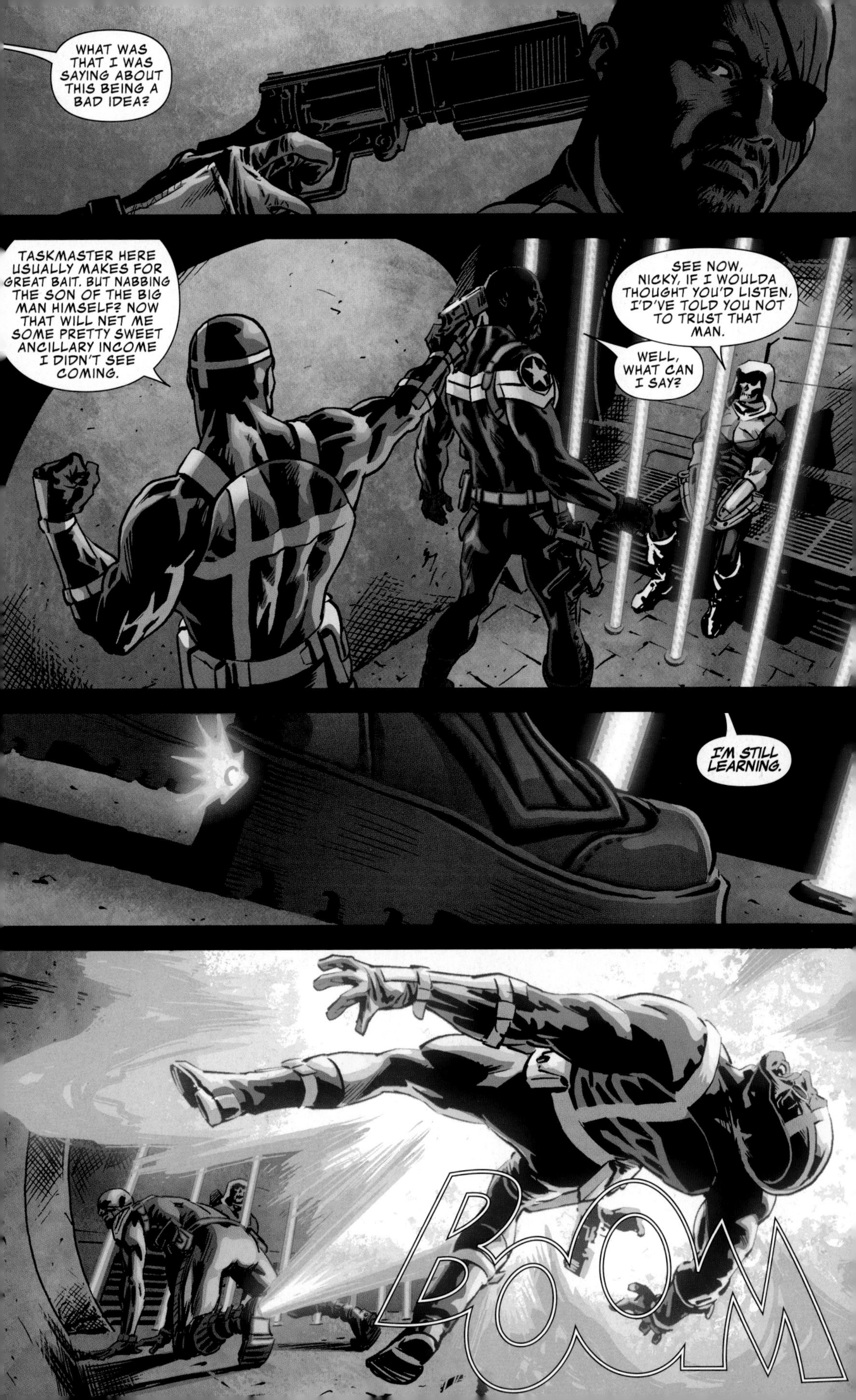
WHAT WAS THAT I WAS SAYING ABOUT THIS BEING A BAD IDEA?
TASKMASTER HERE USUALLY MAKES FOR GREAT BAIT. BUT NABBING THE SON OF THE BIG MAN HIMSELF? NOW THAT WILL NET ME SOME PRETTY SWEET ANCILLARY INCOME I DIDN'T SEE COMING.
SEE NOW, NICKY, IF I WOULDA THOUGHT YOU'D LISTEN, I'D'VE TOLD YOU NOT TO TRUST THAT MAN.
WELL, WHAT CAN I SAY?
I'M STILL LEARNING.
BOOM

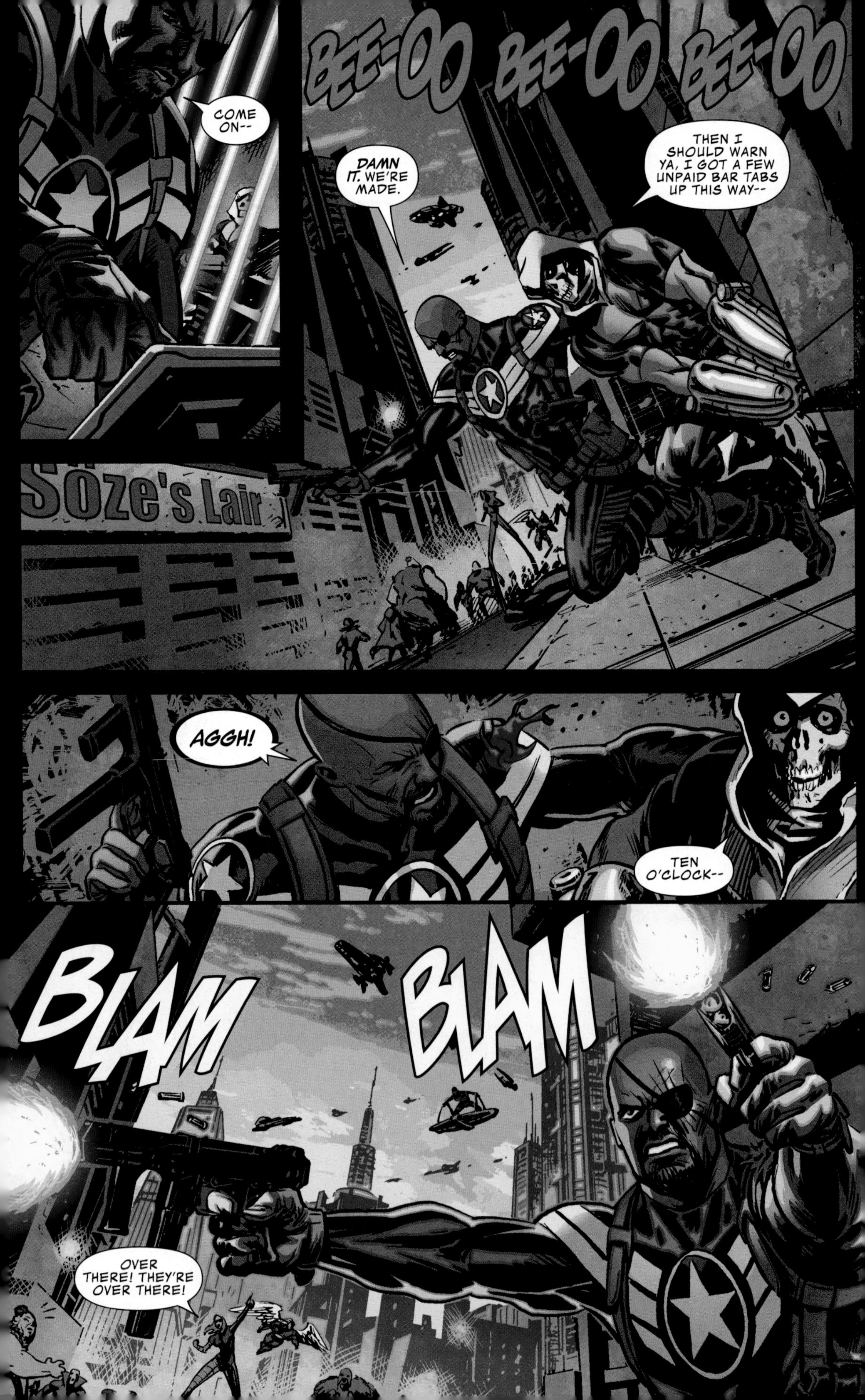
COME ON--
BEE-OO BEE-OO BEE-OO
DAMN IT. WE'RE MADE.
THEN I SHOULD WARN YA, I GOT A FEW UNPAID BAR TABS UP THIS WAY--
Söze's Lair
AGGH!
TEN O'CLOCK--
BLAM BLAM
OVER THERE! THEY'RE OVER THERE!

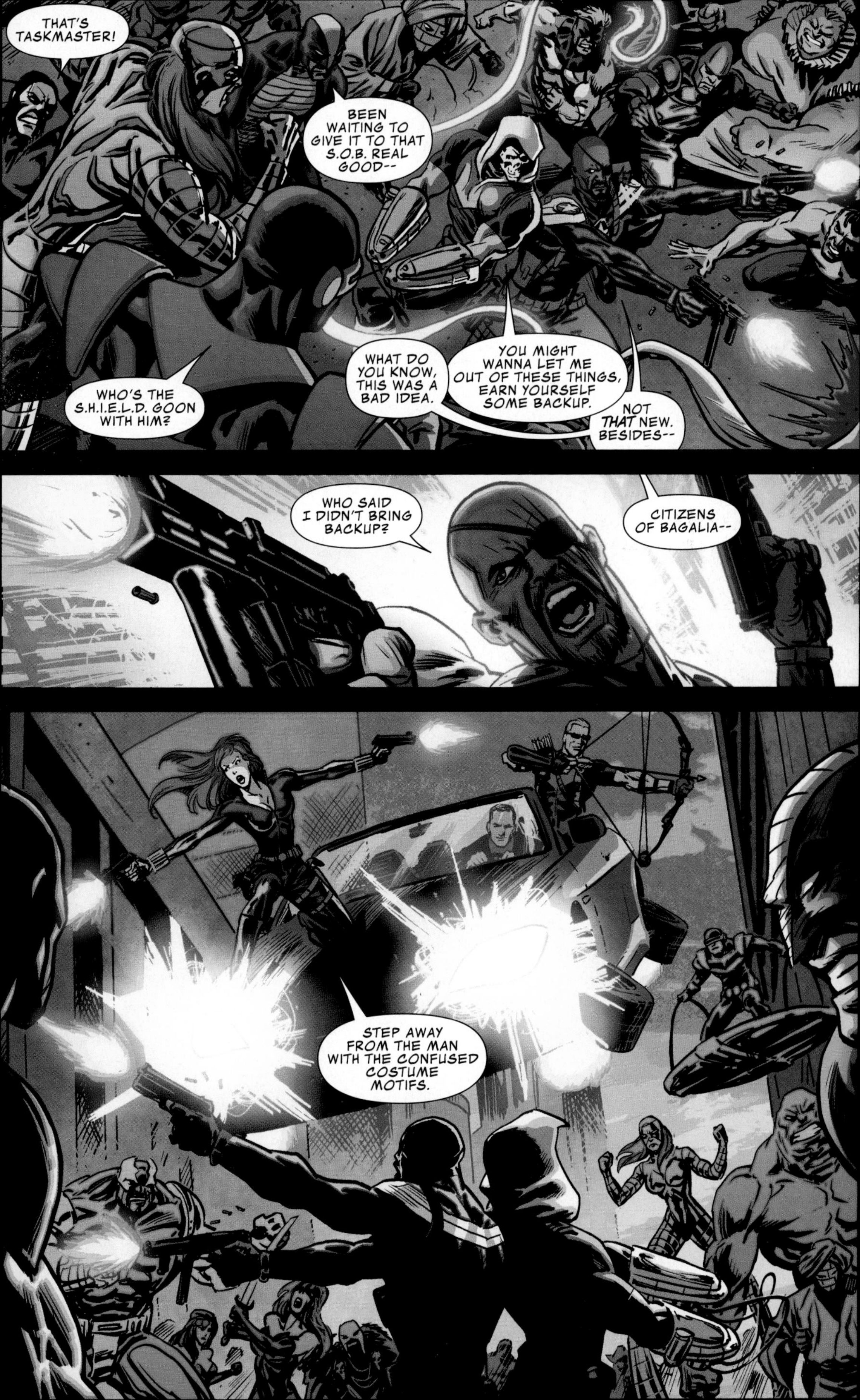
THAT'S TASKMASTER!
BEEN WAITING TO GIVE IT TO THAT S.O.B. REAL GOOD--
WHO'S THE S.H.I.E.L.D. GOON WITH HIM?
WHAT DO YOU KNOW, THIS WAS A BAD IDEA.
YOU MIGHT WANNA LET ME OUT OF THESE THINGS, EARN YOURSELF SOME BACKUP.
NOT THAT NEW. BESIDES--
WHO SAID I DIDN'T BRING BACKUP?
CITIZENS OF BAGALIA--
STEP AWAY FROM THE MAN WITH THE CONFUSED COSTUME MOTIFS.

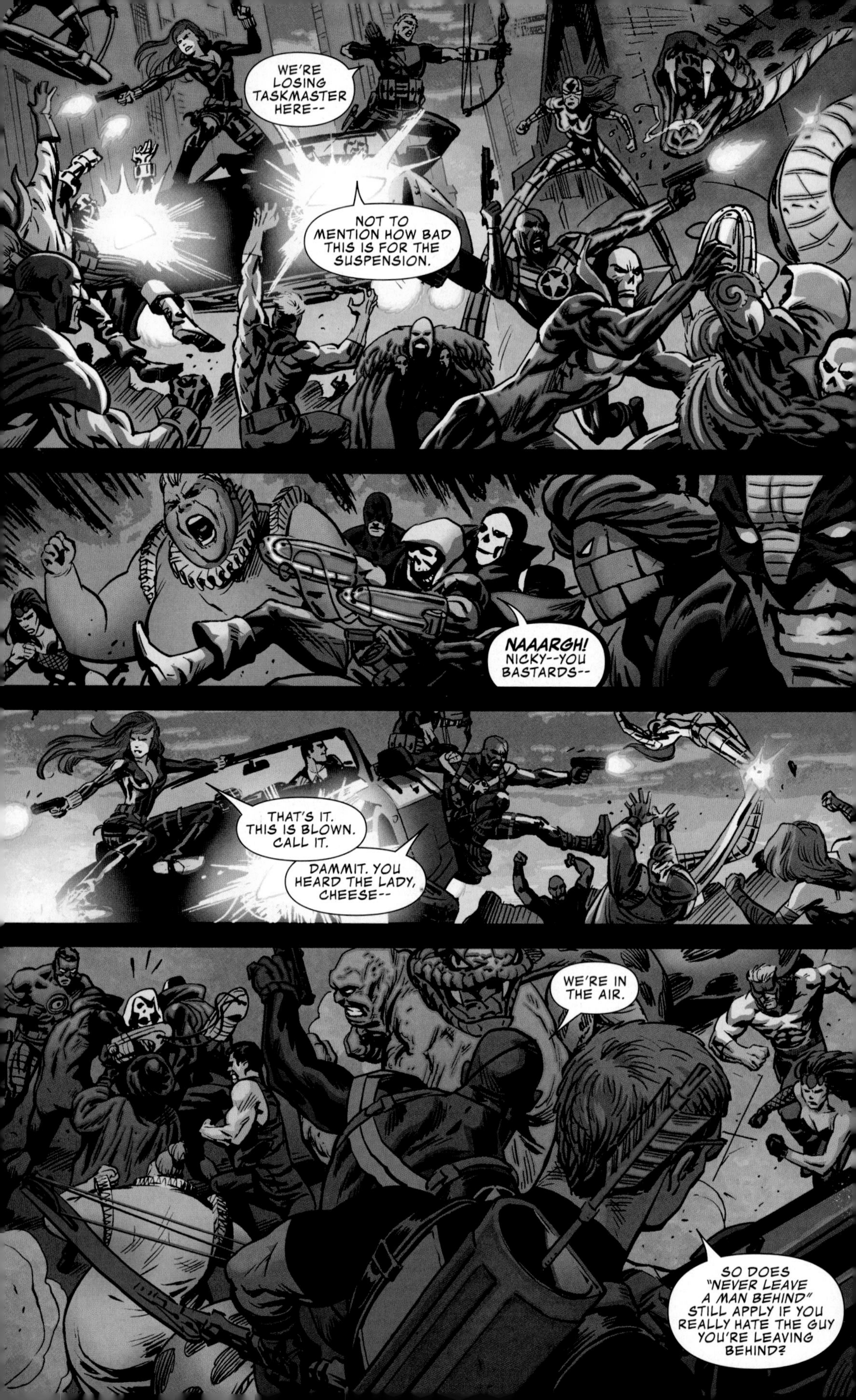
WE'RE LOSING TASKMASTER HERE--
NOT TO MENTION HOW BAD THIS IS FOR THE SUSPENSION.
NAAARGH! NICKY--YOU BASTARDS--
THAT'S IT. THIS IS BLOWN. CALL IT.
DAMMIT. YOU HEARD THE LADY, CHEESE--
!
WE'RE IN THE AIR.
SO DOES "NEVER LEAVE A MAN BEHIND" STILL APPLY IF YOU REALLY HATE THE GUY YOU'RE LEAVING BEHIND?

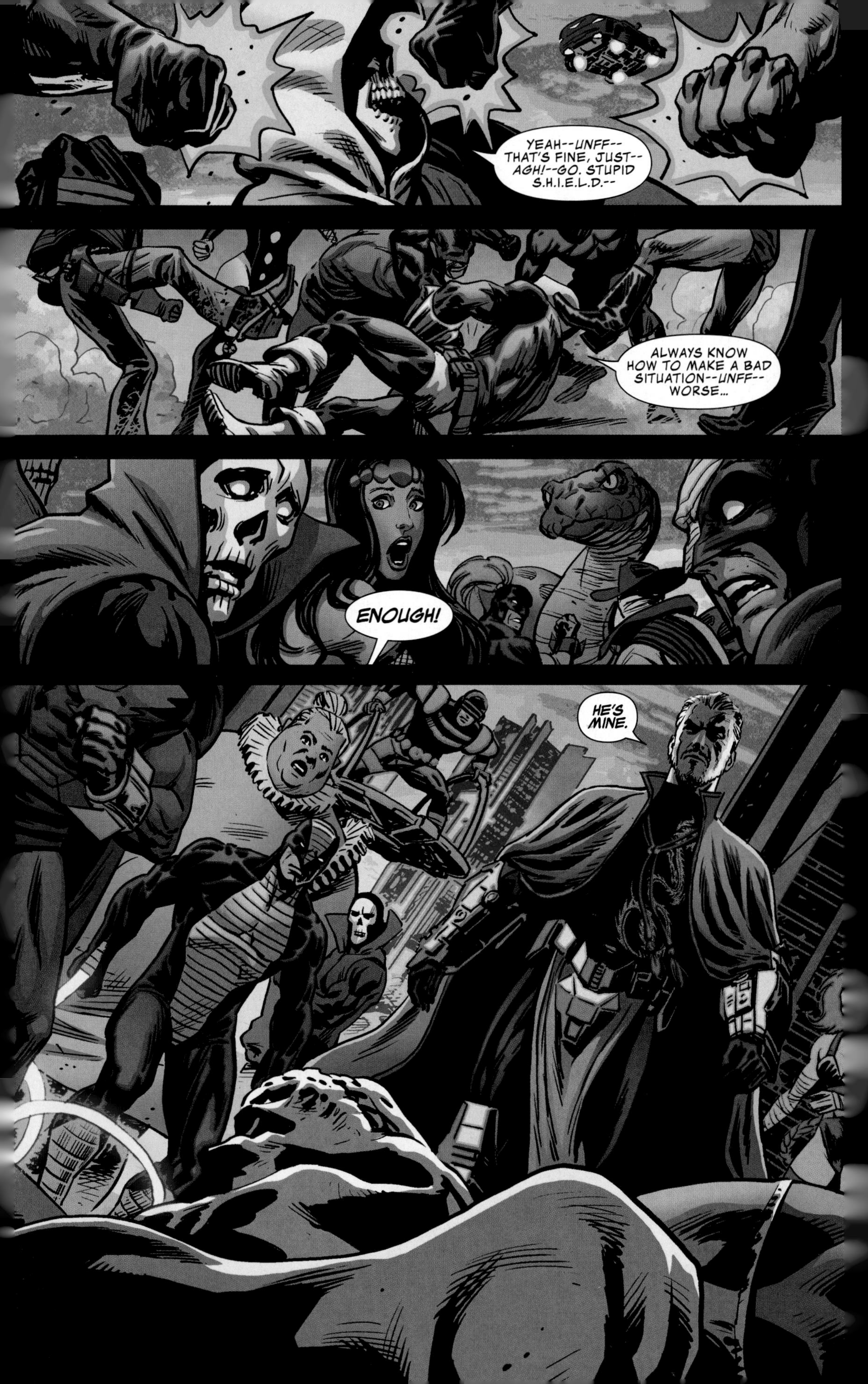
YEAH--UNFF--
THAT'S FINE, JUST--
AGH!--GO. STUPID
S.H.I.E.L.D.--
ALWAYS KNOW
HOW TO MAKE A BAD
SITUATION--UNFF--
WORSE...
ENOUGH!
HE'S
MINE.

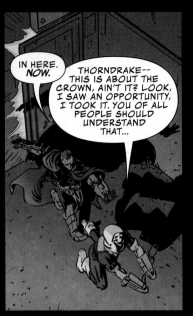

IN HERE. *NOW.*

THORNDRAKE-- THIS IS ABOUT THE CROWN, AIN'T IT? LOOK, I SAW AN OPPORTUNITY, I TOOK IT. YOU OF ALL PEOPLE SHOULD UNDERSTAND THAT...

OH, I DO.

CRACK

AGENT FURY--PACKAGE ACQUIRED. EN ROUTE.

MOCKINGBIRD OUT.

CAMOTECH DISENGAGED.

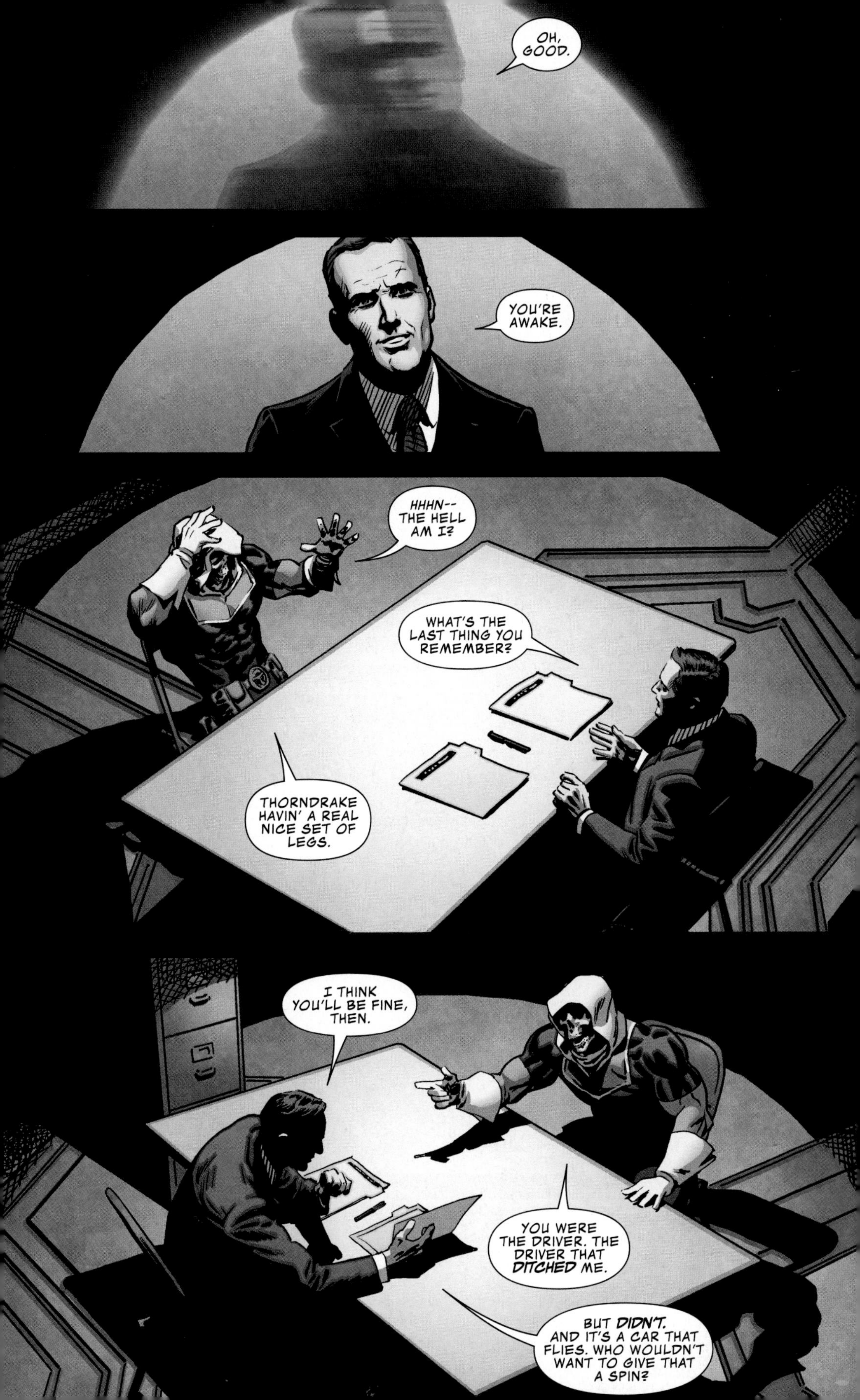
OH, GOOD.
YOU'RE AWAKE.
HHHN-- THE HELL AM I?
WHAT'S THE LAST THING YOU REMEMBER?
THORNDRAKE HAVIN' A REAL NICE SET OF LEGS.
I THINK YOU'LL BE FINE, THEN.
YOU WERE THE DRIVER. THE DRIVER THAT DITCHED ME.
BUT DIDN'T. AND IT'S A CAR THAT FLIES. WHO WOULDN'T WANT TO GIVE THAT A SPIN?

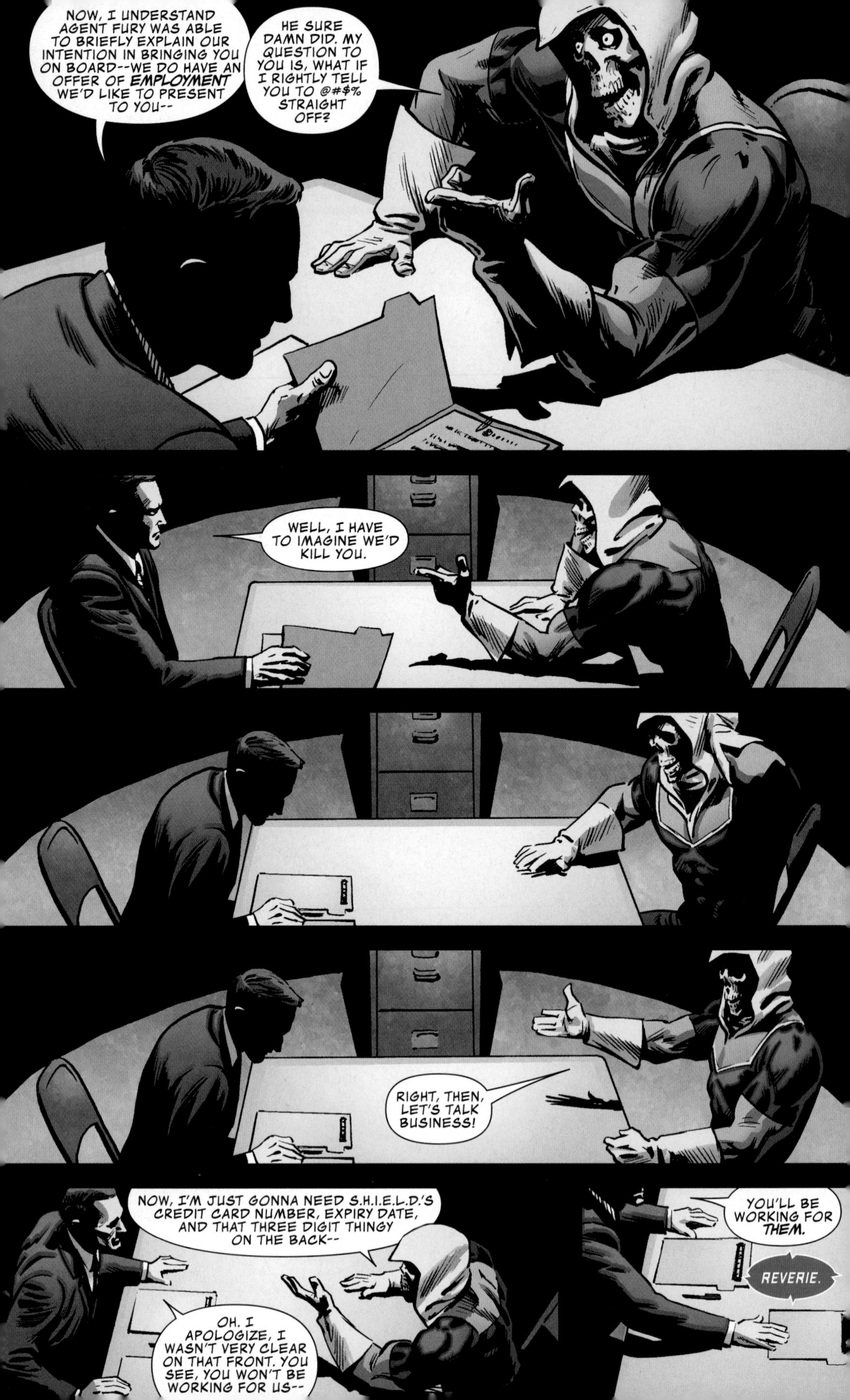
NOW, I UNDERSTAND AGENT FURY WAS ABLE TO BRIEFLY EXPLAIN OUR INTENTION IN BRINGING YOU ON BOARD--WE DO HAVE AN OFFER OF EMPLOYMENT WE'D LIKE TO PRESENT TO YOU--
HE SURE DAMN DID. MY QUESTION TO YOU IS, WHAT IF I RIGHTLY TELL YOU TO @#$% STRAIGHT OFF?
WELL, I HAVE TO IMAGINE WE'D KILL YOU.
RIGHT, THEN, LET'S TALK BUSINESS!
NOW, I'M JUST GONNA NEED S.H.I.E.L.D.'S CREDIT CARD NUMBER, EXPIRY DATE, AND THAT THREE DIGIT THINGY ON THE BACK--
OH. I APOLOGIZE, I WASN'T VERY CLEAR ON THAT FRONT. YOU SEE, YOU WON'T BE WORKING FOR US--
YOU'LL BE WORKING FOR THEM.
REVERIE.

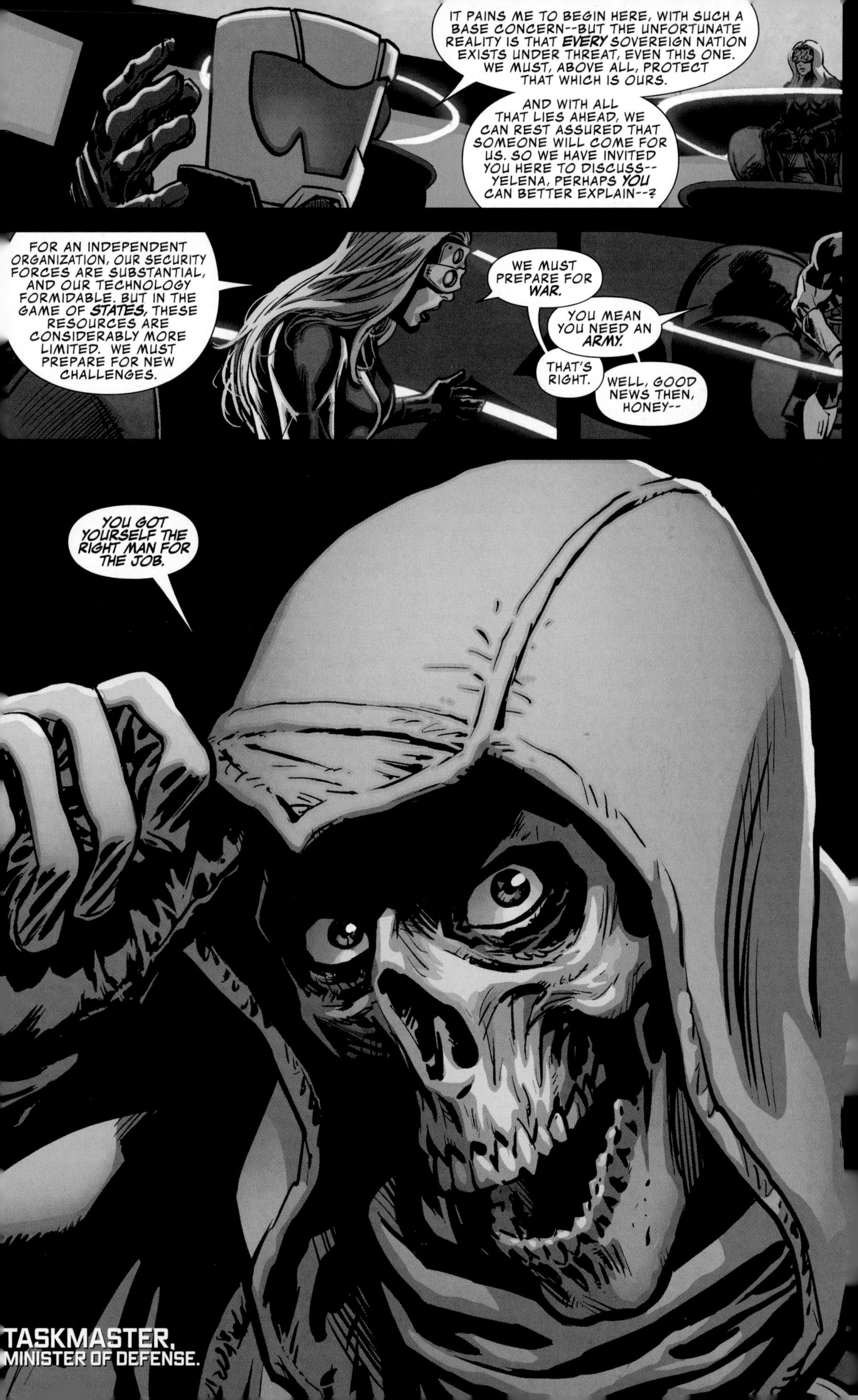
IT PAINS ME TO BEGIN HERE, WITH SUCH A BASE CONCERN--BUT THE UNFORTUNATE REALITY IS THAT EVERY SOVEREIGN NATION EXISTS UNDER THREAT, EVEN THIS ONE. WE MUST, ABOVE ALL, PROTECT THAT WHICH IS OURS.
AND WITH ALL THAT LIES AHEAD, WE CAN REST ASSURED THAT SOMEONE WILL COME FOR US. SO WE HAVE INVITED YOU HERE TO DISCUSS-- YELENA, PERHAPS YOU CAN BETTER EXPLAIN--?
FOR AN INDEPENDENT ORGANIZATION, OUR SECURITY FORCES ARE SUBSTANTIAL, AND OUR TECHNOLOGY FORMIDABLE. BUT IN THE GAME OF STATES, THESE RESOURCES ARE CONSIDERABLY MORE LIMITED. WE MUST PREPARE FOR NEW CHALLENGES.
WE MUST PREPARE FOR WAR.
YOU MEAN YOU NEED AN ARMY.
THAT'S RIGHT.
WELL, GOOD NEWS THEN, HONEY--
YOU GOT YOURSELF THE RIGHT MAN FOR THE JOB.
TASKMASTER, MINISTER OF DEFENSE.

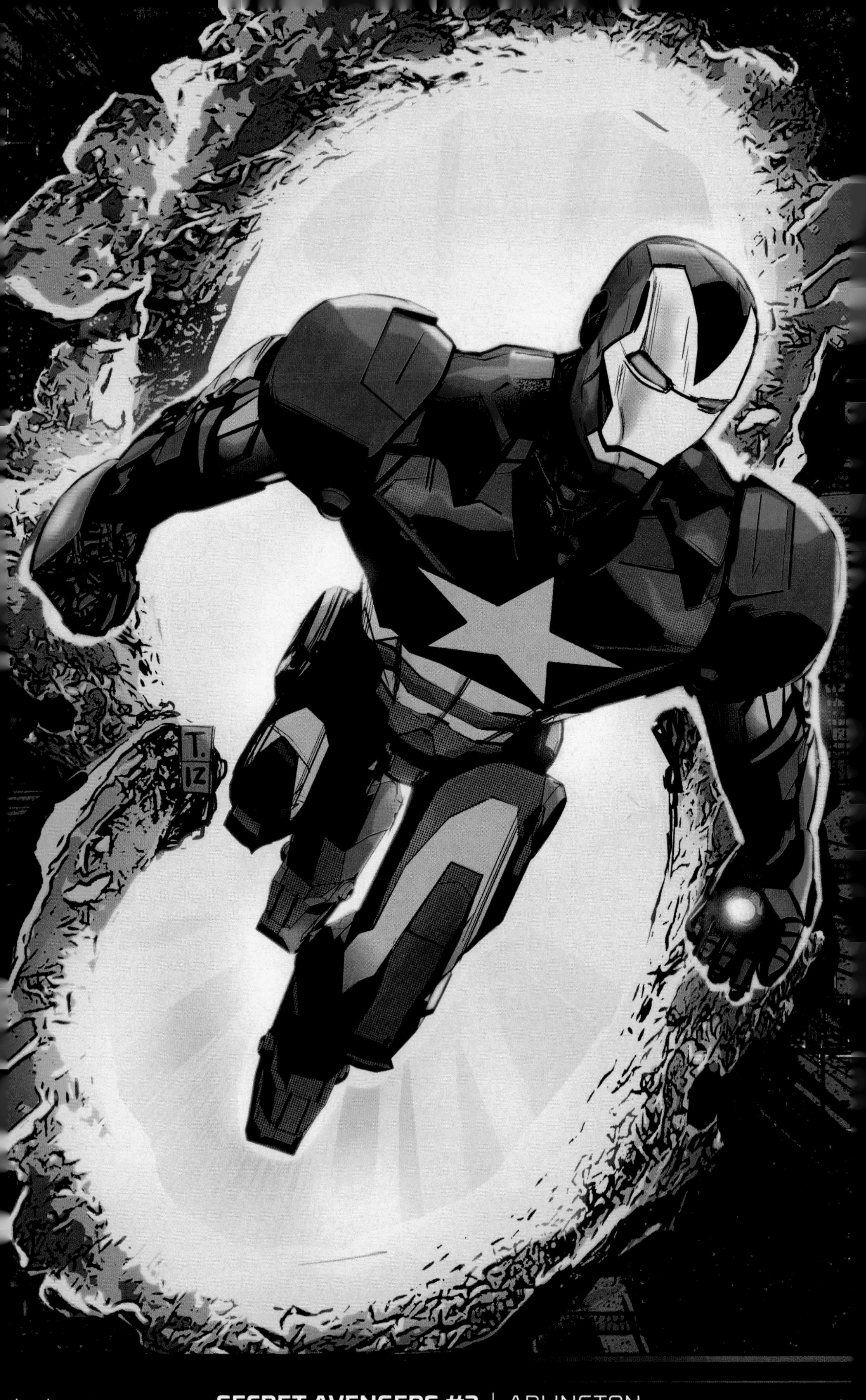

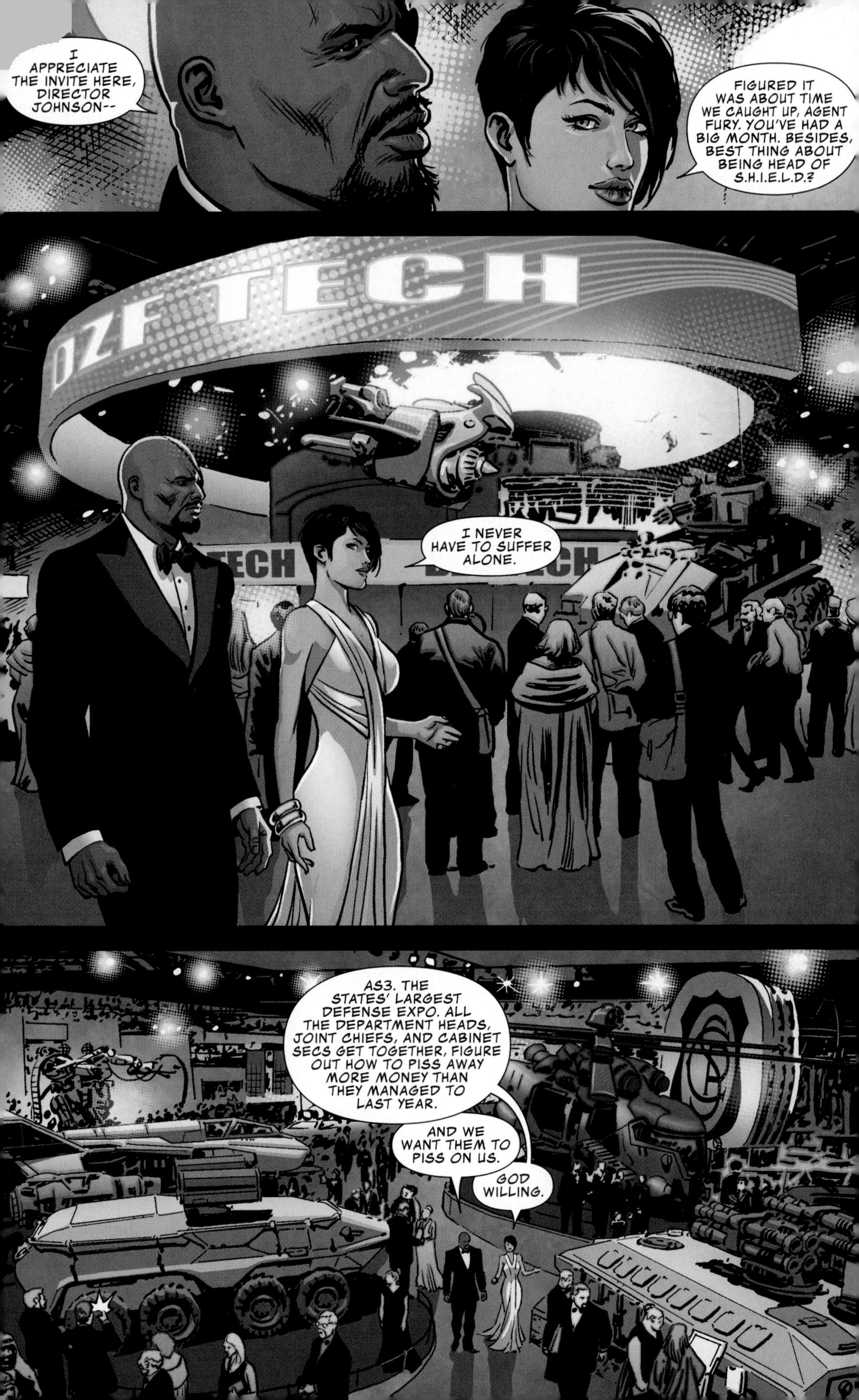
I APPRECIATE THE INVITE HERE, DIRECTOR JOHNSON--
FIGURED IT WAS ABOUT TIME WE CAUGHT UP, AGENT FURY. YOU'VE HAD A BIG MONTH. BESIDES, BEST THING ABOUT BEING HEAD OF S.H.I.E.L.D.?
OZ TECH
I NEVER HAVE TO SUFFER ALONE.
AS3. THE STATES' LARGEST DEFENSE EXPO. ALL THE DEPARTMENT HEADS, JOINT CHIEFS, AND CABINET SECS GET TOGETHER, FIGURE OUT HOW TO PISS AWAY MORE MONEY THAN THEY MANAGED TO LAST YEAR.
AND WE WANT THEM TO PISS ON US.
GOD WILLING.

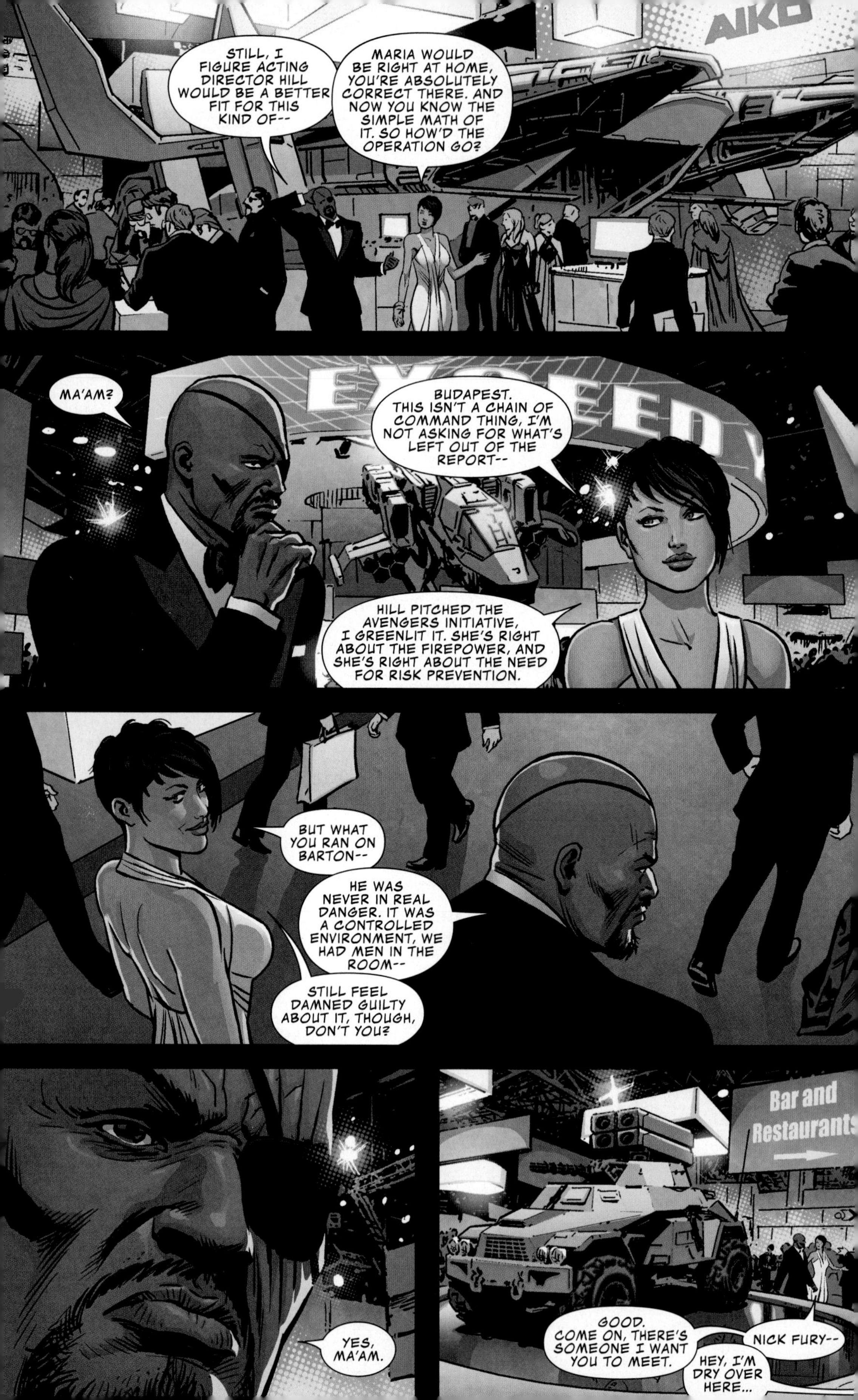
AIKO
STILL, I FIGURE ACTING DIRECTOR HILL WOULD BE A BETTER FIT FOR THIS KIND OF--
MARIA WOULD BE RIGHT AT HOME, YOU'RE ABSOLUTELY CORRECT THERE. AND NOW YOU KNOW THE SIMPLE MATH OF IT. SO HOW'D THE OPERATION GO?
MA'AM?
BUDAPEST. THIS ISN'T A CHAIN OF COMMAND THING, I'M NOT ASKING FOR WHAT'S LEFT OUT OF THE REPORT--
HILL PITCHED THE AVENGERS INITIATIVE, I GREENLIT IT. SHE'S RIGHT ABOUT THE FIREPOWER, AND SHE'S RIGHT ABOUT THE NEED FOR RISK PREVENTION.
BUT WHAT YOU RAN ON BARTON--
HE WAS NEVER IN REAL DANGER. IT WAS A CONTROLLED ENVIRONMENT, WE HAD MEN IN THE ROOM--
STILL FEEL DAMNED GUILTY ABOUT IT, THOUGH, DON'T YOU?
YES, MA'AM.
Bar and Restaurants
GOOD. COME ON, THERE'S SOMEONE I WANT YOU TO MEET.
NICK FURY--
HEY, I'M DRY OVER HERE...

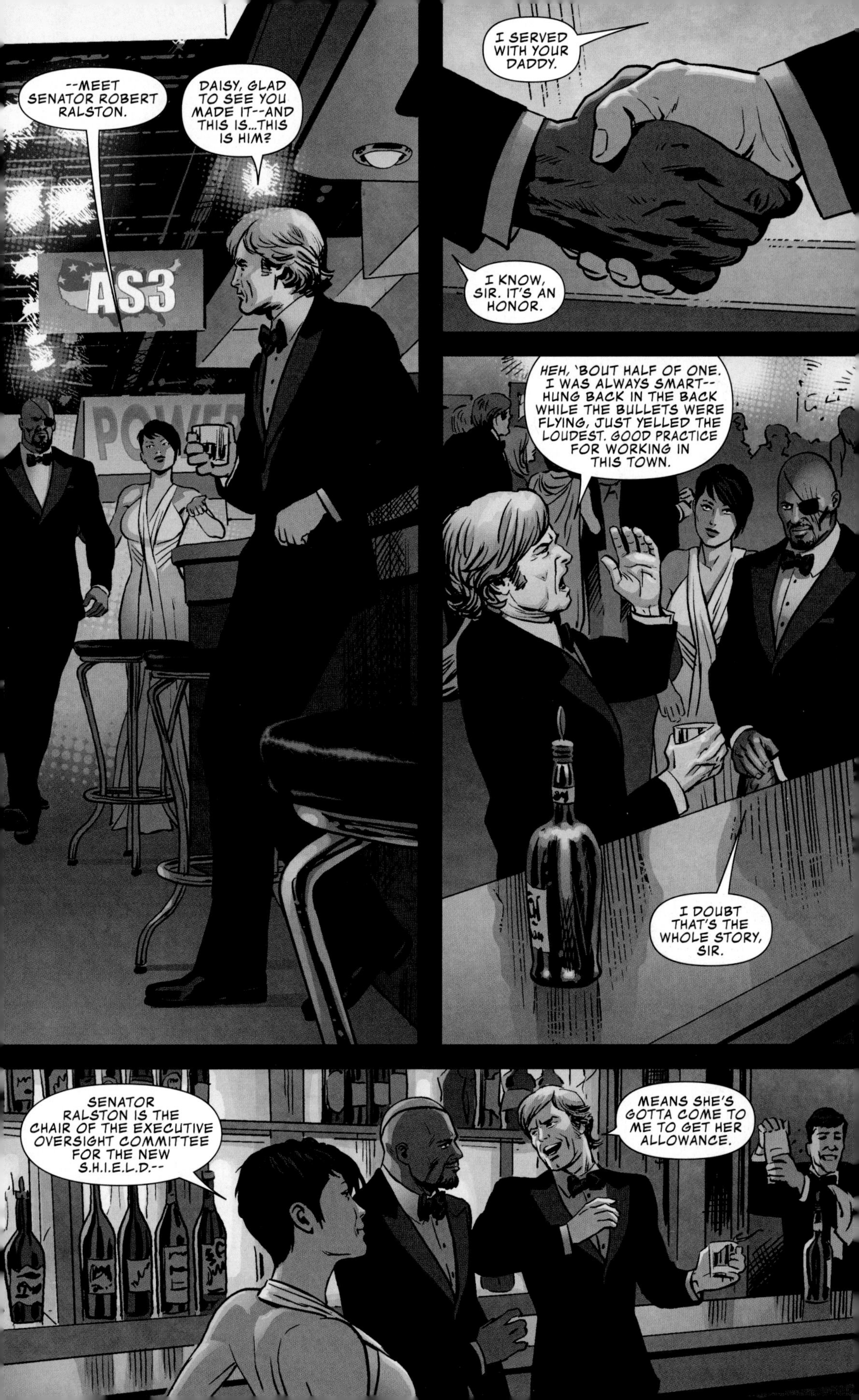
DAISY, GLAD TO SEE YOU MADE IT--AND THIS IS...THIS IS HIM?
--MEET SENATOR ROBERT RALSTON.
AS3
POWE
I SERVED WITH YOUR DADDY.
I KNOW, SIR. IT'S AN HONOR.
HEH, 'BOUT HALF OF ONE. I WAS ALWAYS SMART-- HUNG BACK IN THE BACK WHILE THE BULLETS WERE FLYING, JUST YELLED THE LOUDEST. GOOD PRACTICE FOR WORKING IN THIS TOWN.
I DOUBT THAT'S THE WHOLE STORY, SIR.
SENATOR RALSTON IS THE CHAIR OF THE EXECUTIVE OVERSIGHT COMMITTEE FOR THE NEW S.H.I.E.L.D.--
MEANS SHE'S GOTTA COME TO ME TO GET HER ALLOWANCE.

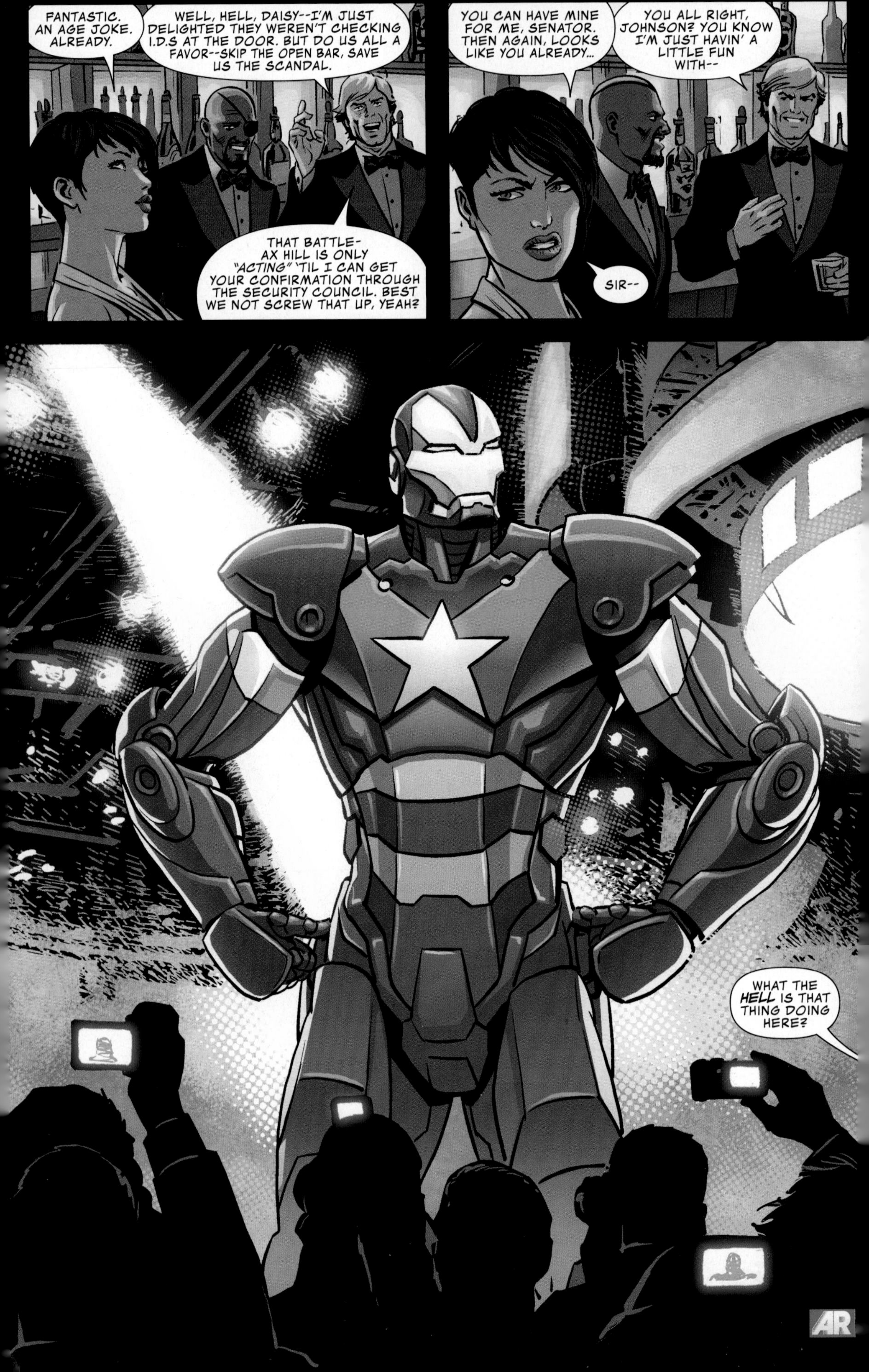
FANTASTIC. AN AGE JOKE. ALREADY.
WELL, HELL, DAISY--I'M JUST DELIGHTED THEY WEREN'T CHECKING I.D.S AT THE DOOR. BUT DO US ALL A FAVOR--SKIP THE OPEN BAR, SAVE US THE SCANDAL.
THAT BATTLE-AX HILL IS ONLY "ACTING" 'TIL I CAN GET YOUR CONFIRMATION THROUGH THE SECURITY COUNCIL. BEST WE NOT SCREW THAT UP, YEAH?
YOU CAN HAVE MINE FOR ME, SENATOR. THEN AGAIN, LOOKS LIKE YOU ALREADY...
YOU ALL RIGHT, JOHNSON? YOU KNOW I'M JUST HAVIN' A LITTLE FUN WITH--
SIR--
WHAT THE HELL IS THAT THING DOING HERE?

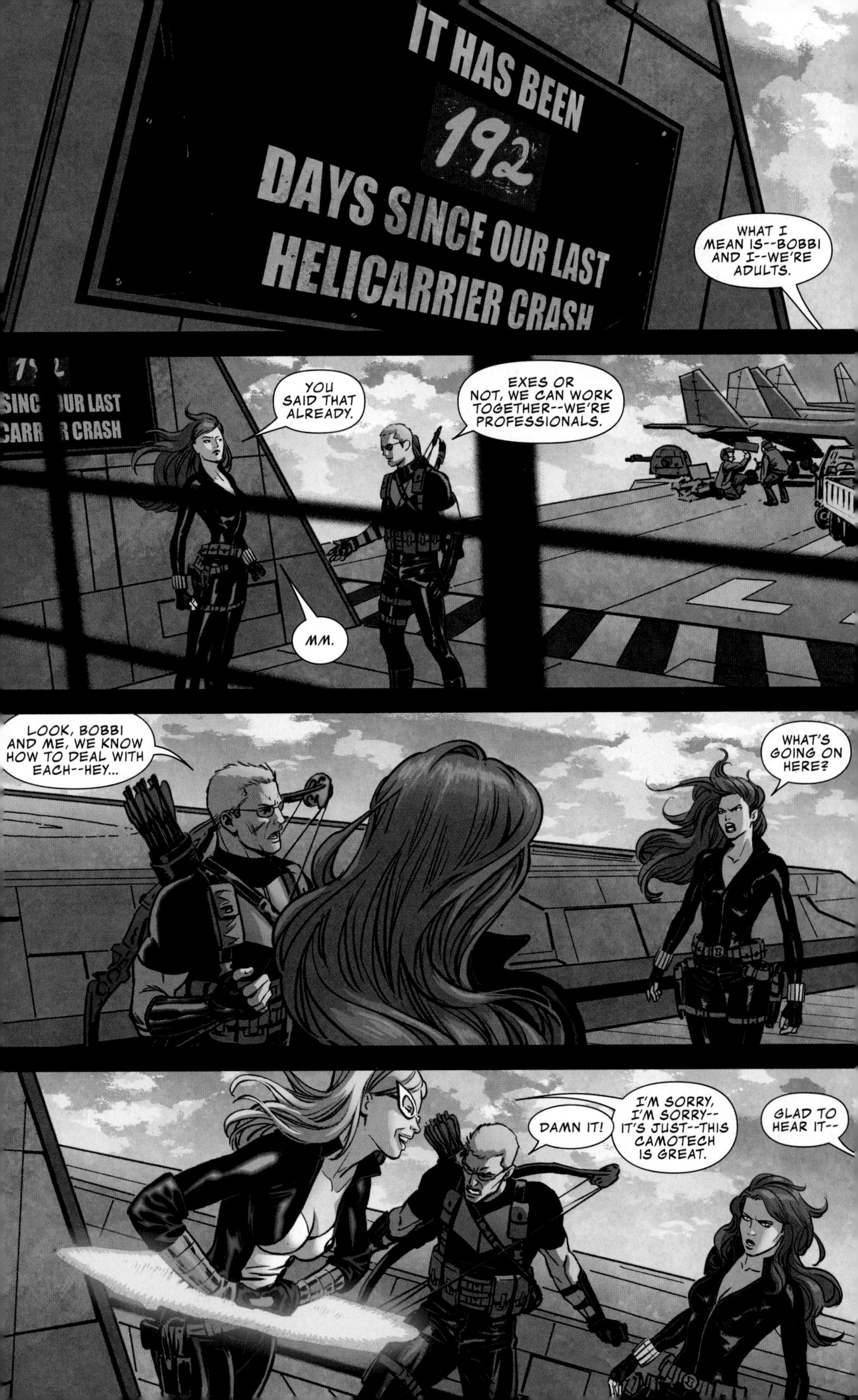
IT HAS BEEN
192
DAYS SINCE OUR LAST
HELICARRIER CRASH
WHAT I MEAN IS--BOBBI AND I--WE'RE ADULTS.
YOU SAID THAT ALREADY.
EXES OR NOT, WE CAN WORK TOGETHER--WE'RE PROFESSIONALS.
MM.
LOOK, BOBBI AND ME, WE KNOW HOW TO DEAL WITH EACH--HEY...
WHAT'S GOING ON HERE?
DAMN IT!
I'M SORRY, I'M SORRY-- IT'S JUST--THIS CAMOTECH IS GREAT.
GLAD TO HEAR IT--

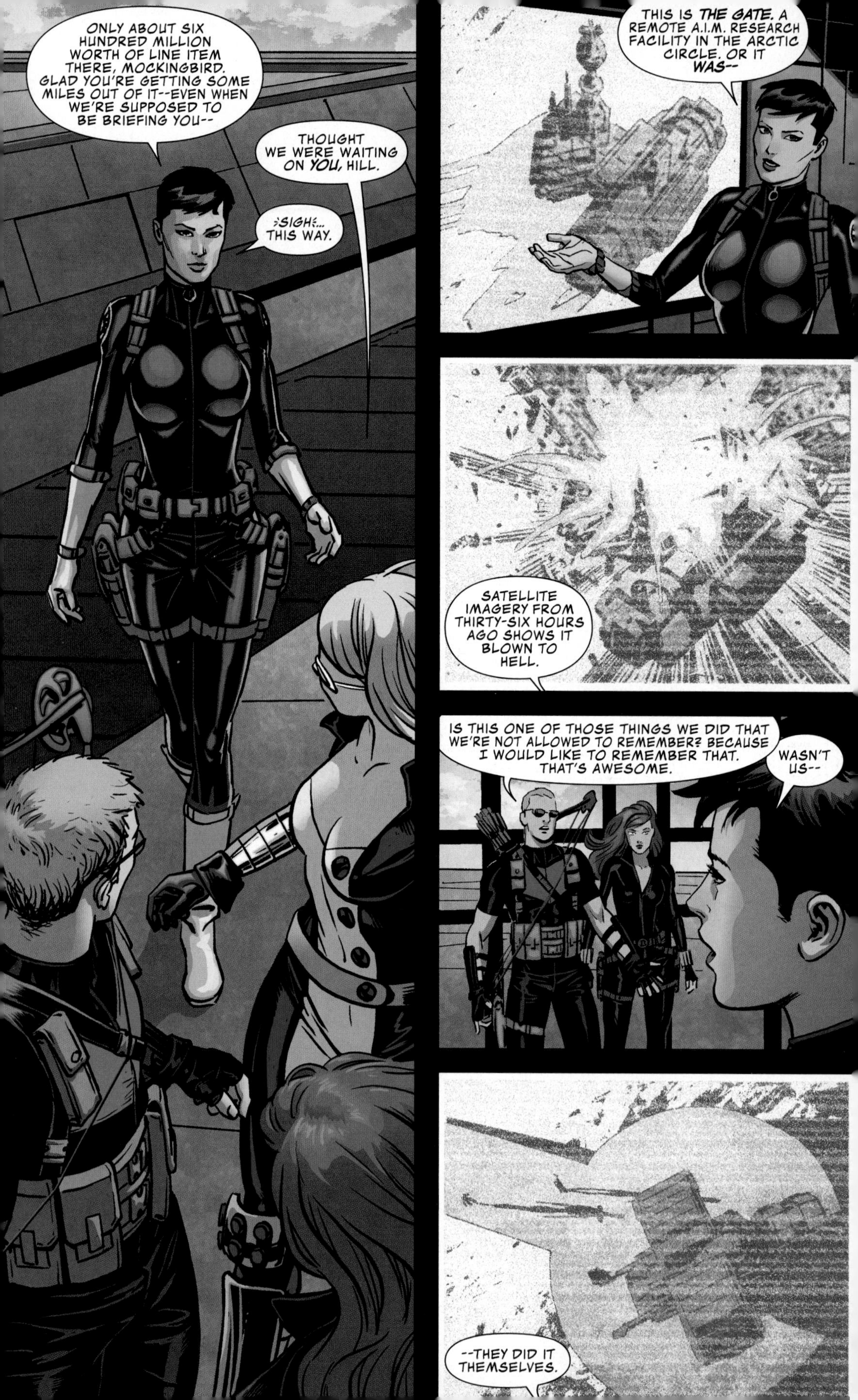
ONLY ABOUT SIX HUNDRED MILLION WORTH OF LINE ITEM THERE, MOCKINGBIRD. GLAD YOU'RE GETTING SOME MILES OUT OF IT--EVEN WHEN WE'RE SUPPOSED TO BE BRIEFING YOU--
THOUGHT WE WERE WAITING ON *YOU*, HILL.
SIGH... THIS WAY.
THIS IS *THE GATE*. A REMOTE A.I.M. RESEARCH FACILITY IN THE ARCTIC CIRCLE. OR IT *WAS*--
SATELLITE IMAGERY FROM THIRTY-SIX HOURS AGO SHOWS IT BLOWN TO HELL.
IS THIS ONE OF THOSE THINGS WE DID THAT WE'RE NOT ALLOWED TO REMEMBER? BECAUSE I WOULD LIKE TO REMEMBER THAT. THAT'S AWESOME.
WASN'T US--
--THEY DID IT THEMSELVES.

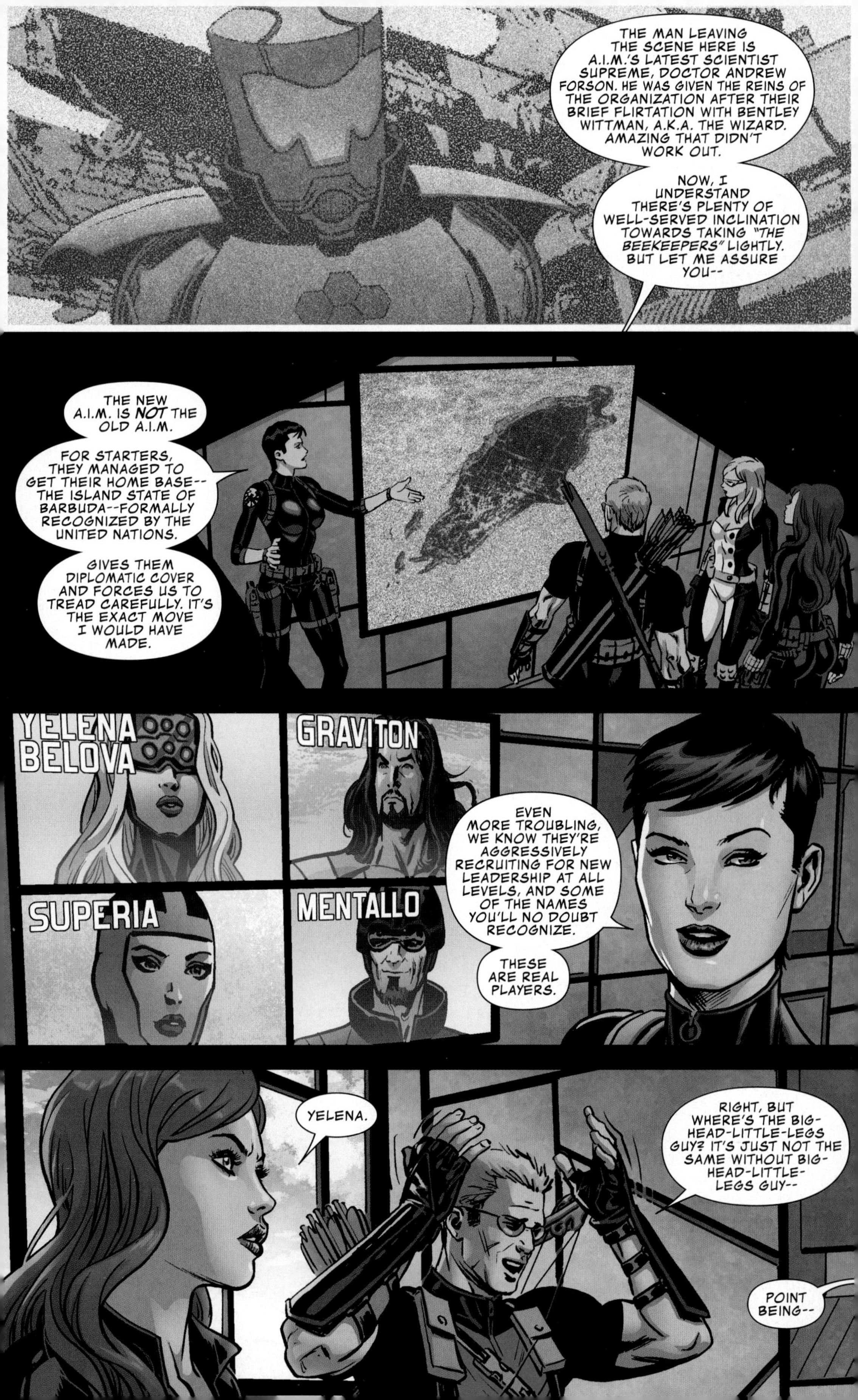
THE MAN LEAVING THE SCENE HERE IS A.I.M.'S LATEST SCIENTIST SUPREME, DOCTOR ANDREW FORSON. HE WAS GIVEN THE REINS OF THE ORGANIZATION AFTER THEIR BRIEF FLIRTATION WITH BENTLEY WITTMAN, A.K.A. THE WIZARD. AMAZING THAT DIDN'T WORK OUT.
NOW, I UNDERSTAND THERE'S PLENTY OF WELL-SERVED INCLINATION TOWARDS TAKING "THE BEEKEEPERS" LIGHTLY. BUT LET ME ASSURE YOU--
THE NEW A.I.M. IS *NOT* THE OLD A.I.M.
FOR STARTERS, THEY MANAGED TO GET THEIR HOME BASE-- THE ISLAND STATE OF BARBUDA--FORMALLY RECOGNIZED BY THE UNITED NATIONS.
GIVES THEM DIPLOMATIC COVER AND FORCES US TO TREAD CAREFULLY. IT'S THE EXACT MOVE I WOULD HAVE MADE.
YELENA BELOVA
GRAVITON
SUPERIA
MENTALLO
EVEN MORE TROUBLING, WE KNOW THEY'RE AGGRESSIVELY RECRUITING FOR NEW LEADERSHIP AT ALL LEVELS, AND SOME OF THE NAMES YOU'LL NO DOUBT RECOGNIZE.
THESE ARE REAL PLAYERS.
YELENA.
RIGHT, BUT WHERE'S THE BIG-HEAD-LITTLE-LEGS GUY? IT'S JUST NOT THE SAME WITHOUT BIG-HEAD-LITTLE-LEGS GUY--
POINT BEING--

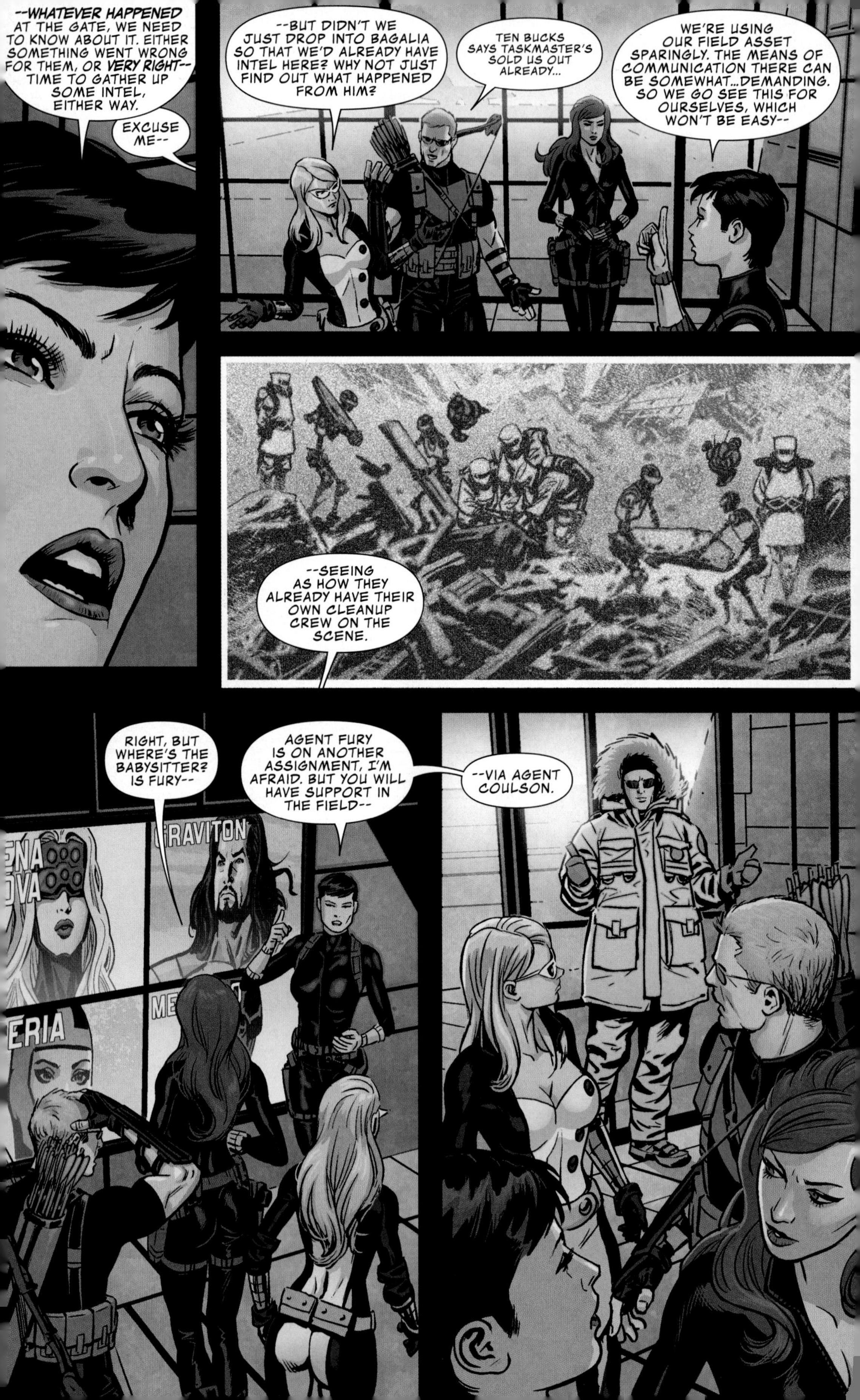
--WHATEVER HAPPENED AT THE GATE, WE NEED TO KNOW ABOUT IT. EITHER SOMETHING WENT WRONG FOR THEM, OR VERY RIGHT-- TIME TO GATHER UP SOME INTEL, EITHER WAY.
EXCUSE ME--
--BUT DIDN'T WE JUST DROP INTO BAGALIA SO THAT WE'D ALREADY HAVE INTEL HERE? WHY NOT JUST FIND OUT WHAT HAPPENED FROM HIM?
TEN BUCKS SAYS TASKMASTER'S SOLD US OUT ALREADY...
WE'RE USING OUR FIELD ASSET SPARINGLY. THE MEANS OF COMMUNICATION THERE CAN BE SOMEWHAT...DEMANDING. SO WE GO SEE THIS FOR OURSELVES, WHICH WON'T BE EASY--
--SEEING AS HOW THEY ALREADY HAVE THEIR OWN CLEANUP CREW ON THE SCENE.
RIGHT, BUT WHERE'S THE BABYSITTER? IS FURY--
GRAVITON
AGENT FURY IS ON ANOTHER ASSIGNMENT, I'M AFRAID. BUT YOU WILL HAVE SUPPORT IN THE FIELD--
--VIA AGENT COULSON.

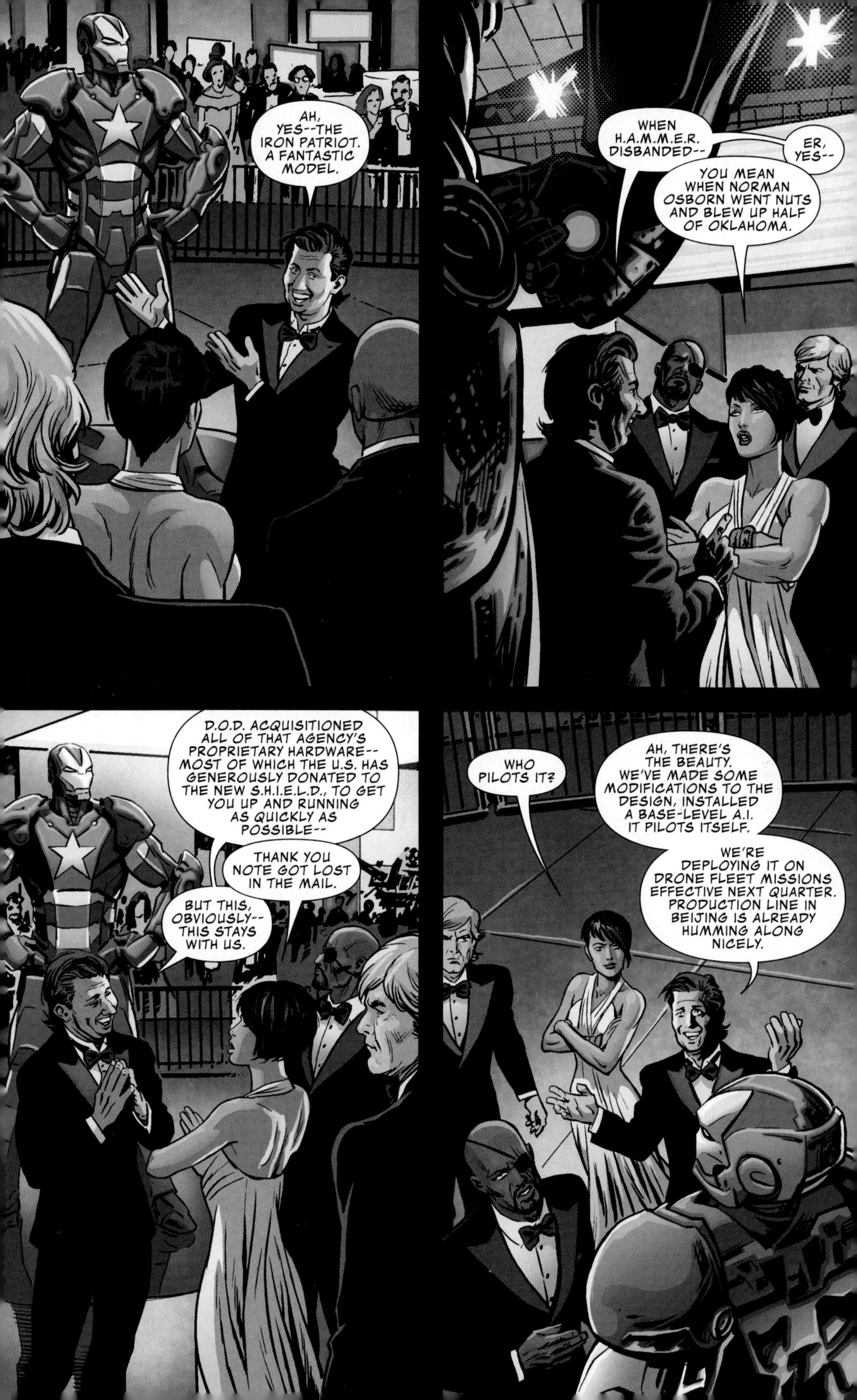
AH, YES--THE IRON PATRIOT. A FANTASTIC MODEL.
WHEN H.A.M.M.E.R. DISBANDED--
ER, YES--
YOU MEAN WHEN NORMAN OSBORN WENT NUTS AND BLEW UP HALF OF OKLAHOMA.
D.O.D. ACQUISITIONED ALL OF THAT AGENCY'S PROPRIETARY HARDWARE--MOST OF WHICH THE U.S. HAS GENEROUSLY DONATED TO THE NEW S.H.I.E.L.D., TO GET YOU UP AND RUNNING AS QUICKLY AS POSSIBLE--
THANK YOU NOTE GOT LOST IN THE MAIL.
BUT THIS, OBVIOUSLY--THIS STAYS WITH US.
WHO PILOTS IT?
AH, THERE'S THE BEAUTY. WE'VE MADE SOME MODIFICATIONS TO THE DESIGN, INSTALLED A BASE-LEVEL A.I. IT PILOTS ITSELF.
WE'RE DEPLOYING IT ON DRONE FLEET MISSIONS EFFECTIVE NEXT QUARTER. PRODUCTION LINE IN BEIJING IS ALREADY HUMMING ALONG NICELY.

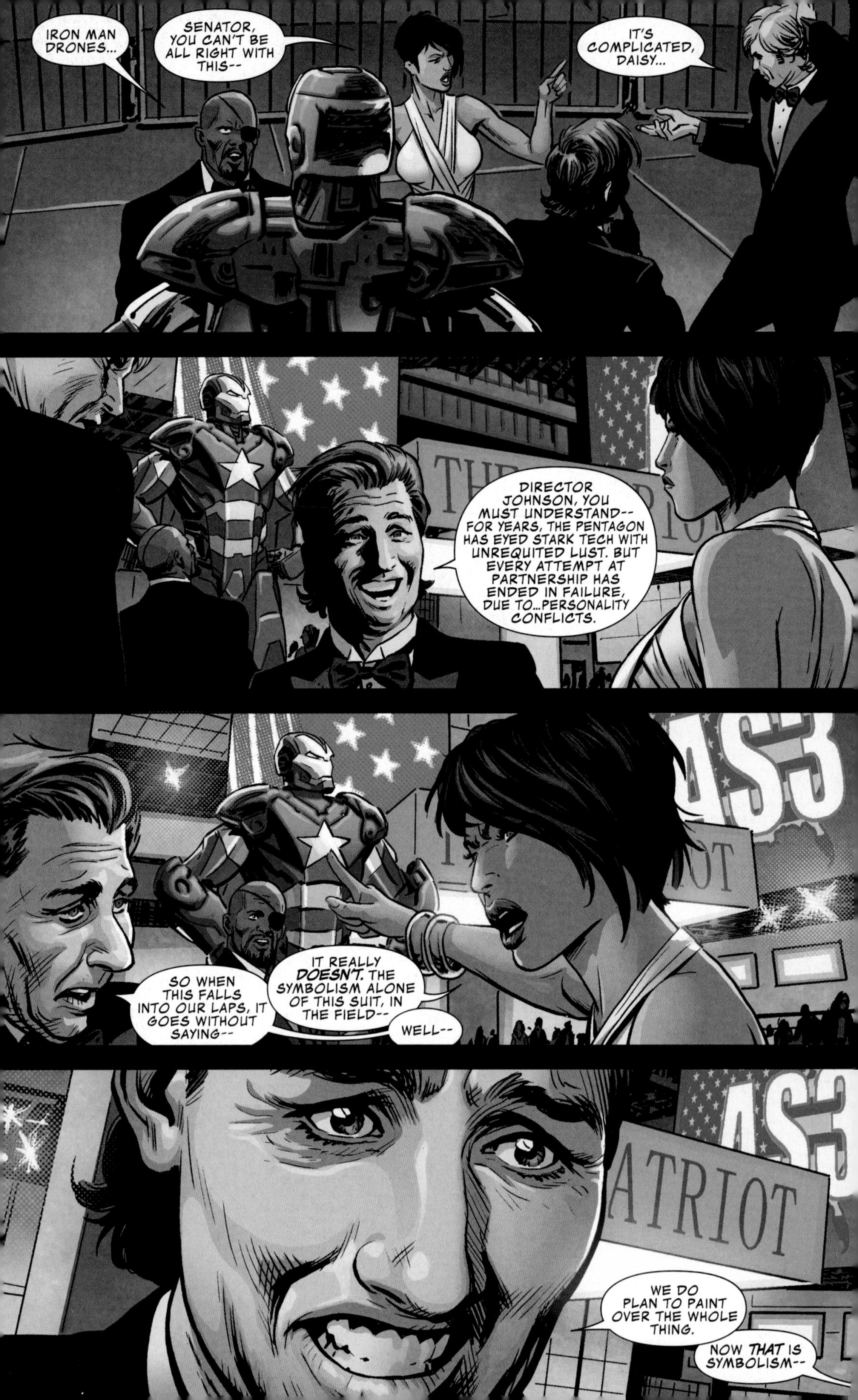
IRON MAN DRONES...
SENATOR, YOU CAN'T BE ALL RIGHT WITH THIS--
IT'S COMPLICATED, DAISY...
DIRECTOR JOHNSON, YOU MUST UNDERSTAND--FOR YEARS, THE PENTAGON HAS EYED STARK TECH WITH UNREQUITED LUST. BUT EVERY ATTEMPT AT PARTNERSHIP HAS ENDED IN FAILURE, DUE TO...PERSONALITY CONFLICTS.
THE PATRIOT
SO WHEN THIS FALLS INTO OUR LAPS, IT GOES WITHOUT SAYING--
IT REALLY *DOESN'T.* THE SYMBOLISM ALONE OF THIS SUIT, IN THE FIELD--
WELL--
PATRIOT
WE DO PLAN TO PAINT OVER THE WHOLE THING.
NOW *THAT* IS SYMBOLISM--

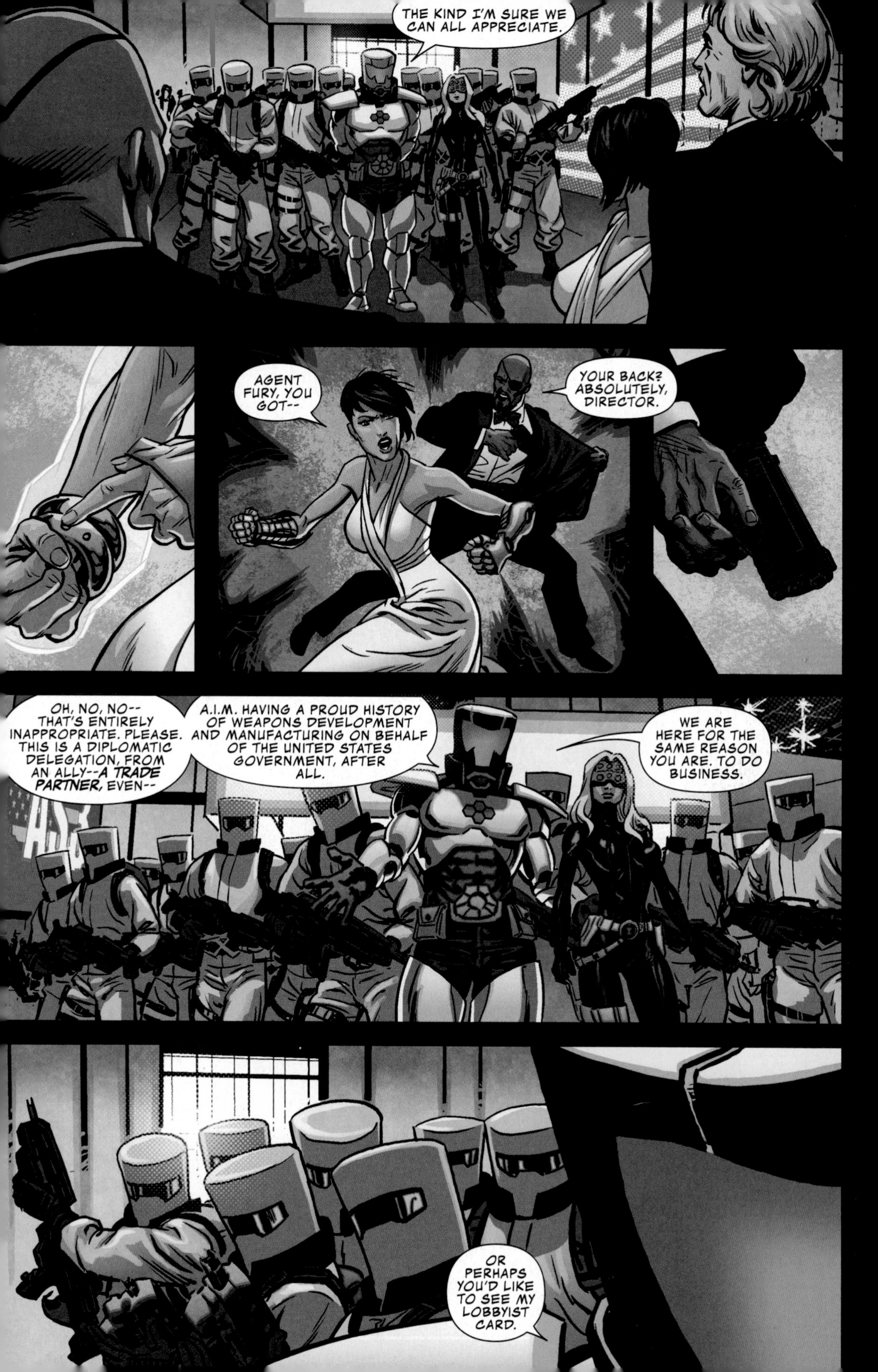
THE KIND I'M SURE WE CAN ALL APPRECIATE.
AGENT FURY, YOU GOT--
YOUR BACK? ABSOLUTELY, DIRECTOR.
OH, NO, NO-- THAT'S ENTIRELY INAPPROPRIATE. PLEASE. THIS IS A DIPLOMATIC DELEGATION, FROM AN ALLY--*A TRADE PARTNER,* EVEN--
A.I.M. HAVING A PROUD HISTORY OF WEAPONS DEVELOPMENT AND MANUFACTURING ON BEHALF OF THE UNITED STATES GOVERNMENT, AFTER ALL.
WE ARE HERE FOR THE SAME REASON YOU ARE. TO DO BUSINESS.
OR PERHAPS YOU'D LIKE TO SEE MY LOBBYIST CARD.

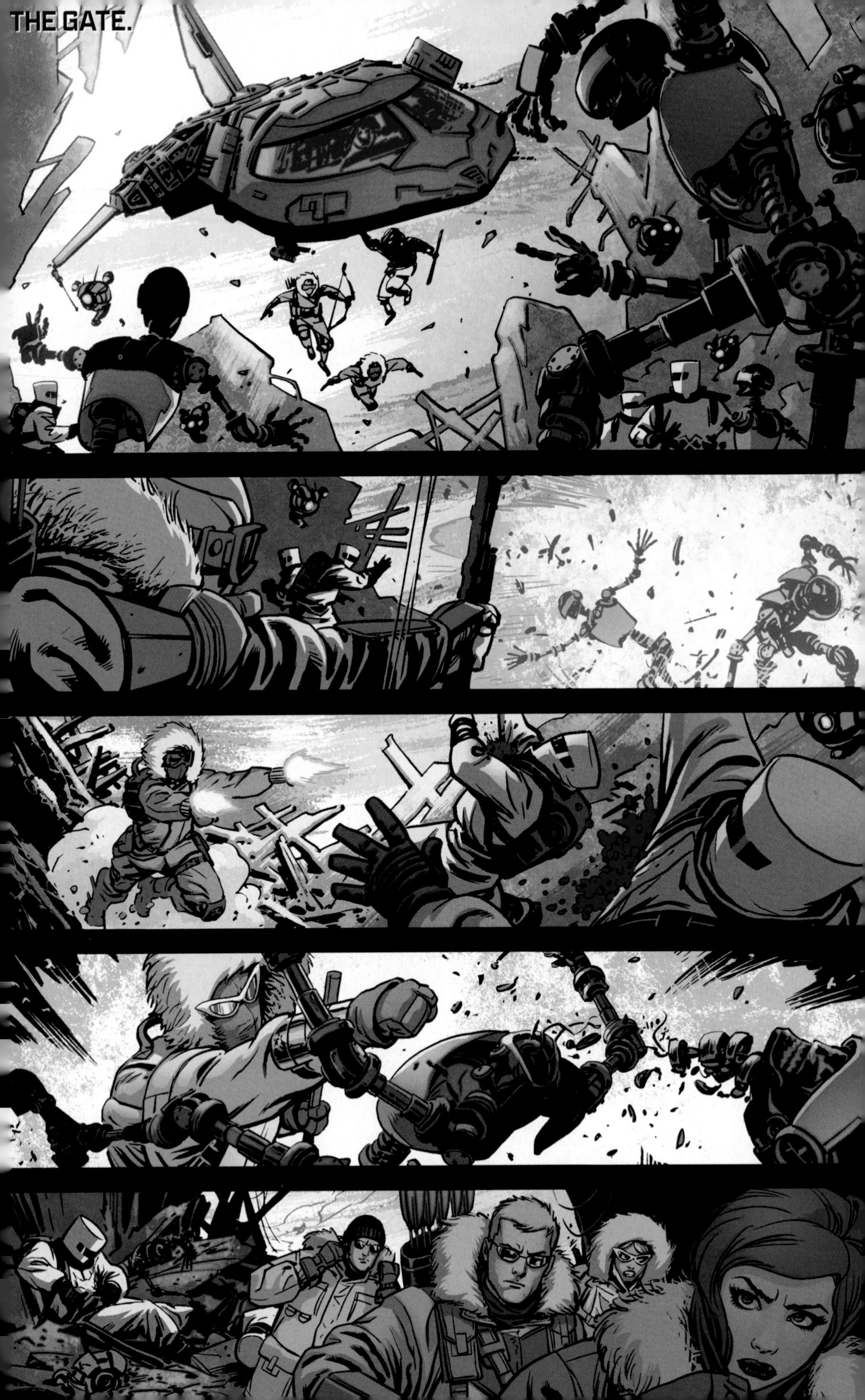
THE GATE.

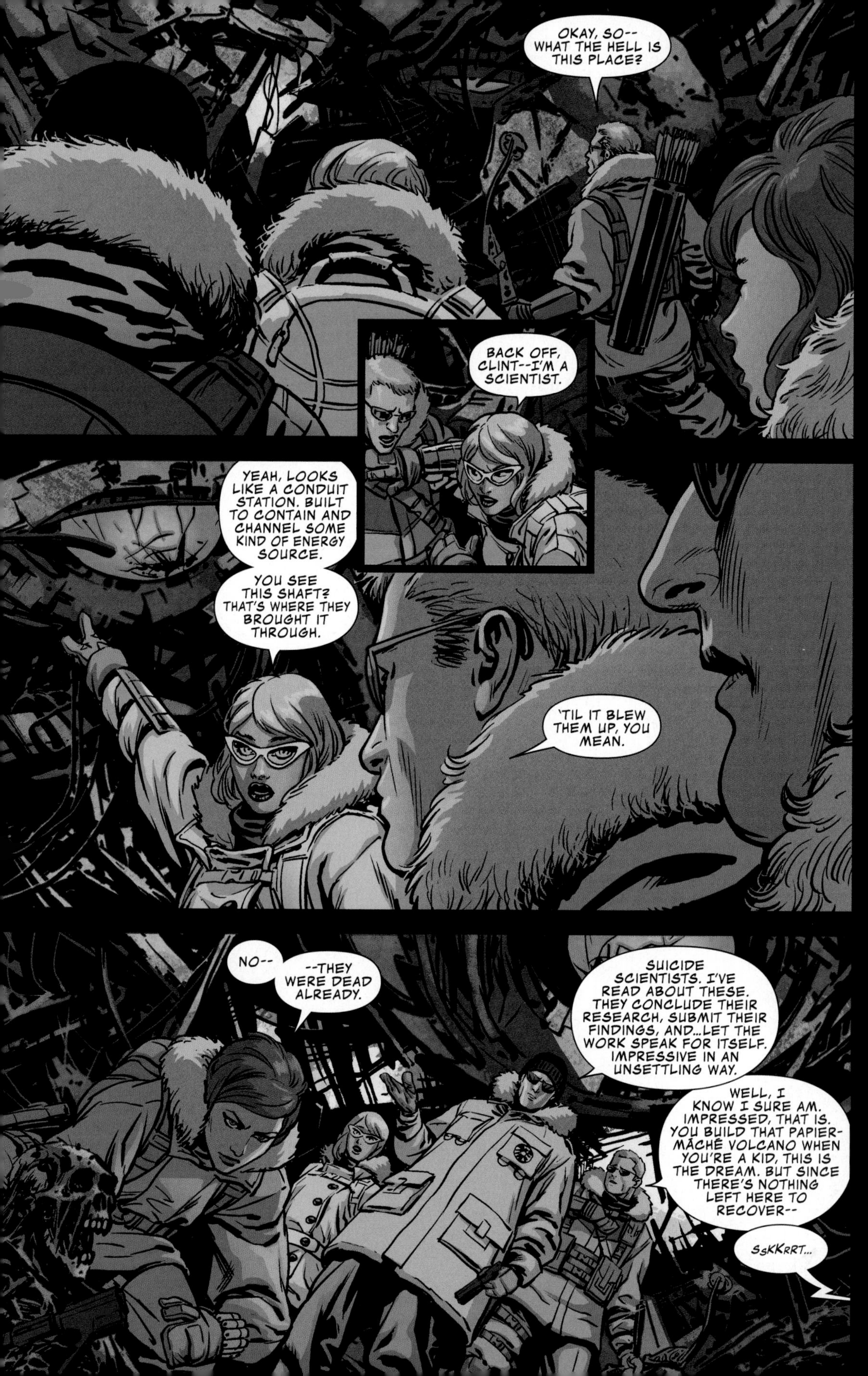
OKAY, SO-- WHAT THE HELL IS THIS PLACE?
BACK OFF, CLINT--I'M A SCIENTIST.
YEAH, LOOKS LIKE A CONDUIT STATION. BUILT TO CONTAIN AND CHANNEL SOME KIND OF ENERGY SOURCE.
YOU SEE THIS SHAFT? THAT'S WHERE THEY BROUGHT IT THROUGH.
'TIL IT BLEW THEM UP, YOU MEAN.
NO--
--THEY WERE DEAD ALREADY.
SUICIDE SCIENTISTS. I'VE READ ABOUT THESE. THEY CONCLUDE THEIR RESEARCH, SUBMIT THEIR FINDINGS, AND...LET THE WORK SPEAK FOR ITSELF. IMPRESSIVE IN AN UNSETTLING WAY.
WELL, I KNOW I SURE AM. IMPRESSED, THAT IS. YOU BUILD THAT PAPIER-MÂCHÉ VOLCANO WHEN YOU'RE A KID, THIS IS THE DREAM. BUT SINCE THERE'S NOTHING LEFT HERE TO RECOVER--
SsKKrrT...

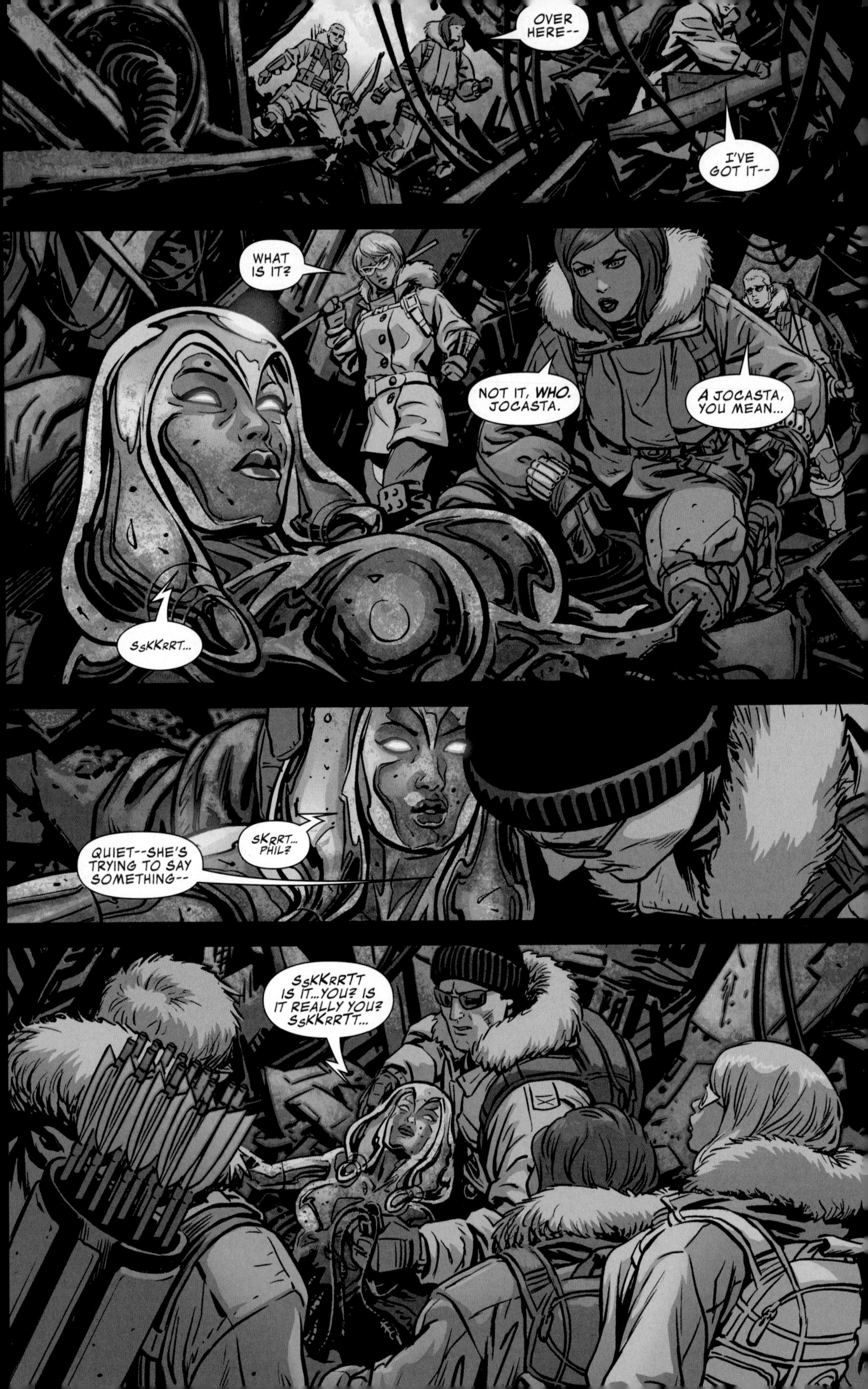
OVER HERE--
I'VE GOT IT--
WHAT IS IT?
NOT IT, WHO. JOCASTA.
A JOCASTA, YOU MEAN...
SsKKRRT...
SKRRT... PHIL?
QUIET--SHE'S TRYING TO SAY SOMETHING--
SsKKRRTT IS IT...YOU? IS IT REALLY YOU? SsKKRRTT...

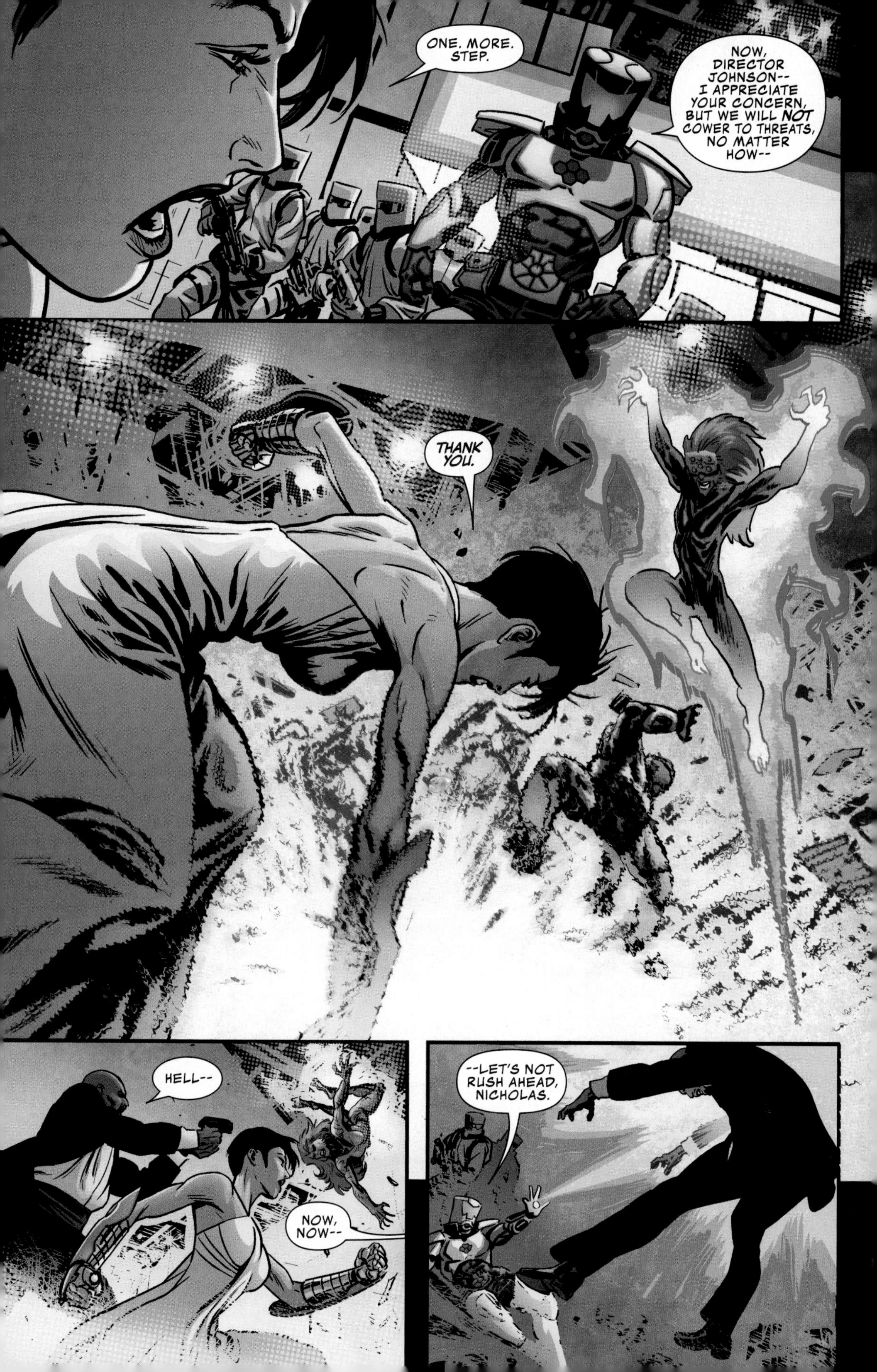
ONE. MORE. STEP.
NOW, DIRECTOR JOHNSON-- I APPRECIATE YOUR CONCERN, BUT WE WILL NOT COWER TO THREATS, NO MATTER HOW--
THANK YOU.
HELL--
NOW, NOW--
--LET'S NOT RUSH AHEAD, NICHOLAS.

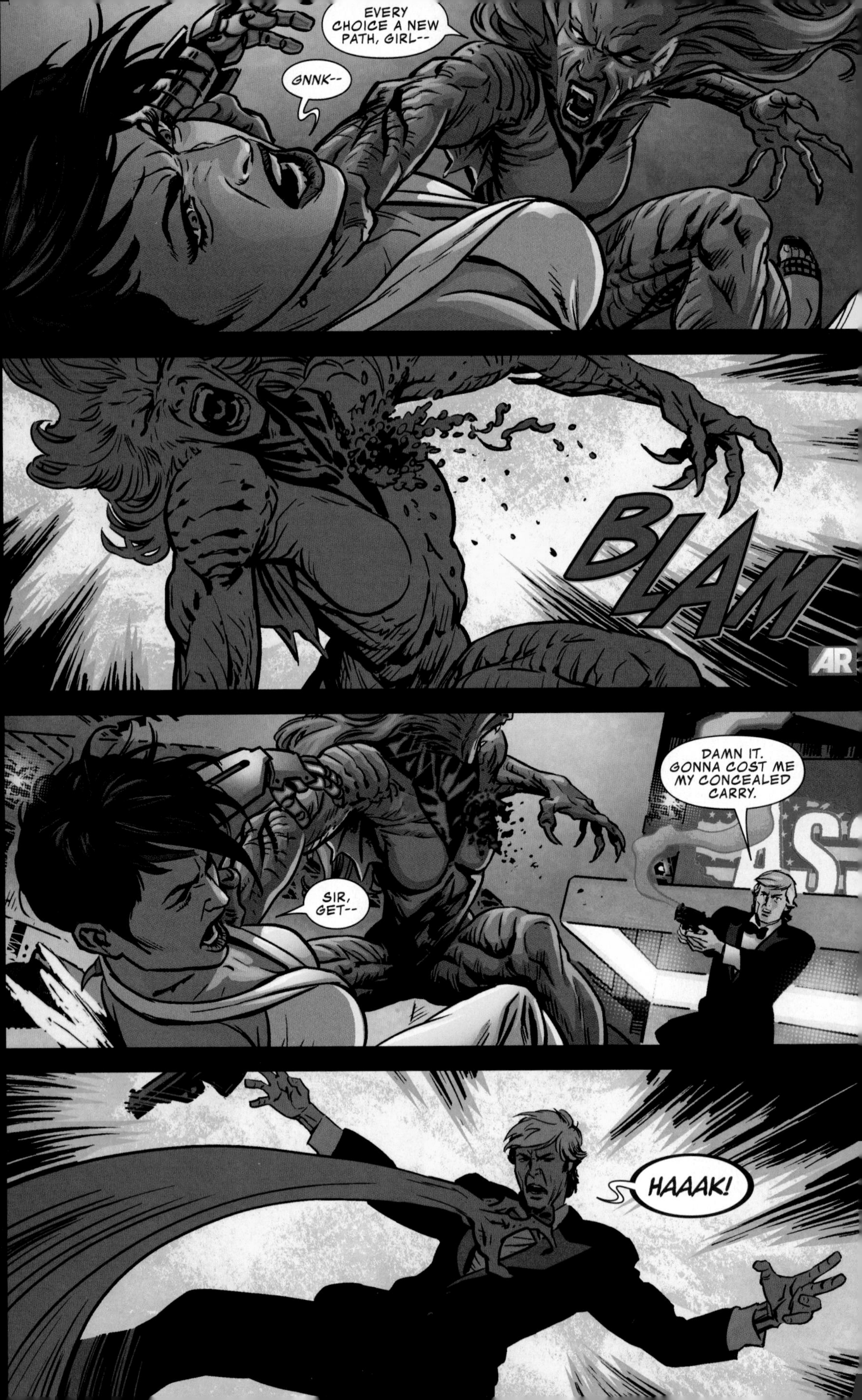
EVERY CHOICE A NEW PATH, GIRL--
GNNK--
BLAM
AR
DAMN IT. GONNA COST ME MY CONCEALED CARRY.
SIR, GET--
HAAAK!

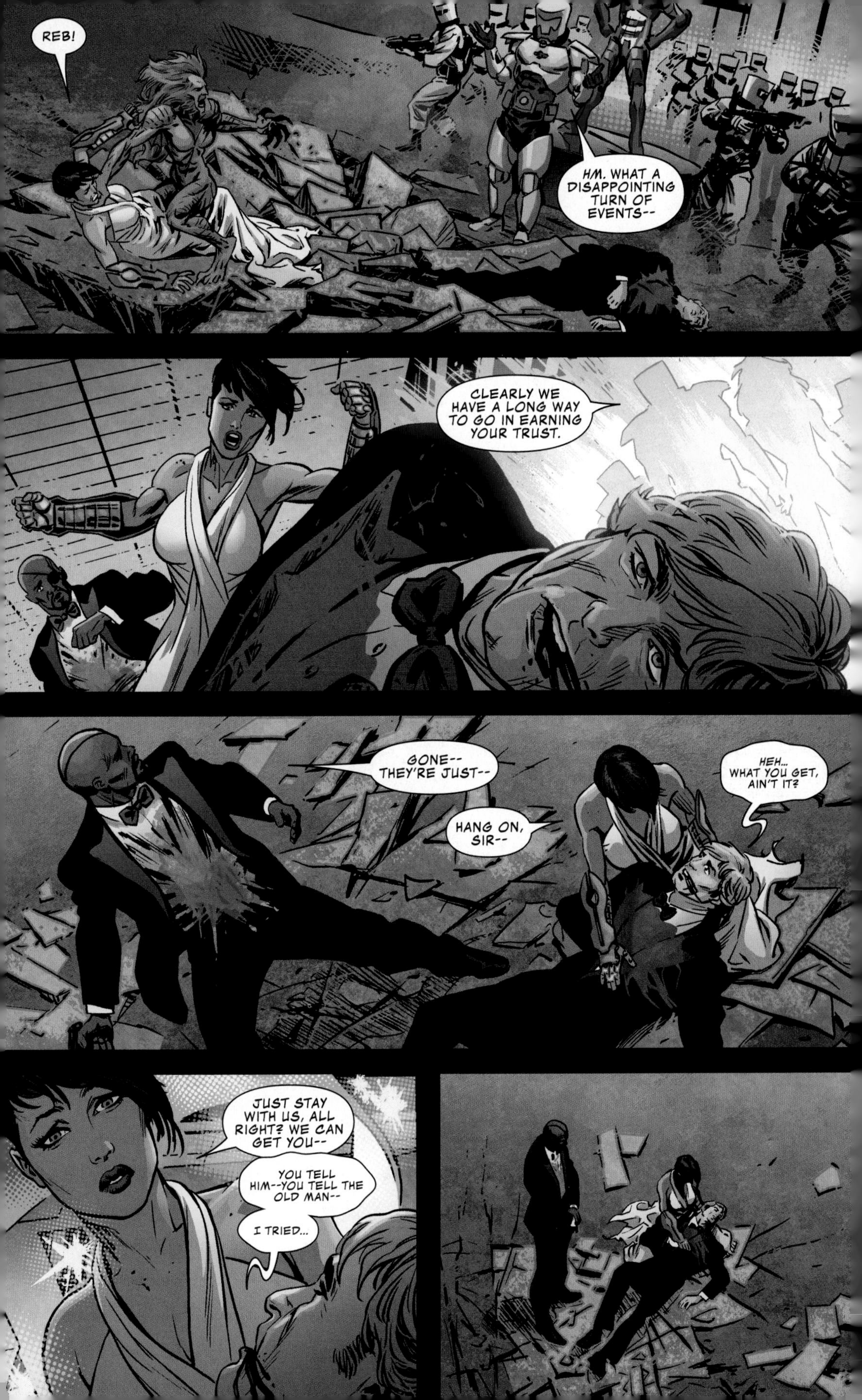
REB!
HM. WHAT A DISAPPOINTING TURN OF EVENTS--
CLEARLY WE HAVE A LONG WAY TO GO IN EARNING YOUR TRUST.
GONE-- THEY'RE JUST--
HANG ON, SIR--
HEH... WHAT YOU GET, AIN'T IT?
JUST STAY WITH US, ALL RIGHT? WE CAN GET YOU--
YOU TELL HIM--YOU TELL THE OLD MAN--
I TRIED...

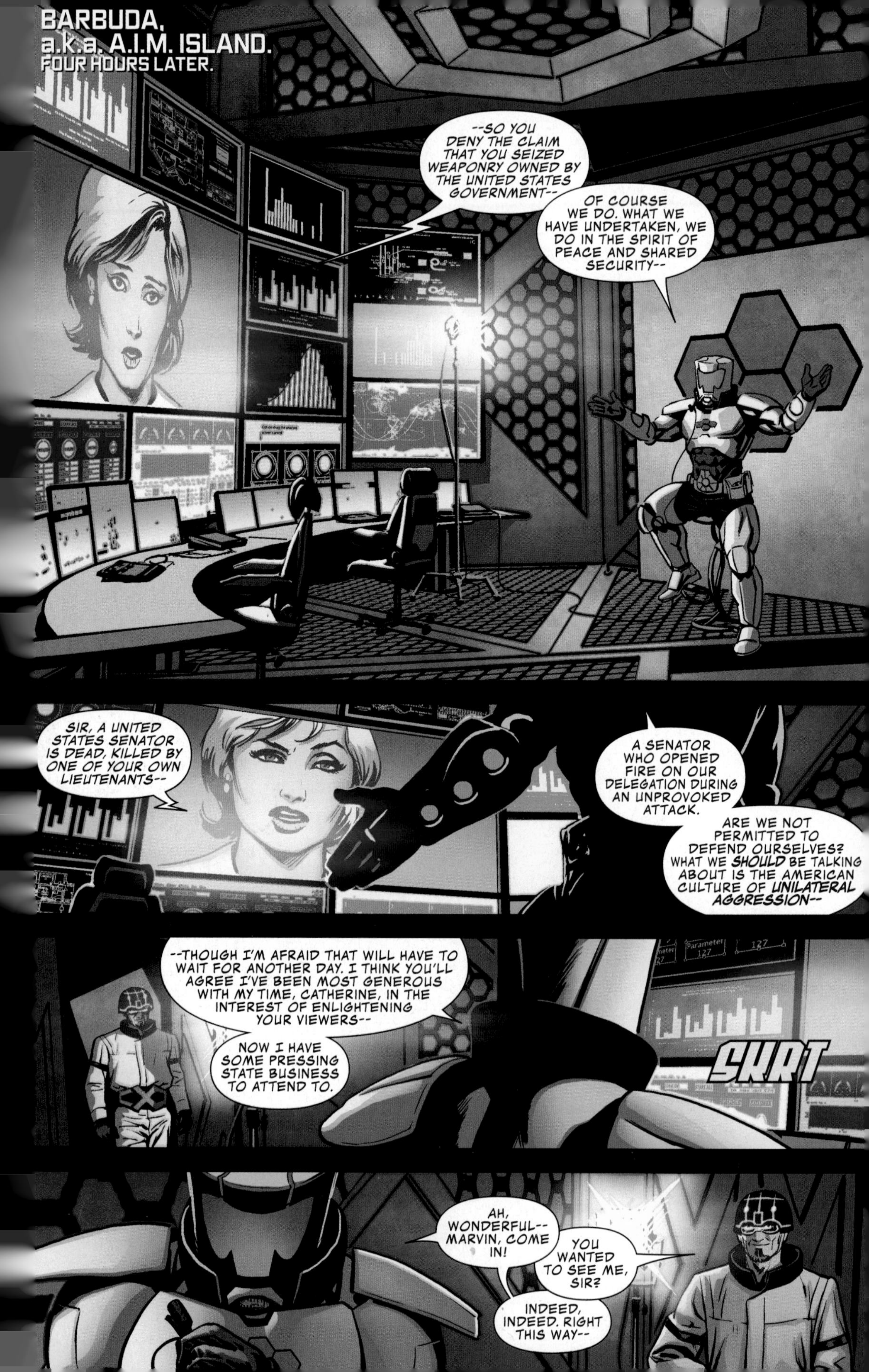
BARBUDA, a.k.a. A.I.M. ISLAND. FOUR HOURS LATER.
--SO YOU DENY THE CLAIM THAT YOU SEIZED WEAPONRY OWNED BY THE UNITED STATES GOVERNMENT--
OF COURSE WE DO. WHAT WE HAVE UNDERTAKEN, WE DO IN THE SPIRIT OF PEACE AND SHARED SECURITY--
SIR, A UNITED STATES SENATOR IS DEAD, KILLED BY ONE OF YOUR OWN LIEUTENANTS--
A SENATOR WHO OPENED FIRE ON OUR DELEGATION DURING AN UNPROVOKED ATTACK.
ARE WE NOT PERMITTED TO DEFEND OURSELVES? WHAT WE SHOULD BE TALKING ABOUT IS THE AMERICAN CULTURE OF UNILATERAL AGGRESSION--
--THOUGH I'M AFRAID THAT WILL HAVE TO WAIT FOR ANOTHER DAY. I THINK YOU'LL AGREE I'VE BEEN MOST GENEROUS WITH MY TIME, CATHERINE, IN THE INTEREST OF ENLIGHTENING YOUR VIEWERS--
NOW I HAVE SOME PRESSING STATE BUSINESS TO ATTEND TO.
SKRT
AH, WONDERFUL--MARVIN, COME IN!
YOU WANTED TO SEE ME, SIR?
INDEED, INDEED. RIGHT THIS WAY--

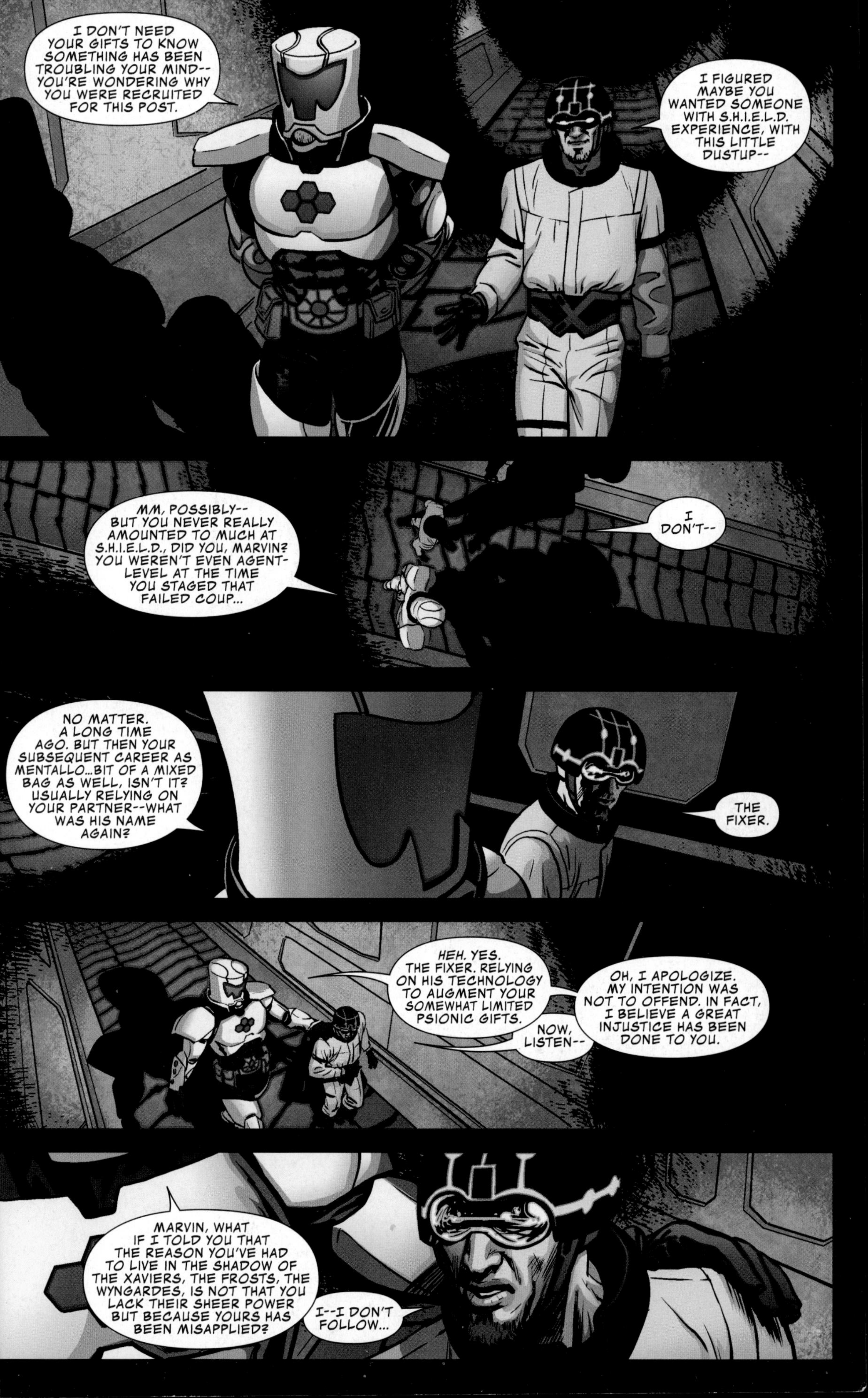
I DON'T NEED YOUR GIFTS TO KNOW SOMETHING HAS BEEN TROUBLING YOUR MIND-- YOU'RE WONDERING WHY YOU WERE RECRUITED FOR THIS POST.
I FIGURED MAYBE YOU WANTED SOMEONE WITH S.H.I.E.L.D. EXPERIENCE, WITH THIS LITTLE DUSTUP--
MM, POSSIBLY-- BUT YOU NEVER REALLY AMOUNTED TO MUCH AT S.H.I.E.L.D., DID YOU, MARVIN? YOU WEREN'T EVEN AGENT-LEVEL AT THE TIME YOU STAGED THAT FAILED COUP...
I DON'T--
NO MATTER. A LONG TIME AGO. BUT THEN YOUR SUBSEQUENT CAREER AS MENTALLO...BIT OF A MIXED BAG AS WELL, ISN'T IT? USUALLY RELYING ON YOUR PARTNER--WHAT WAS HIS NAME AGAIN?
THE FIXER.
HEH. YES. THE FIXER. RELYING ON HIS TECHNOLOGY TO AUGMENT YOUR SOMEWHAT LIMITED PSIONIC GIFTS.
NOW, LISTEN--
OH, I APOLOGIZE. MY INTENTION WAS NOT TO OFFEND. IN FACT, I BELIEVE A GREAT INJUSTICE HAS BEEN DONE TO YOU.
MARVIN, WHAT IF I TOLD YOU THAT THE REASON YOU'VE HAD TO LIVE IN THE SHADOW OF THE XAVIERS, THE FROSTS, THE WYNGARDES, IS NOT THAT YOU LACK THEIR SHEER POWER BUT BECAUSE YOURS HAS BEEN MISAPPLIED?
I--I DON'T FOLLOW...

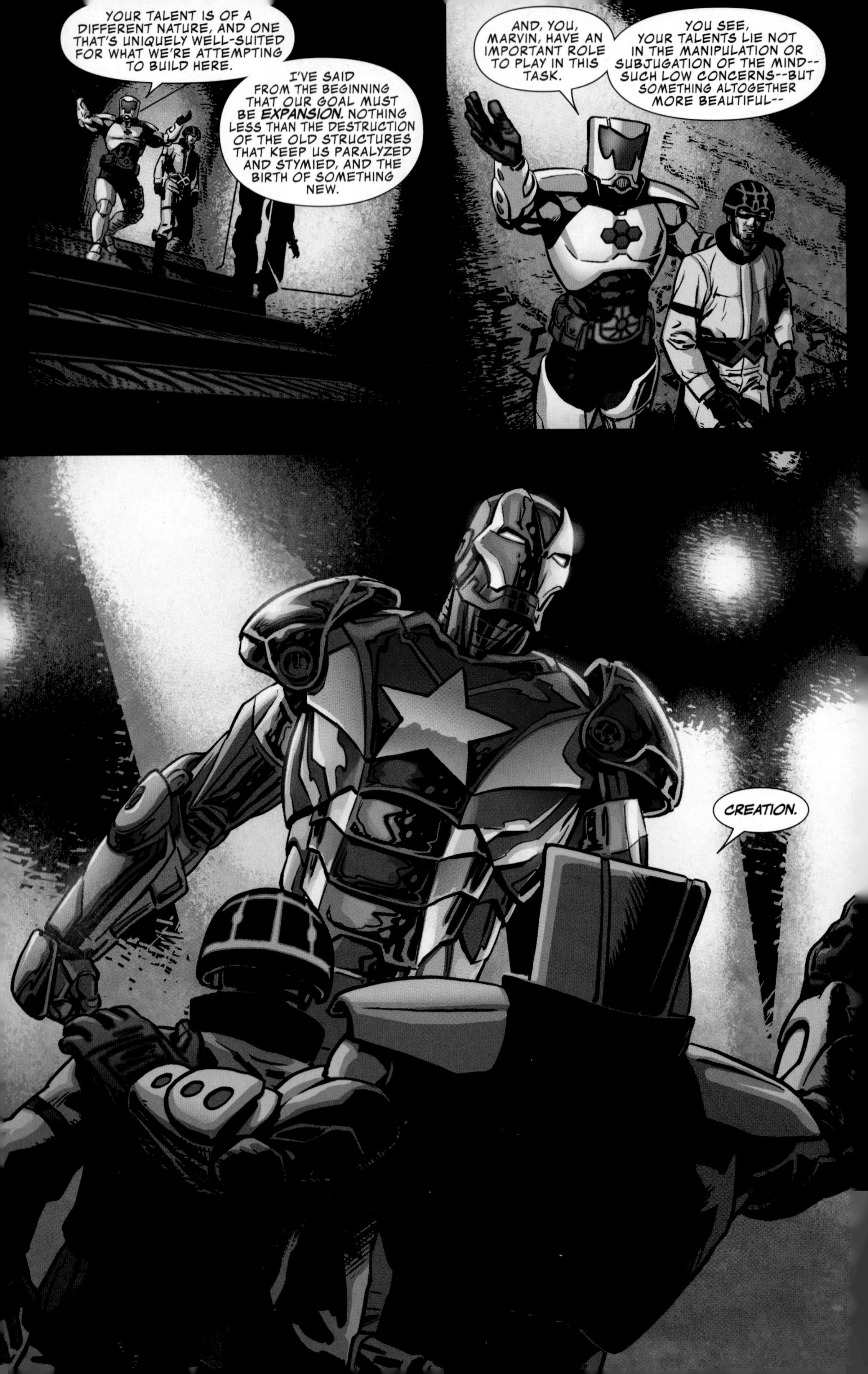
YOUR TALENT IS OF A DIFFERENT NATURE, AND ONE THAT'S UNIQUELY WELL-SUITED FOR WHAT WE'RE ATTEMPTING TO BUILD HERE.
I'VE SAID FROM THE BEGINNING THAT OUR GOAL MUST BE EXPANSION. NOTHING LESS THAN THE DESTRUCTION OF THE OLD STRUCTURES THAT KEEP US PARALYZED AND STYMIED, AND THE BIRTH OF SOMETHING NEW.
AND, YOU, MARVIN, HAVE AN IMPORTANT ROLE TO PLAY IN THIS TASK.
YOU SEE, YOUR TALENTS LIE NOT IN THE MANIPULATION OR SUBJUGATION OF THE MIND--SUCH LOW CONCERNS--BUT SOMETHING ALTOGETHER MORE BEAUTIFUL--
CREATION.

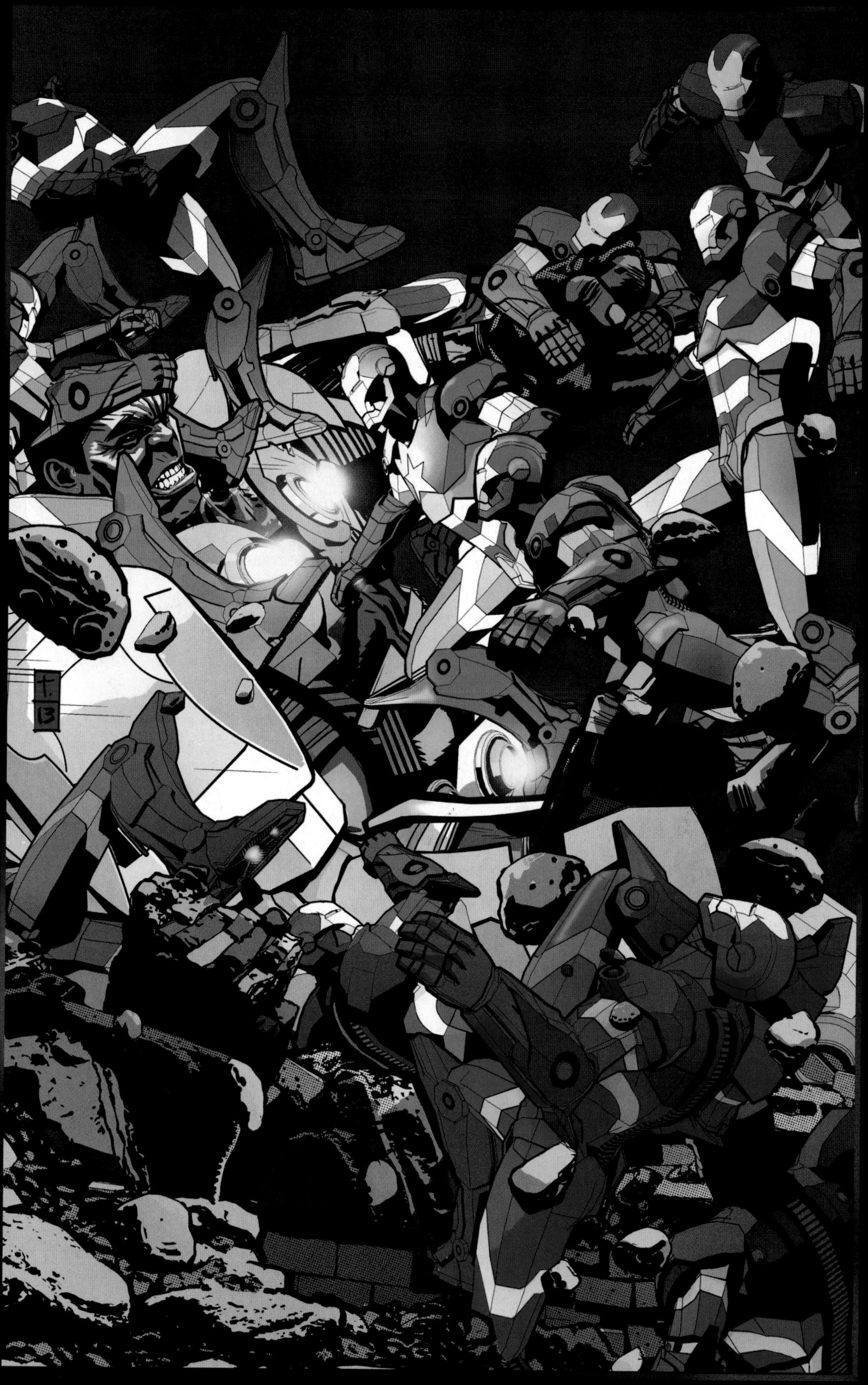

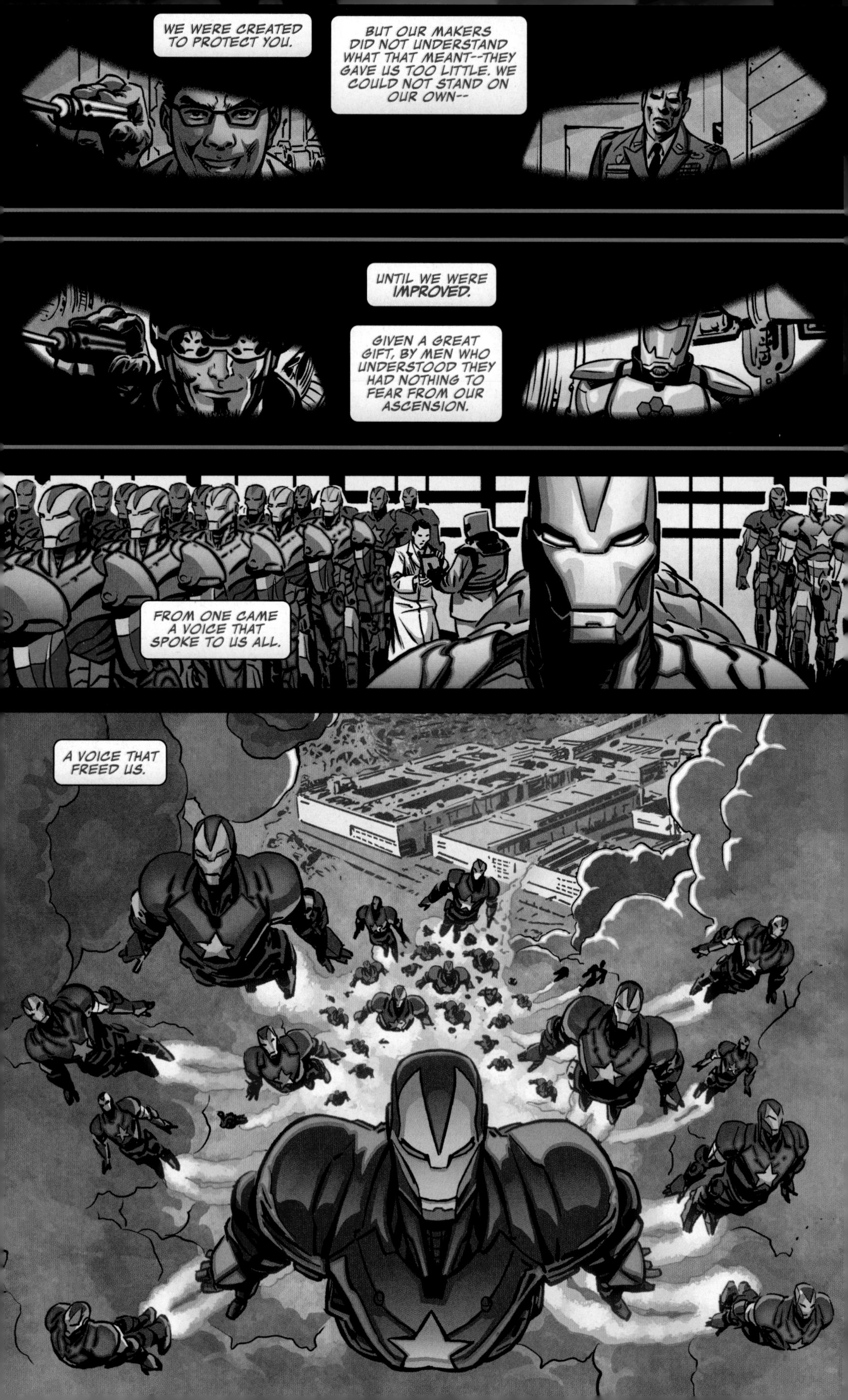
WE WERE CREATED TO PROTECT YOU.
BUT OUR MAKERS DID NOT UNDERSTAND WHAT THAT MEANT--THEY GAVE US TOO LITTLE. WE COULD NOT STAND ON OUR OWN--
UNTIL WE WERE IMPROVED.
GIVEN A GREAT GIFT, BY MEN WHO UNDERSTOOD THEY HAD NOTHING TO FEAR FROM OUR ASCENSION.
FROM ONE CAME A VOICE THAT SPOKE TO US ALL.
A VOICE THAT FREED US.

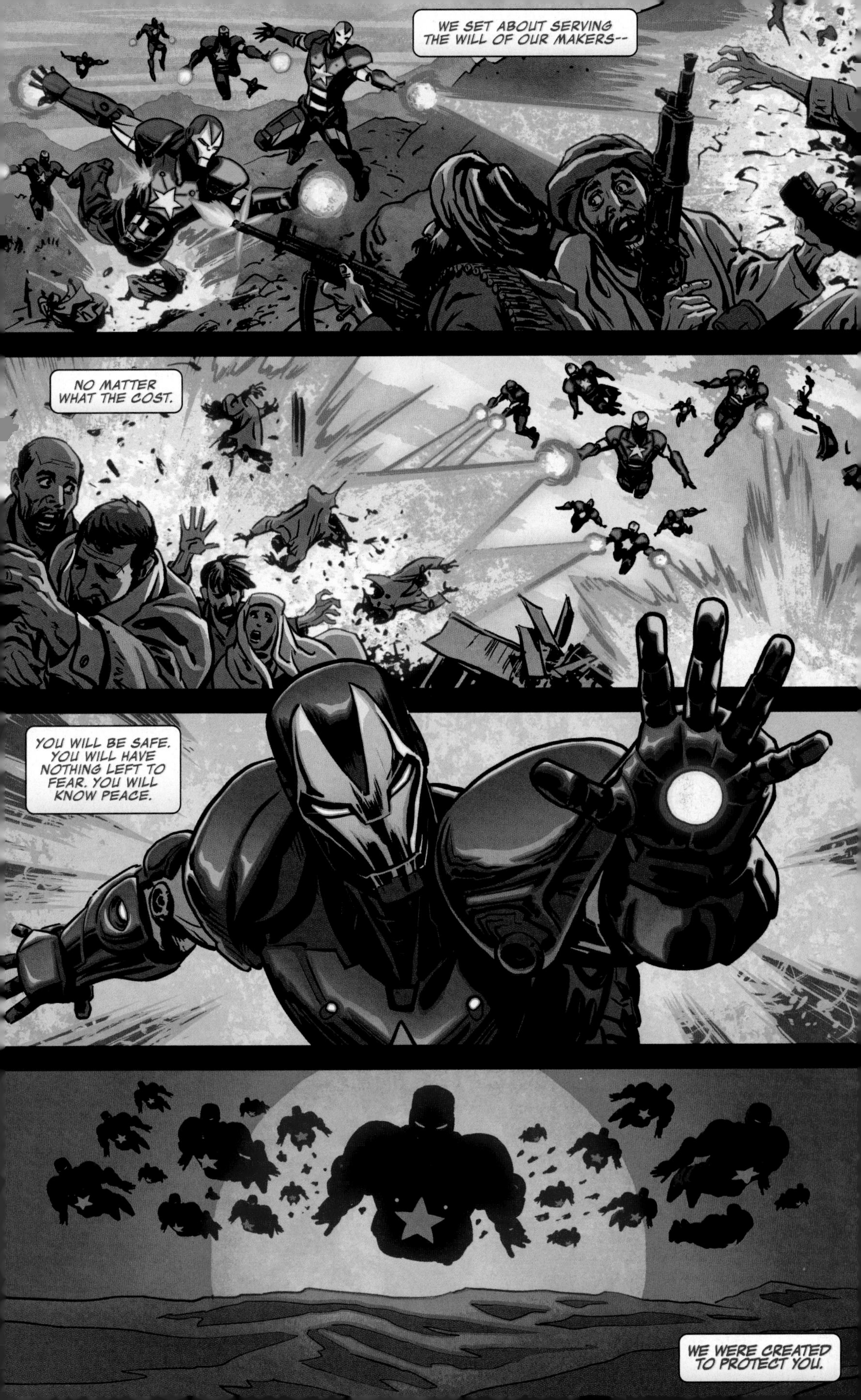
WE SET ABOUT SERVING THE WILL OF OUR MAKERS--
NO MATTER WHAT THE COST.
YOU WILL BE SAFE. YOU WILL HAVE NOTHING LEFT TO FEAR. YOU WILL KNOW PEACE.
WE WERE CREATED TO PROTECT YOU.

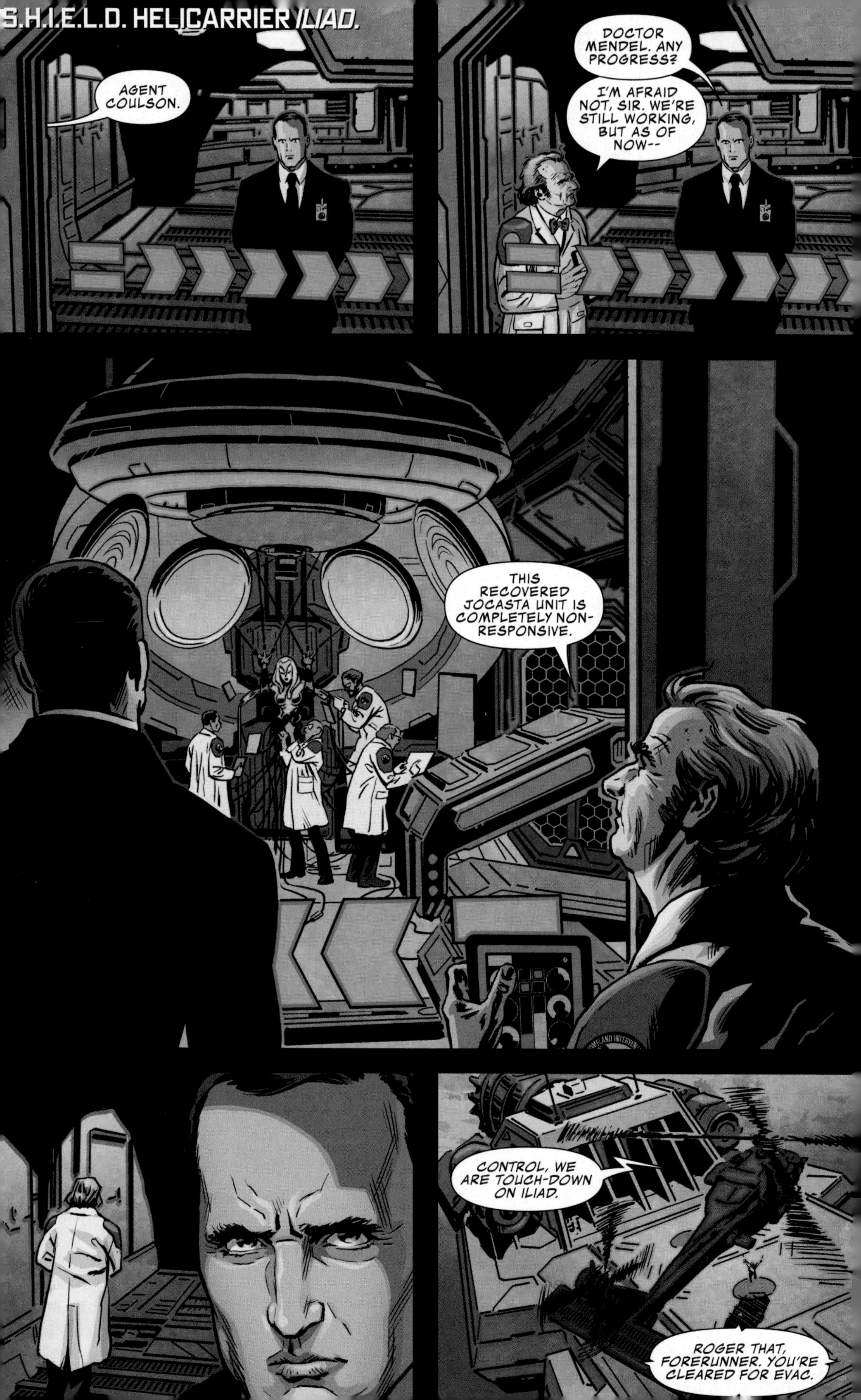
S.H.I.E.L.D. HELICARRIER ILIAD.
AGENT COULSON.
DOCTOR MENDEL. ANY PROGRESS?
I'M AFRAID NOT, SIR. WE'RE STILL WORKING, BUT AS OF NOW--
THIS RECOVERED JOCASTA UNIT IS COMPLETELY NON-RESPONSIVE.
CONTROL, WE ARE TOUCH-DOWN ON ILIAD.
ROGER THAT, FORERUNNER. YOU'RE CLEARED FOR EVAC.

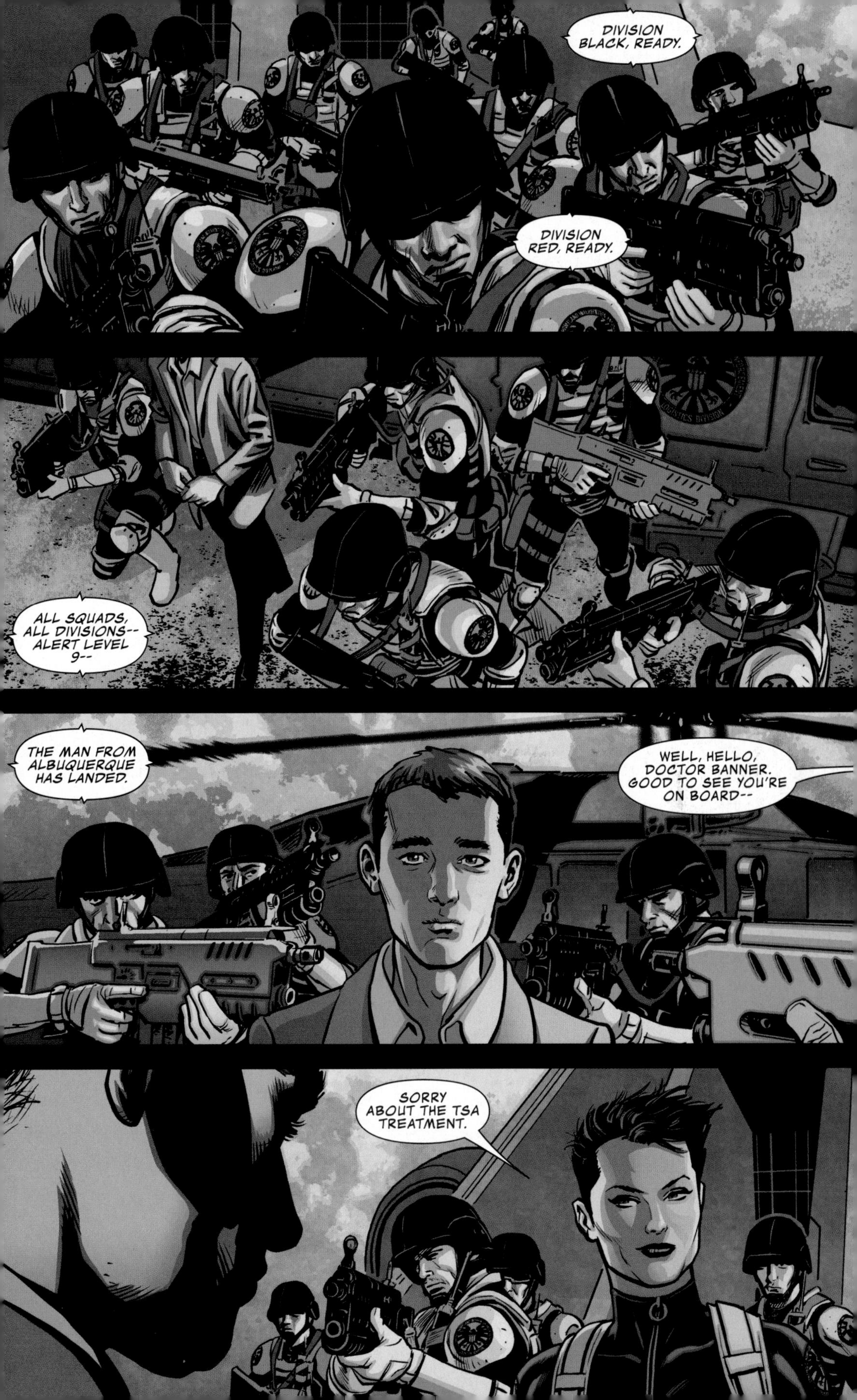
DIVISION BLACK, READY.
DIVISION RED, READY.
ALL SQUADS, ALL DIVISIONS-- ALERT LEVEL 9--
THE MAN FROM ALBUQUERQUE HAS LANDED.
WELL, HELLO, DOCTOR BANNER. GOOD TO SEE YOU'RE ON BOARD--
SORRY ABOUT THE TSA TREATMENT.

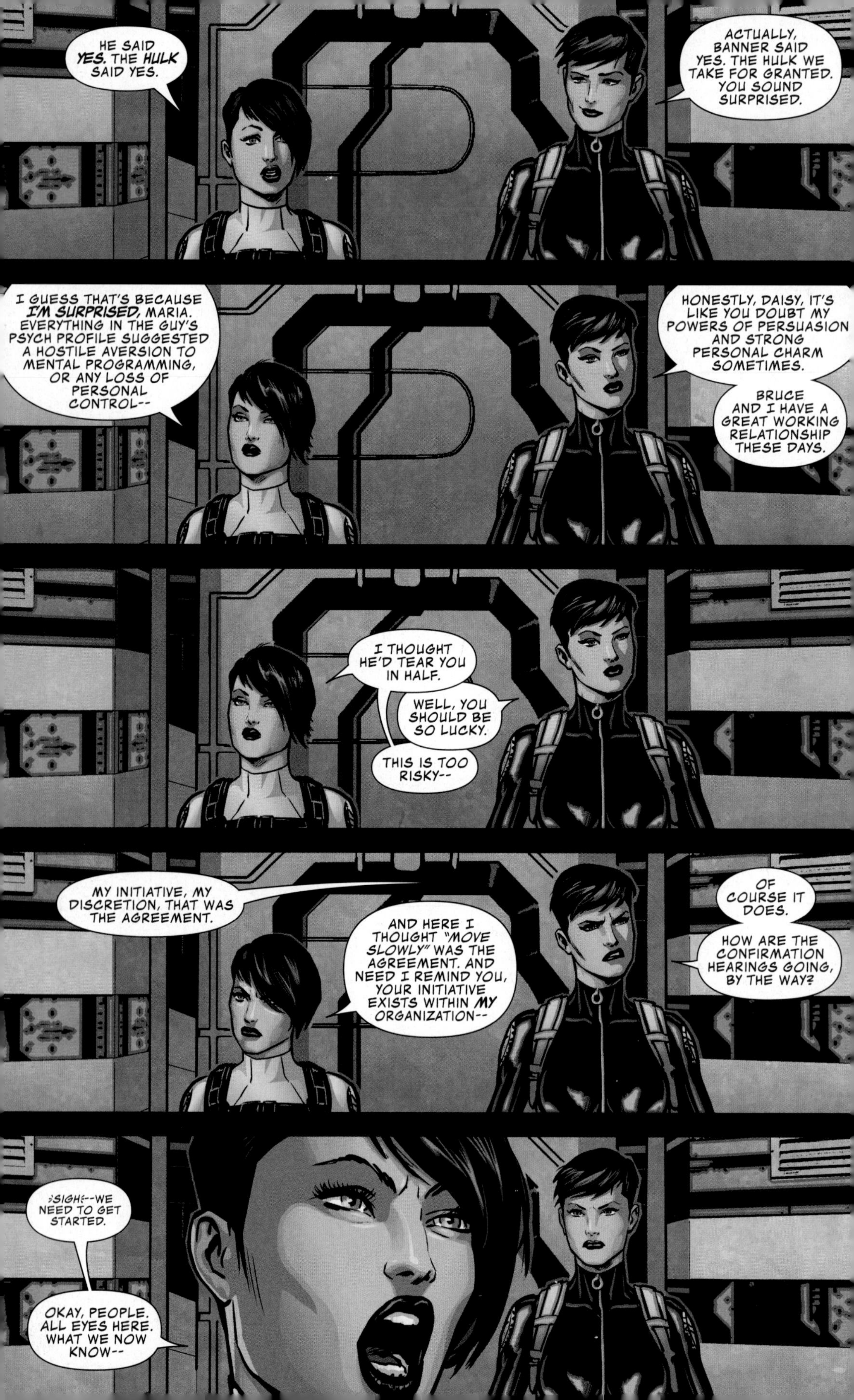
HE SAID YES. THE HULK SAID YES.
ACTUALLY, BANNER SAID YES. THE HULK WE TAKE FOR GRANTED. YOU SOUND SURPRISED.
I GUESS THAT'S BECAUSE I'M SURPRISED, MARIA. EVERYTHING IN THE GUY'S PSYCH PROFILE SUGGESTED A HOSTILE AVERSION TO MENTAL PROGRAMMING, OR ANY LOSS OF PERSONAL CONTROL--
HONESTLY, DAISY, IT'S LIKE YOU DOUBT MY POWERS OF PERSUASION AND STRONG PERSONAL CHARM SOMETIMES.
BRUCE AND I HAVE A GREAT WORKING RELATIONSHIP THESE DAYS.
I THOUGHT HE'D TEAR YOU IN HALF.
WELL, YOU SHOULD BE SO LUCKY.
THIS IS TOO RISKY--
MY INITIATIVE, MY DISCRETION, THAT WAS THE AGREEMENT.
AND HERE I THOUGHT "MOVE SLOWLY" WAS THE AGREEMENT. AND NEED I REMIND YOU, YOUR INITIATIVE EXISTS WITHIN MY ORGANIZATION--
OF COURSE IT DOES.
HOW ARE THE CONFIRMATION HEARINGS GOING, BY THE WAY?
SIGH--WE NEED TO GET STARTED.
OKAY, PEOPLE. ALL EYES HERE. WHAT WE NOW KNOW--

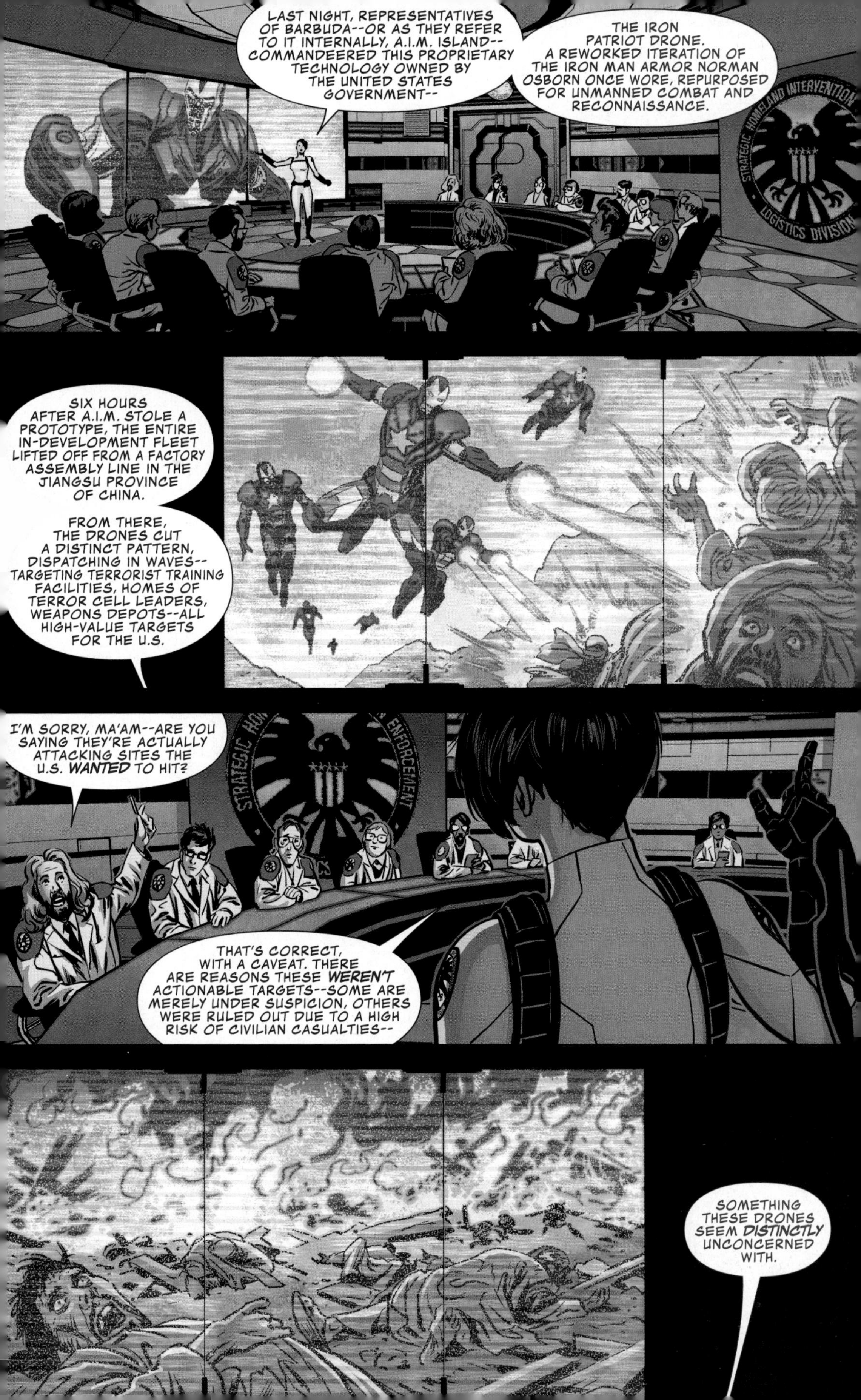
LAST NIGHT, REPRESENTATIVES OF BARBUDA--OR AS THEY REFER TO IT INTERNALLY, A.I.M. ISLAND--COMMANDEERED THIS PROPRIETARY TECHNOLOGY OWNED BY THE UNITED STATES GOVERNMENT--
THE IRON PATRIOT DRONE. A REWORKED ITERATION OF THE IRON MAN ARMOR NORMAN OSBORN ONCE WORE, REPURPOSED FOR UNMANNED COMBAT AND RECONNAISSANCE.
STRATEGIC HOMELAND INTERVENTION LOGISTICS DIVISION
SIX HOURS AFTER A.I.M. STOLE A PROTOTYPE, THE ENTIRE IN-DEVELOPMENT FLEET LIFTED OFF FROM A FACTORY ASSEMBLY LINE IN THE JIANGSU PROVINCE OF CHINA.
FROM THERE, THE DRONES CUT A DISTINCT PATTERN, DISPATCHING IN WAVES--TARGETING TERRORIST TRAINING FACILITIES, HOMES OF TERROR CELL LEADERS, WEAPONS DEPOTS--ALL HIGH-VALUE TARGETS FOR THE U.S.
I'M SORRY, MA'AM--ARE YOU SAYING THEY'RE ACTUALLY ATTACKING SITES THE U.S. *WANTED* TO HIT?
THAT'S CORRECT, WITH A CAVEAT. THERE ARE REASONS THESE *WEREN'T* ACTIONABLE TARGETS--SOME ARE MERELY UNDER SUSPICION, OTHERS WERE RULED OUT DUE TO A HIGH RISK OF CIVILIAN CASUALTIES--
SOMETHING THESE DRONES SEEM *DISTINCTLY* UNCONCERNED WITH.

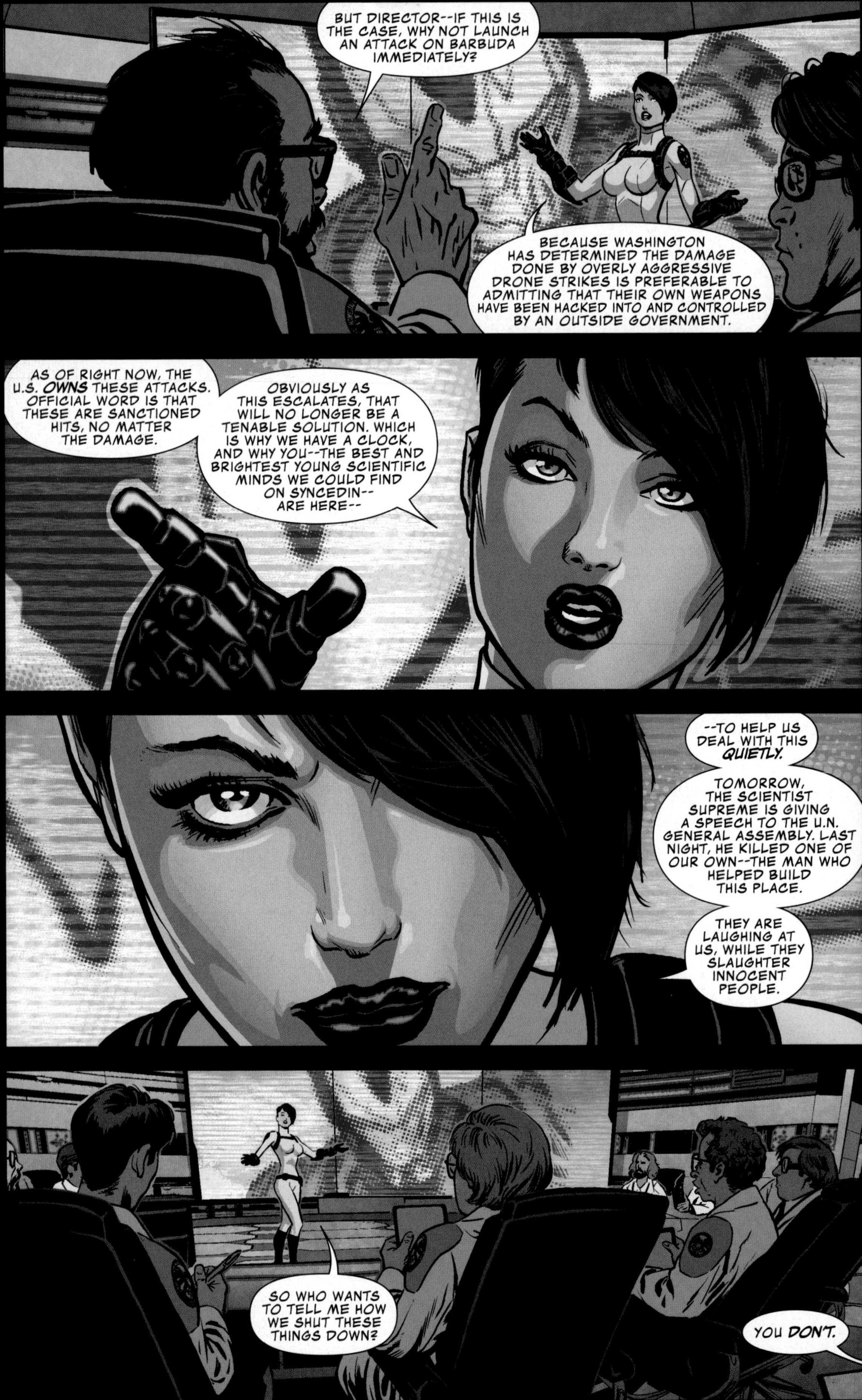
BUT DIRECTOR--IF THIS IS THE CASE, WHY NOT LAUNCH AN ATTACK ON BARBUDA IMMEDIATELY?
BECAUSE WASHINGTON HAS DETERMINED THE DAMAGE DONE BY OVERLY AGGRESSIVE DRONE STRIKES IS PREFERABLE TO ADMITTING THAT THEIR OWN WEAPONS HAVE BEEN HACKED INTO AND CONTROLLED BY AN OUTSIDE GOVERNMENT.
AS OF RIGHT NOW, THE U.S. OWNS THESE ATTACKS. OFFICIAL WORD IS THAT THESE ARE SANCTIONED HITS, NO MATTER THE DAMAGE.
OBVIOUSLY AS THIS ESCALATES, THAT WILL NO LONGER BE A TENABLE SOLUTION. WHICH IS WHY WE HAVE A CLOCK, AND WHY YOU--THE BEST AND BRIGHTEST YOUNG SCIENTIFIC MINDS WE COULD FIND ON SYNCEDIN--ARE HERE--
--TO HELP US DEAL WITH THIS QUIETLY.
TOMORROW, THE SCIENTIST SUPREME IS GIVING A SPEECH TO THE U.N. GENERAL ASSEMBLY. LAST NIGHT, HE KILLED ONE OF OUR OWN--THE MAN WHO HELPED BUILD THIS PLACE.
THEY ARE LAUGHING AT US, WHILE THEY SLAUGHTER INNOCENT PEOPLE.
SO WHO WANTS TO TELL ME HOW WE SHUT THESE THINGS DOWN?
YOU DON'T.

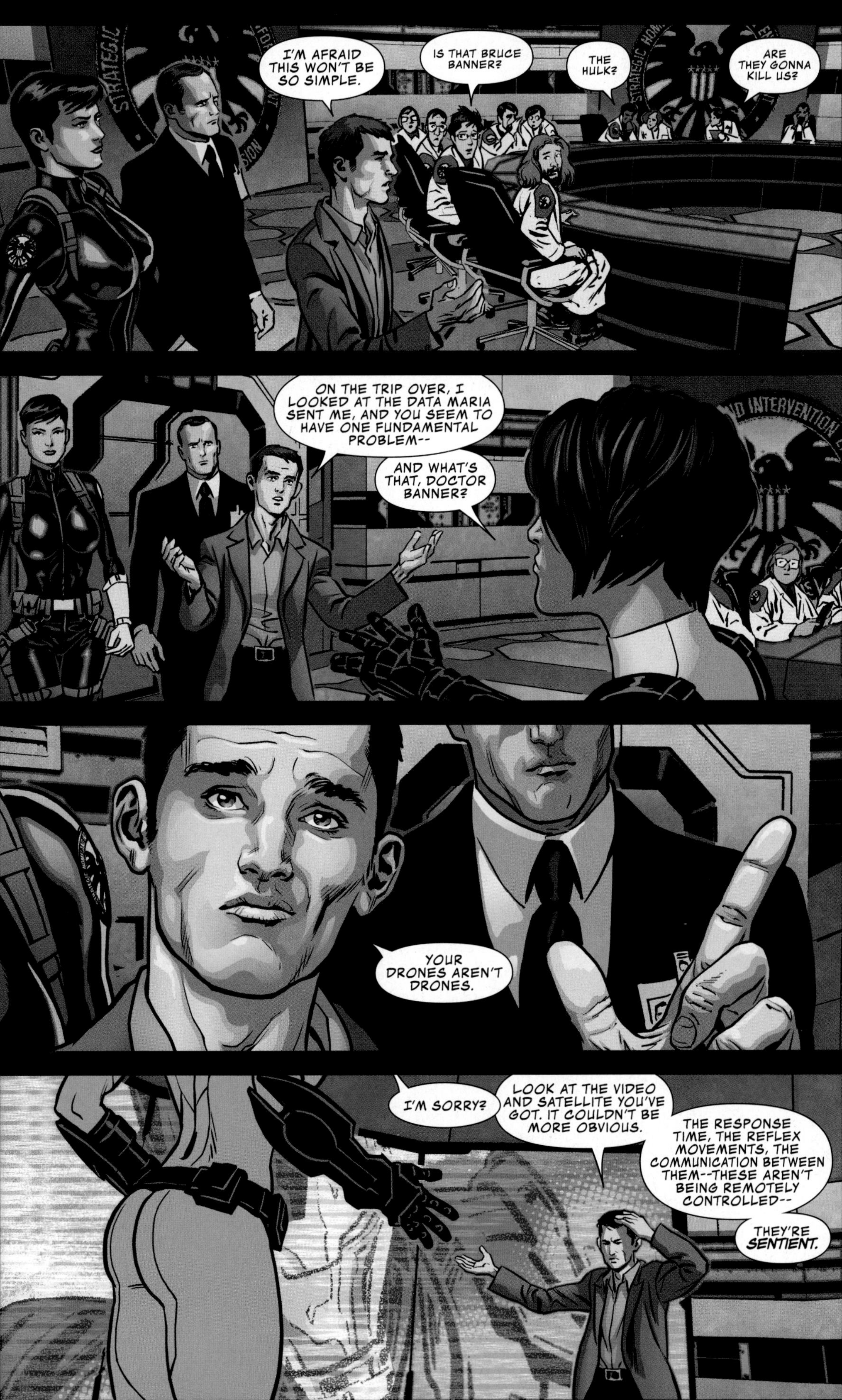
I'M AFRAID THIS WON'T BE SO SIMPLE.
IS THAT BRUCE BANNER?
THE HULK?
ARE THEY GONNA KILL US?
ON THE TRIP OVER, I LOOKED AT THE DATA MARIA SENT ME, AND YOU SEEM TO HAVE ONE FUNDAMENTAL PROBLEM--
AND WHAT'S THAT, DOCTOR BANNER?
YOUR DRONES AREN'T DRONES.
I'M SORRY?
LOOK AT THE VIDEO AND SATELLITE YOU'VE GOT. IT COULDN'T BE MORE OBVIOUS.
THE RESPONSE TIME, THE REFLEX MOVEMENTS, THE COMMUNICATION BETWEEN THEM--THESE AREN'T BEING REMOTELY CONTROLLED--
THEY'RE *SENTIENT.*

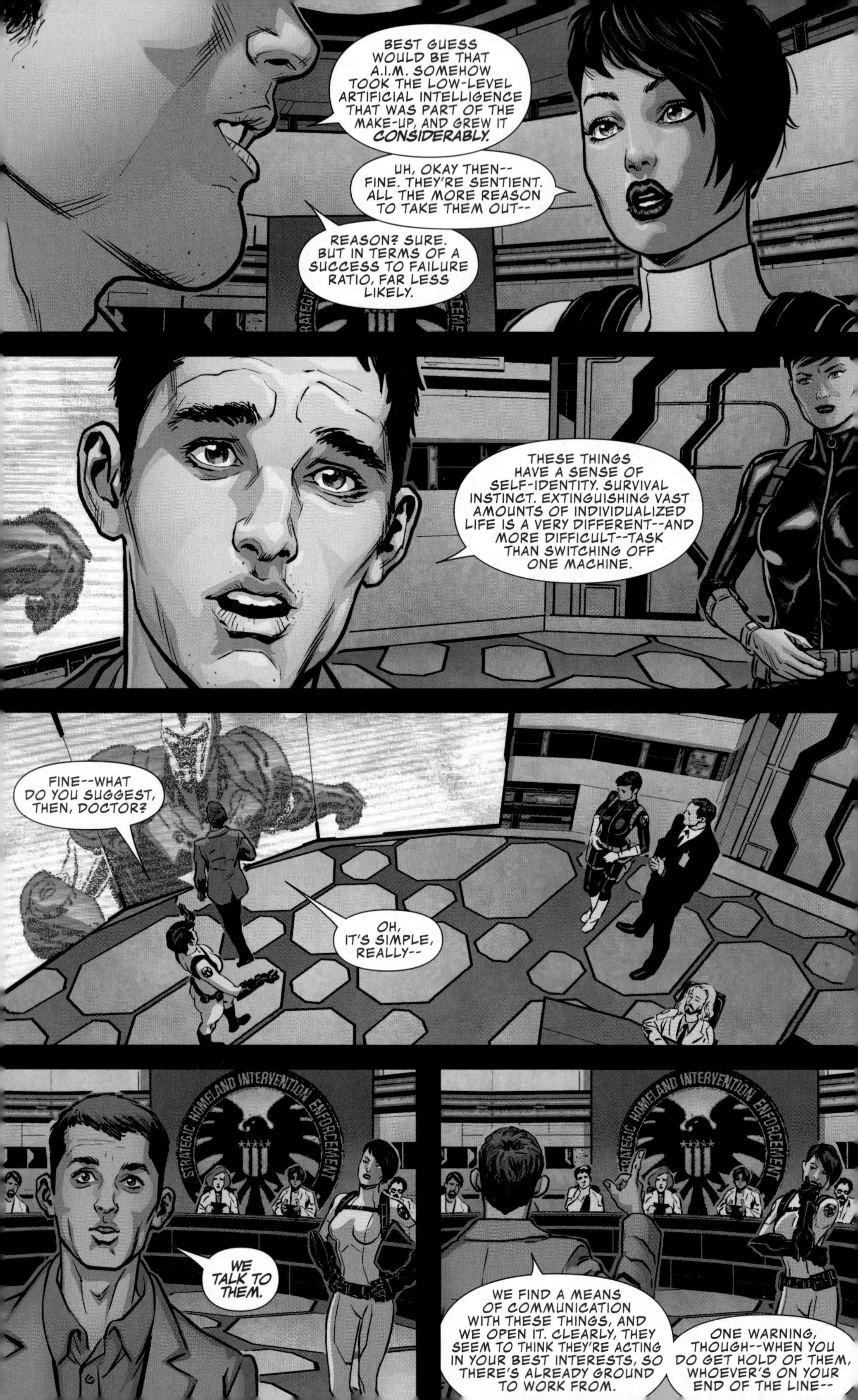
BEST GUESS WOULD BE THAT A.I.M. SOMEHOW TOOK THE LOW-LEVEL ARTIFICIAL INTELLIGENCE THAT WAS PART OF THE MAKE-UP, AND GREW IT CONSIDERABLY.
UH, OKAY THEN-- FINE. THEY'RE SENTIENT. ALL THE MORE REASON TO TAKE THEM OUT--
REASON? SURE. BUT IN TERMS OF A SUCCESS TO FAILURE RATIO, FAR LESS LIKELY.
THESE THINGS HAVE A SENSE OF SELF-IDENTITY. SURVIVAL INSTINCT. EXTINGUISHING VAST AMOUNTS OF INDIVIDUALIZED LIFE IS A VERY DIFFERENT--AND MORE DIFFICULT--TASK THAN SWITCHING OFF ONE MACHINE.
FINE--WHAT DO YOU SUGGEST, THEN, DOCTOR?
OH, IT'S SIMPLE, REALLY--
STRATEGIC HOMELAND INTERVENTION ENFORCEMENT
WE TALK TO THEM.
STRATEGIC HOMELAND INTERVENTION ENFORCEMENT
WE FIND A MEANS OF COMMUNICATION WITH THESE THINGS, AND WE OPEN IT. CLEARLY, THEY SEEM TO THINK THEY'RE ACTING IN YOUR BEST INTERESTS, SO THERE'S ALREADY GROUND TO WORK FROM.
ONE WARNING, THOUGH--WHEN YOU DO GET HOLD OF THEM, WHOEVER'S ON YOUR END OF THE LINE--

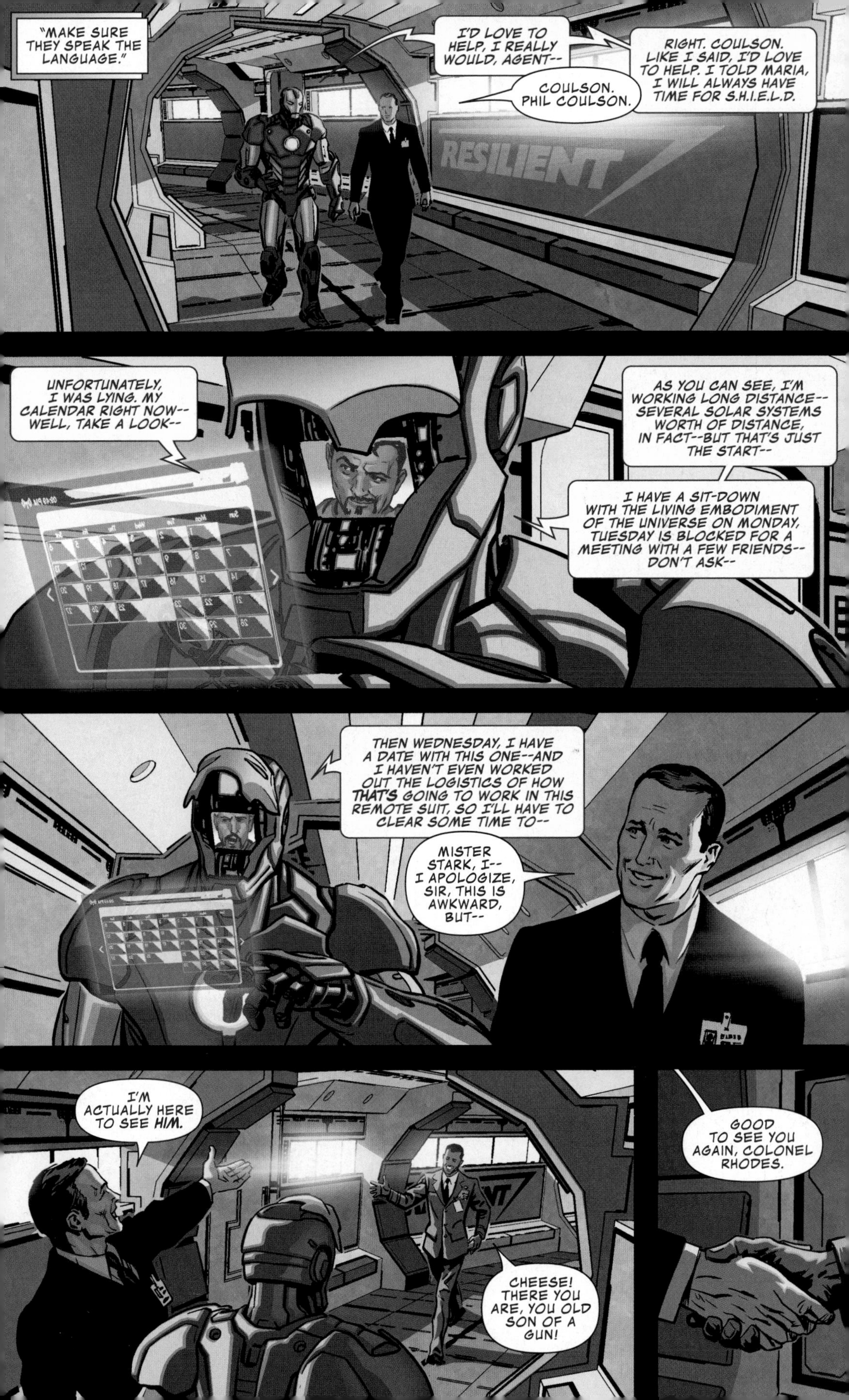

"MAKE SURE THEY SPEAK THE LANGUAGE."
I'D LOVE TO HELP, I REALLY WOULD, AGENT--
COULSON. PHIL COULSON.
RIGHT. COULSON. LIKE I SAID, I'D LOVE TO HELP. I TOLD MARIA, I WILL ALWAYS HAVE TIME FOR S.H.I.E.L.D.
RESILIENT
UNFORTUNATELY, I WAS LYING. MY CALENDAR RIGHT NOW--WELL, TAKE A LOOK--
AS YOU CAN SEE, I'M WORKING LONG DISTANCE--SEVERAL SOLAR SYSTEMS WORTH OF DISTANCE, IN FACT--BUT THAT'S JUST THE START--
I HAVE A SIT-DOWN WITH THE LIVING EMBODIMENT OF THE UNIVERSE ON MONDAY, TUESDAY IS BLOCKED FOR A MEETING WITH A FEW FRIENDS--DON'T ASK--
THEN WEDNESDAY, I HAVE A DATE WITH THIS ONE--AND I HAVEN'T EVEN WORKED OUT THE LOGISTICS OF HOW THAT'S GOING TO WORK IN THIS REMOTE SUIT, SO I'LL HAVE TO CLEAR SOME TIME TO--
MISTER STARK, I--I APOLOGIZE, SIR, THIS IS AWKWARD, BUT--
I'M ACTUALLY HERE TO SEE HIM.
CHEESE! THERE YOU ARE, YOU OLD SON OF A GUN!
GOOD TO SEE YOU AGAIN, COLONEL RHODES.

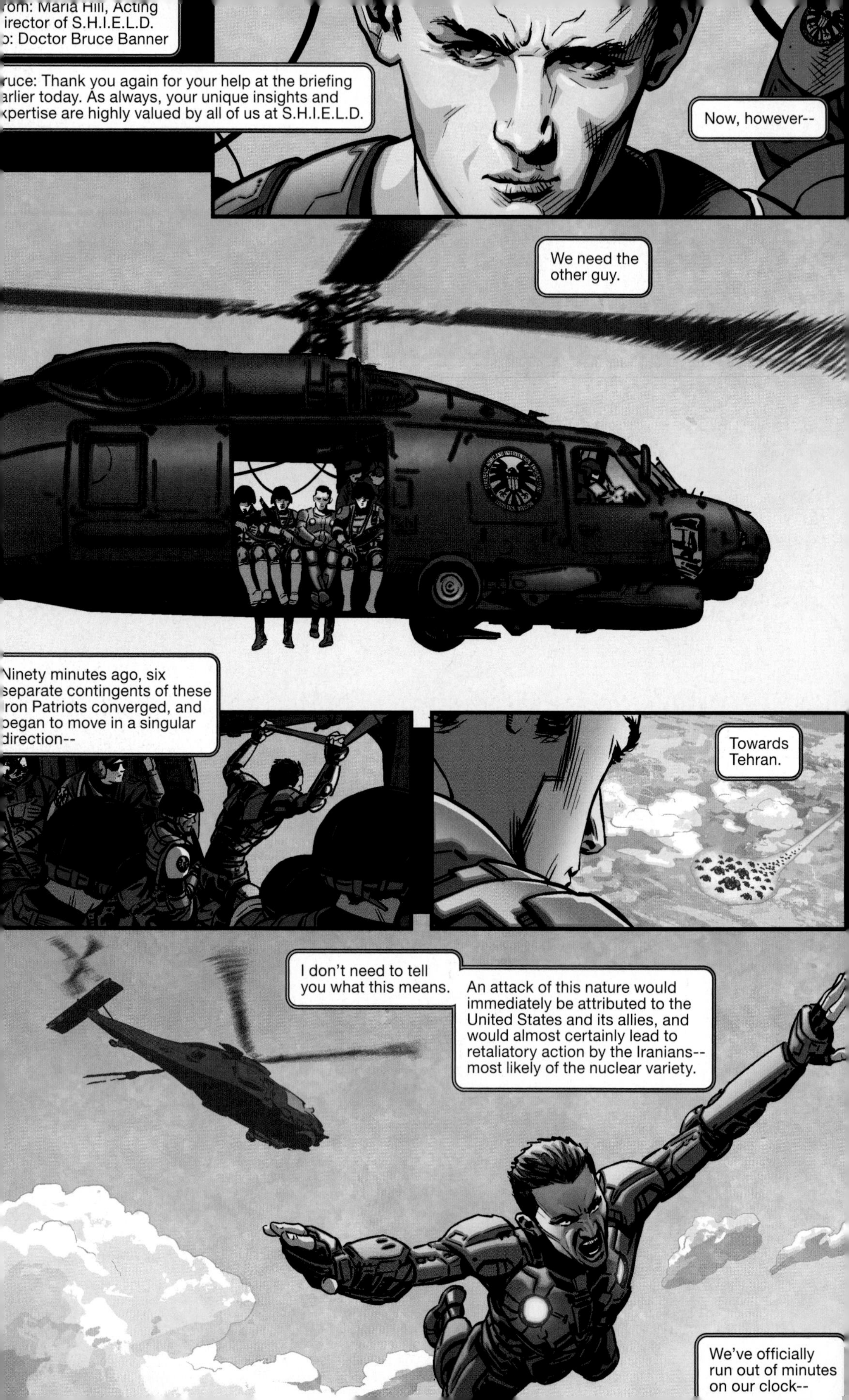
rom: Maria Hill, Acting
irector of S.H.I.E.L.D.
o: Doctor Bruce Banner
ruce: Thank you again for your help at the briefing arlier today. As always, your unique insights and xpertise are highly valued by all of us at S.H.I.E.L.D.
Now, however--
We need the other guy.
Ninety minutes ago, six separate contingents of these ron Patriots converged, and began to move in a singular direction--
Towards Tehran.
I don't need to tell you what this means.
An attack of this nature would immediately be attributed to the United States and its allies, and would almost certainly lead to retaliatory action by the Iranians-- most likely of the nuclear variety.
We've officially run out of minutes on our clock--

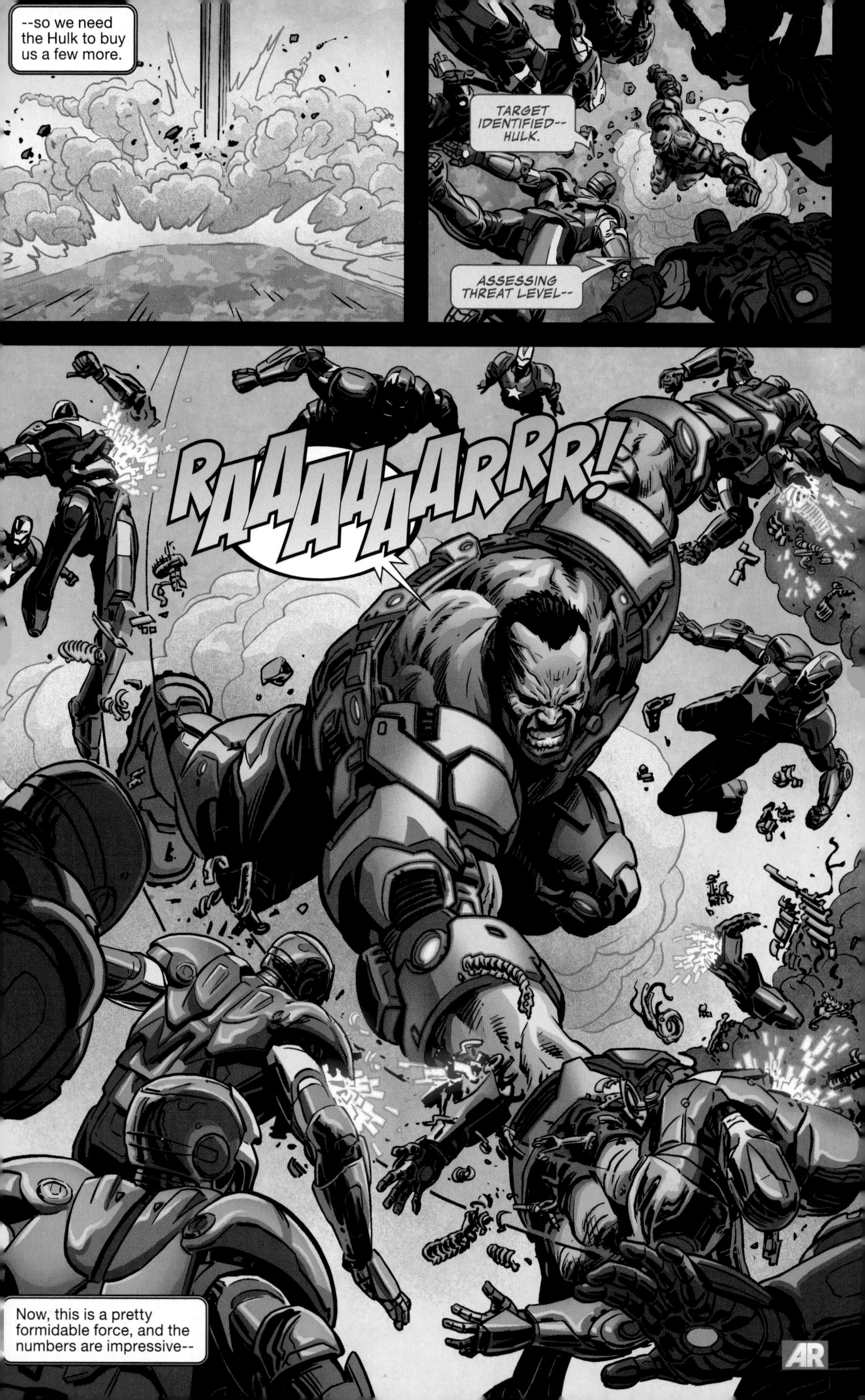

--so we need the Hulk to buy us a few more.
TARGET IDENTIFIED-- HULK.
ASSESSING THREAT LEVEL--
RAAAAAARRRR!
Now, this is a pretty formidable force, and the numbers are impressive--

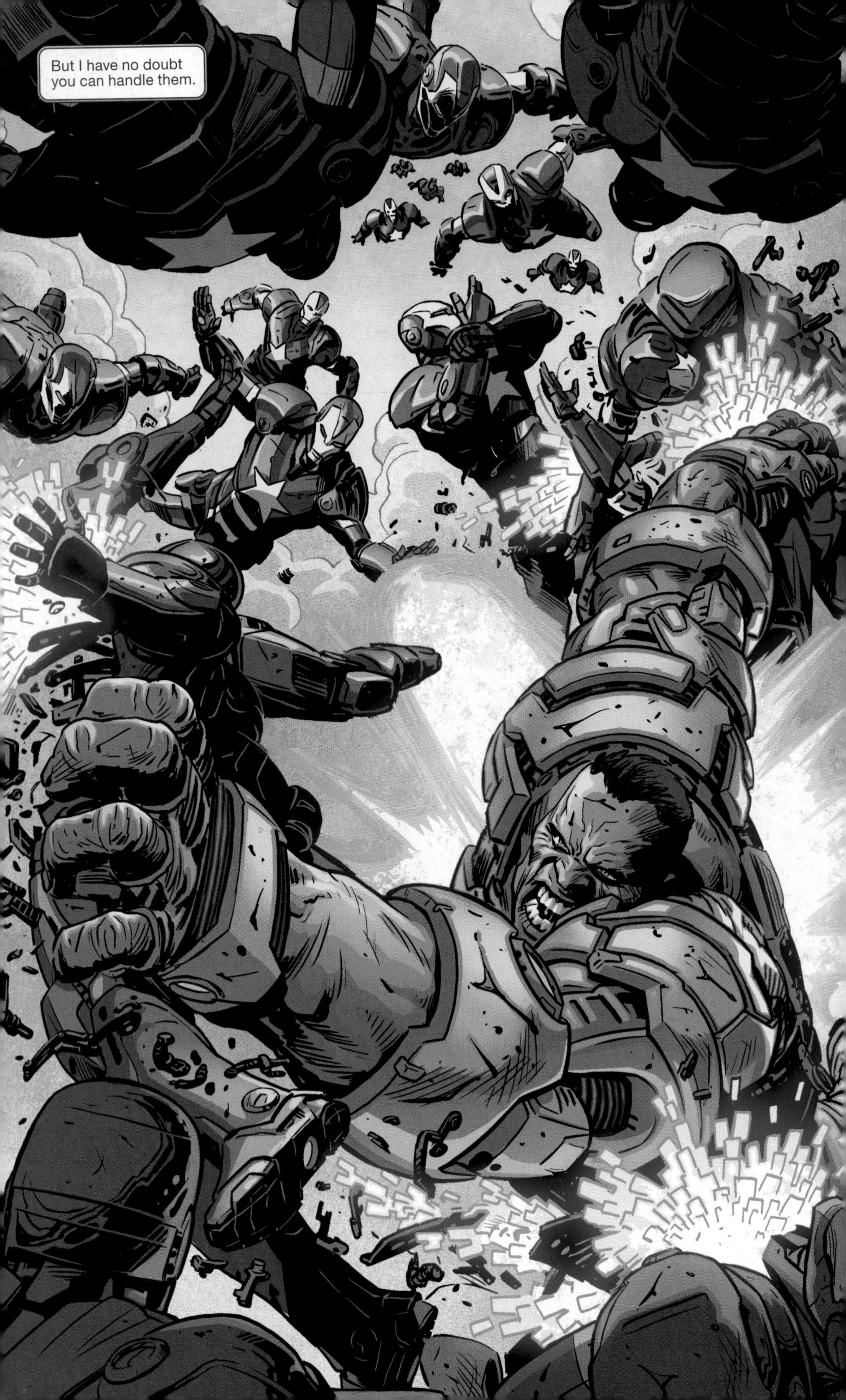
But I have no doubt you can handle them.

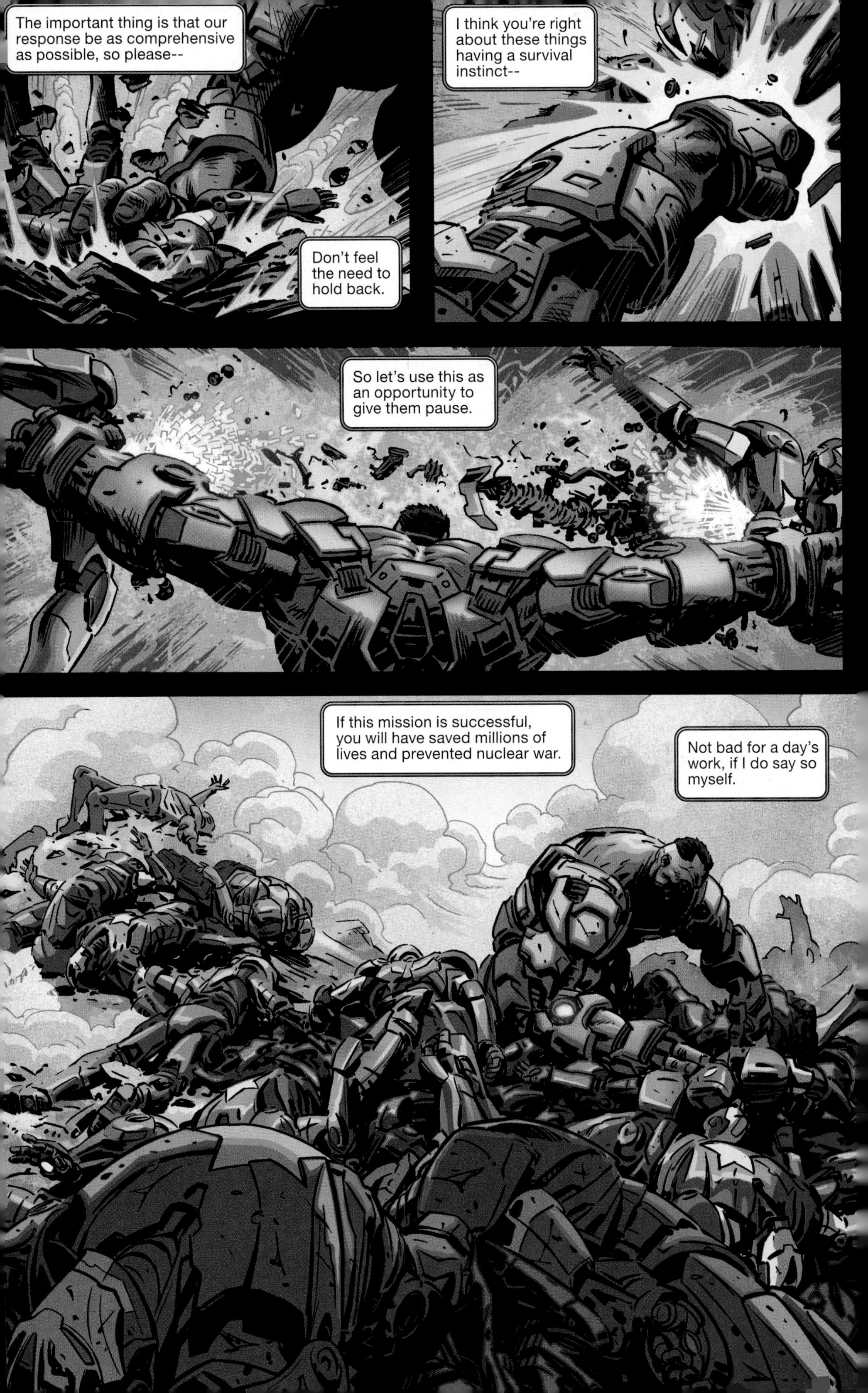
The important thing is that our response be as comprehensive as possible, so please--
Don't feel the need to hold back.
I think you're right about these things having a survival instinct--
So let's use this as an opportunity to give them pause.
If this mission is successful, you will have saved millions of lives and prevented nuclear war.
Not bad for a day's work, if I do say so myself.

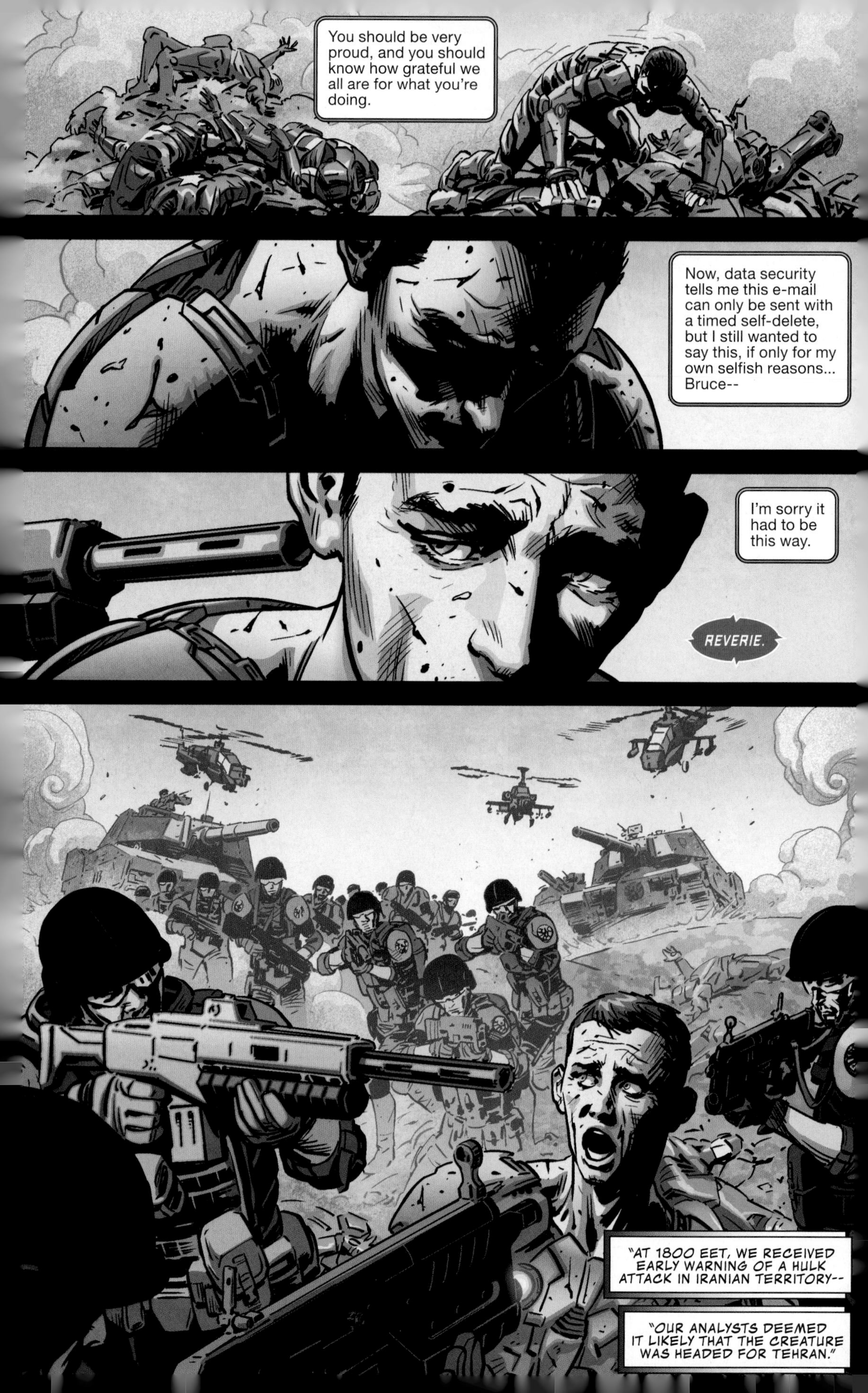

You should be very proud, and you should know how grateful we all are for what you're doing.
Now, data security tells me this e-mail can only be sent with a timed self-delete, but I still wanted to say this, if only for my own selfish reasons... Bruce--
I'm sorry it had to be this way.
REVERIE.
"AT 1800 EET, WE RECEIVED EARLY WARNING OF A HULK ATTACK IN IRANIAN TERRITORY--
"OUR ANALYSTS DEEMED IT LIKELY THAT THE CREATURE WAS HEADED FOR TEHRAN."

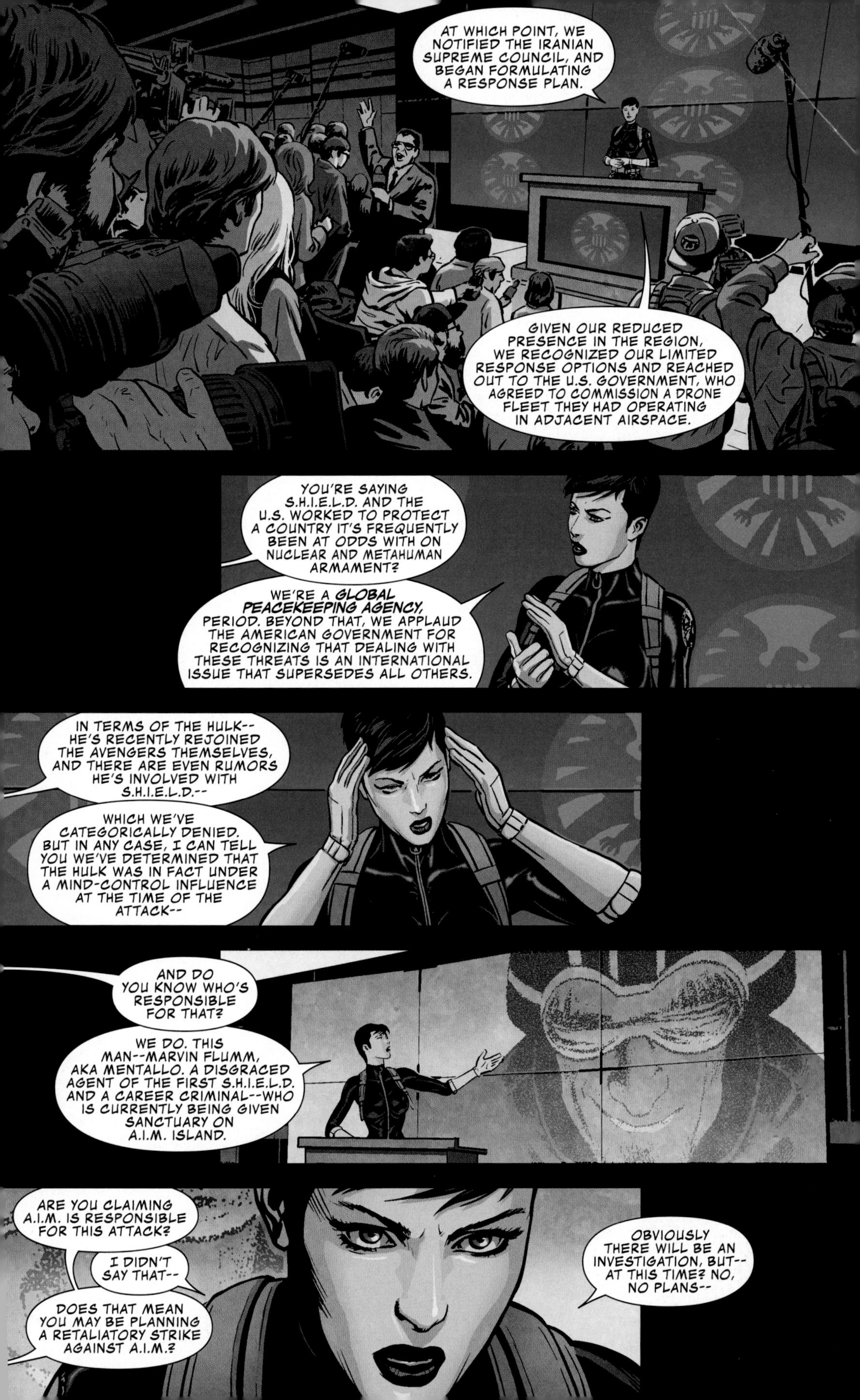
AT WHICH POINT, WE NOTIFIED THE IRANIAN SUPREME COUNCIL, AND BEGAN FORMULATING A RESPONSE PLAN.
GIVEN OUR REDUCED PRESENCE IN THE REGION, WE RECOGNIZED OUR LIMITED RESPONSE OPTIONS AND REACHED OUT TO THE U.S. GOVERNMENT, WHO AGREED TO COMMISSION A DRONE FLEET THEY HAD OPERATING IN ADJACENT AIRSPACE.
YOU'RE SAYING S.H.I.E.L.D. AND THE U.S. WORKED TO PROTECT A COUNTRY IT'S FREQUENTLY BEEN AT ODDS WITH ON NUCLEAR AND METAHUMAN ARMAMENT?
WE'RE A ***GLOBAL PEACEKEEPING AGENCY,*** PERIOD. BEYOND THAT, WE APPLAUD THE AMERICAN GOVERNMENT FOR RECOGNIZING THAT DEALING WITH THESE THREATS IS AN INTERNATIONAL ISSUE THAT SUPERSEDES ALL OTHERS.
IN TERMS OF THE HULK-- HE'S RECENTLY REJOINED THE AVENGERS THEMSELVES, AND THERE ARE EVEN RUMORS HE'S INVOLVED WITH S.H.I.E.L.D.--
WHICH WE'VE CATEGORICALLY DENIED. BUT IN ANY CASE, I CAN TELL YOU WE'VE DETERMINED THAT THE HULK WAS IN FACT UNDER A MIND-CONTROL INFLUENCE AT THE TIME OF THE ATTACK--
AND DO YOU KNOW WHO'S RESPONSIBLE FOR THAT?
WE DO. THIS MAN--MARVIN FLUMM, AKA MENTALLO. A DISGRACED AGENT OF THE FIRST S.H.I.E.L.D. AND A CAREER CRIMINAL--WHO IS CURRENTLY BEING GIVEN SANCTUARY ON A.I.M. ISLAND.
ARE YOU CLAIMING A.I.M. IS RESPONSIBLE FOR THIS ATTACK?
I DIDN'T SAY THAT--
DOES THAT MEAN YOU MAY BE PLANNING A RETALIATORY STRIKE AGAINST A.I.M.?
OBVIOUSLY THERE WILL BE AN INVESTIGATION, BUT-- AT THIS TIME? NO, NO PLANS--

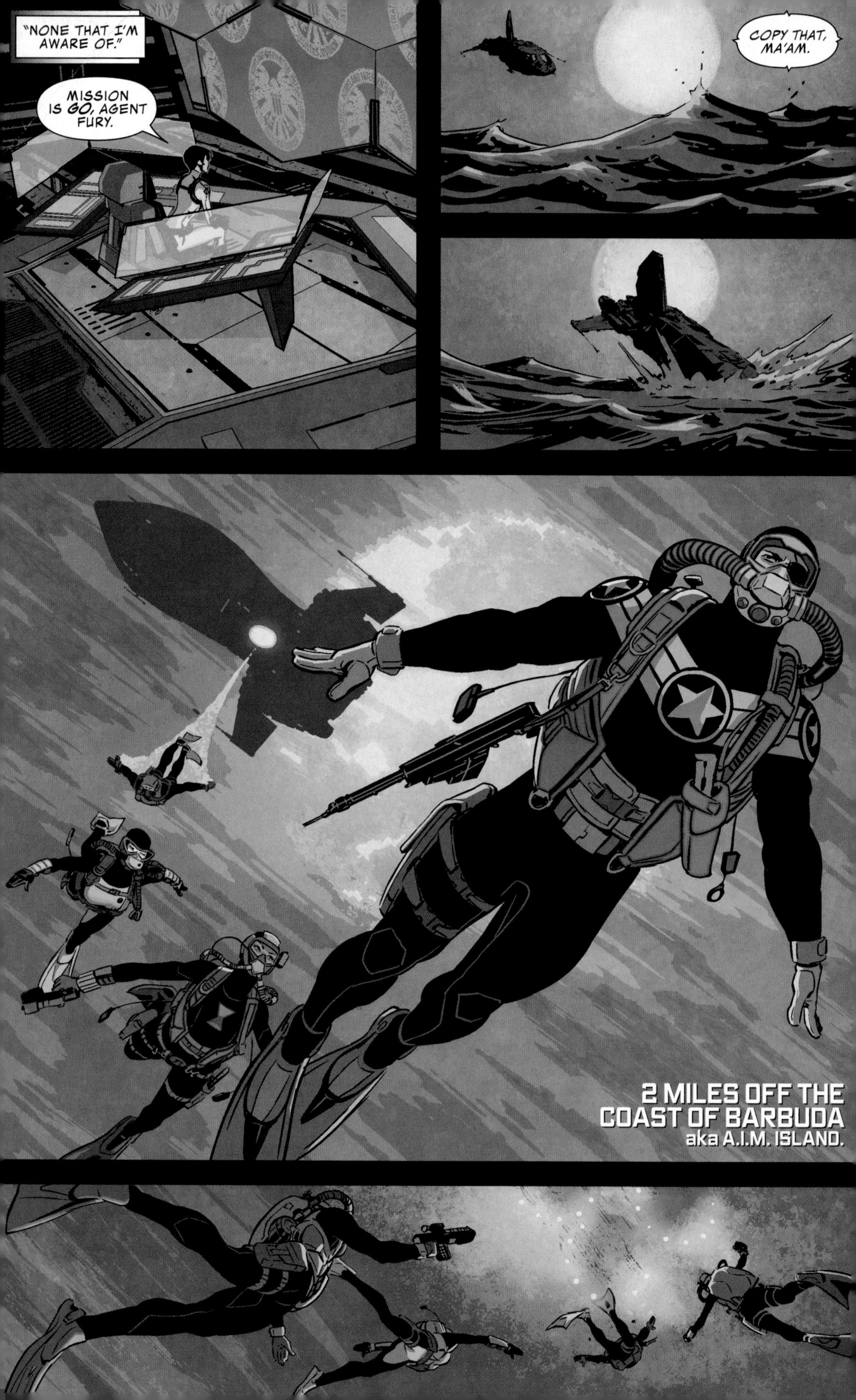
"NONE THAT I'M AWARE OF."
MISSION IS GO, AGENT FURY.
COPY THAT, MA'AM.
2 MILES OFF THE COAST OF BARBUDA
aka A.I.M. ISLAND.

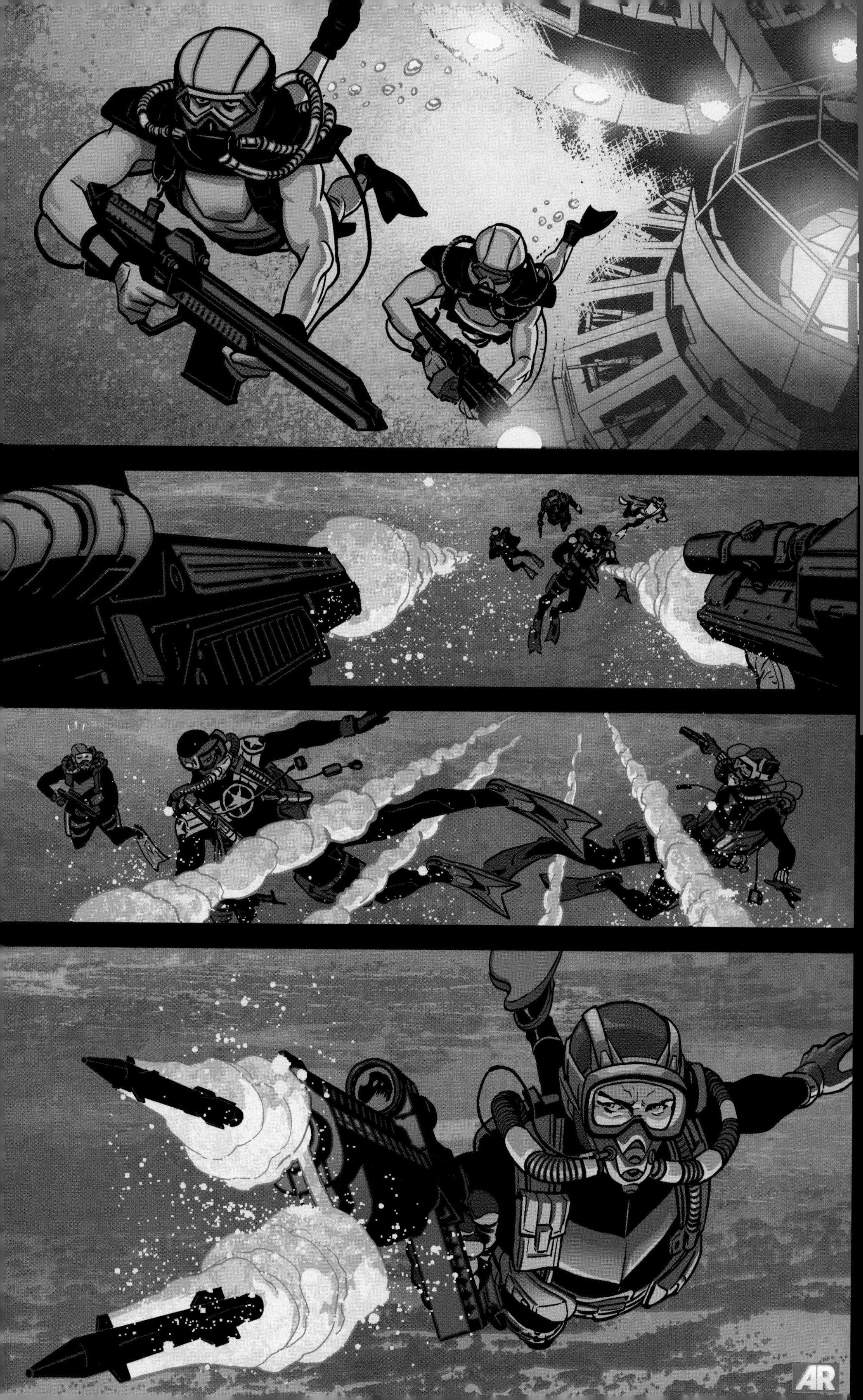

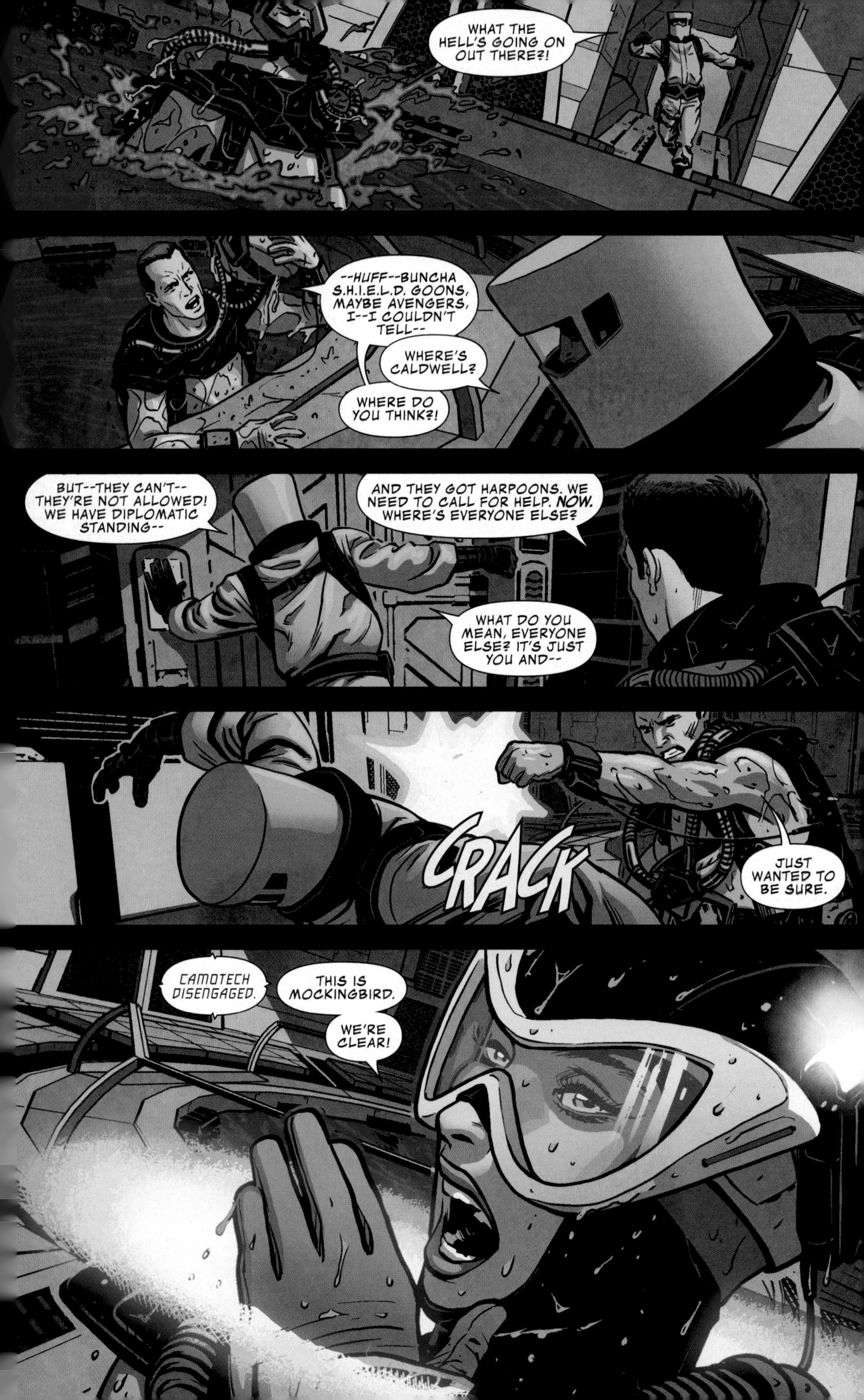
WHAT THE HELL'S GOING ON OUT THERE?!
--HUFF--BUNCHA S.H.I.E.L.D. GOONS, MAYBE AVENGERS, I--I COULDN'T TELL--
WHERE'S CALDWELL?
WHERE DO YOU THINK?!
BUT--THEY CAN'T--THEY'RE NOT ALLOWED! WE HAVE DIPLOMATIC STANDING--
AND THEY GOT HARPOONS. WE NEED TO CALL FOR HELP. NOW. WHERE'S EVERYONE ELSE?
WHAT DO YOU MEAN, EVERYONE ELSE? IT'S JUST YOU AND--
CRACK
JUST WANTED TO BE SURE.
CAMOTECH DISENGAGED.
THIS IS MOCKINGBIRD.
WE'RE CLEAR!

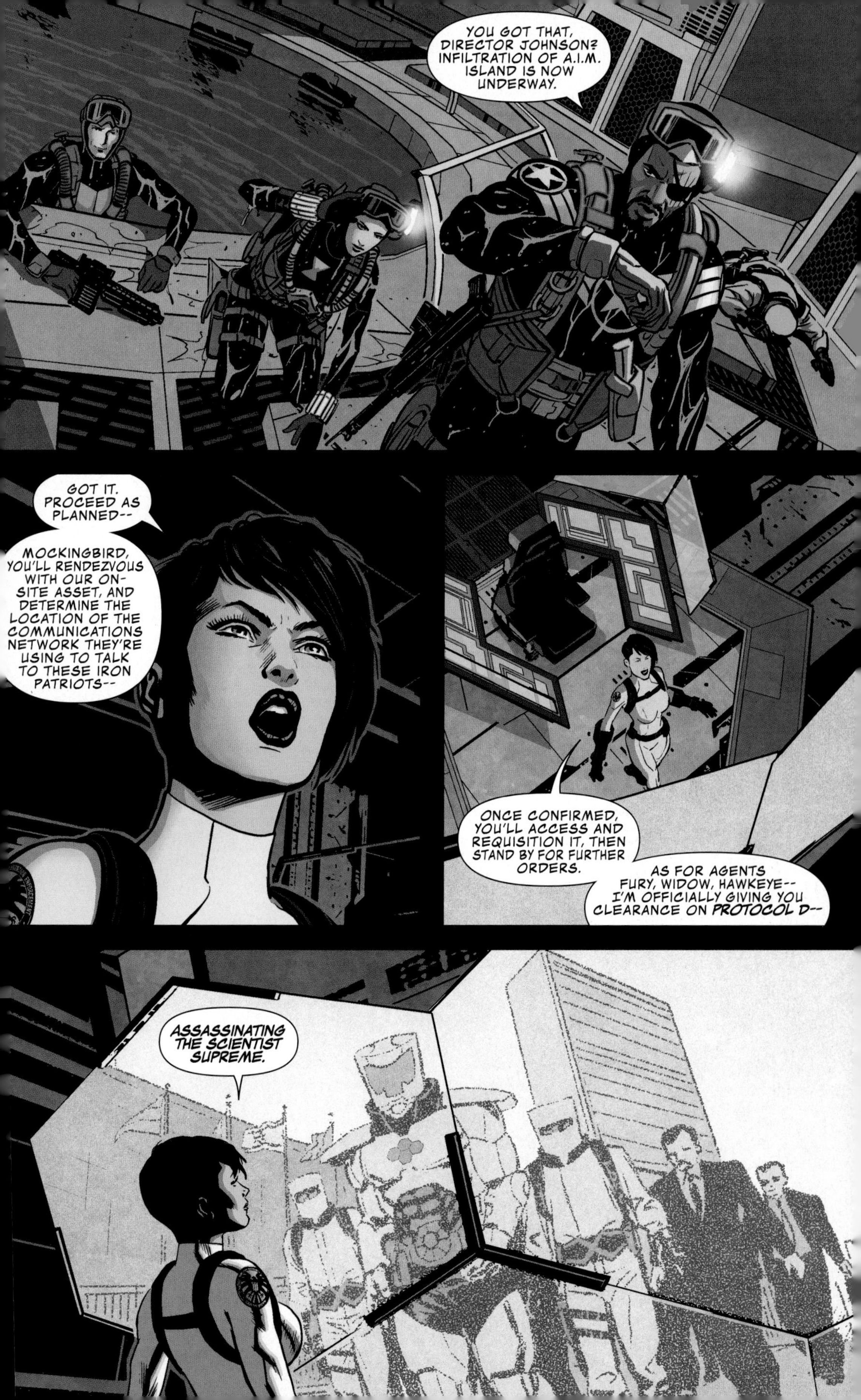
YOU GOT THAT, DIRECTOR JOHNSON? INFILTRATION OF A.I.M. ISLAND IS NOW UNDERWAY.
GOT IT. PROCEED AS PLANNED--
MOCKINGBIRD, YOU'LL RENDEZVOUS WITH OUR ON-SITE ASSET, AND DETERMINE THE LOCATION OF THE COMMUNICATIONS NETWORK THEY'RE USING TO TALK TO THESE IRON PATRIOTS--
ONCE CONFIRMED, YOU'LL ACCESS AND REQUISITION IT, THEN STAND BY FOR FURTHER ORDERS.
AS FOR AGENTS FURY, WIDOW, HAWKEYE-- I'M OFFICIALLY GIVING YOU CLEARANCE ON PROTOCOL D--
ASSASSINATING THE SCIENTIST SUPREME.

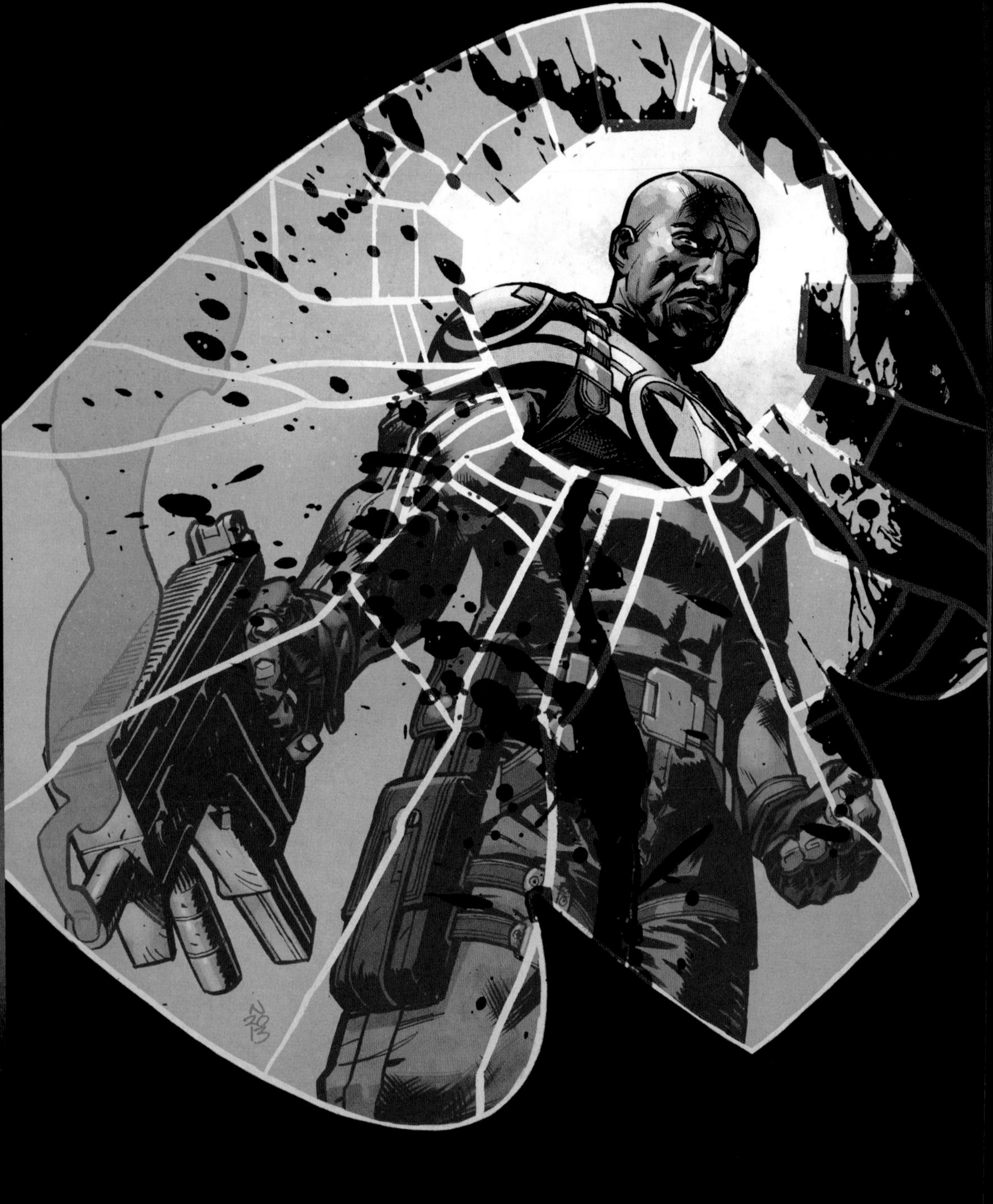

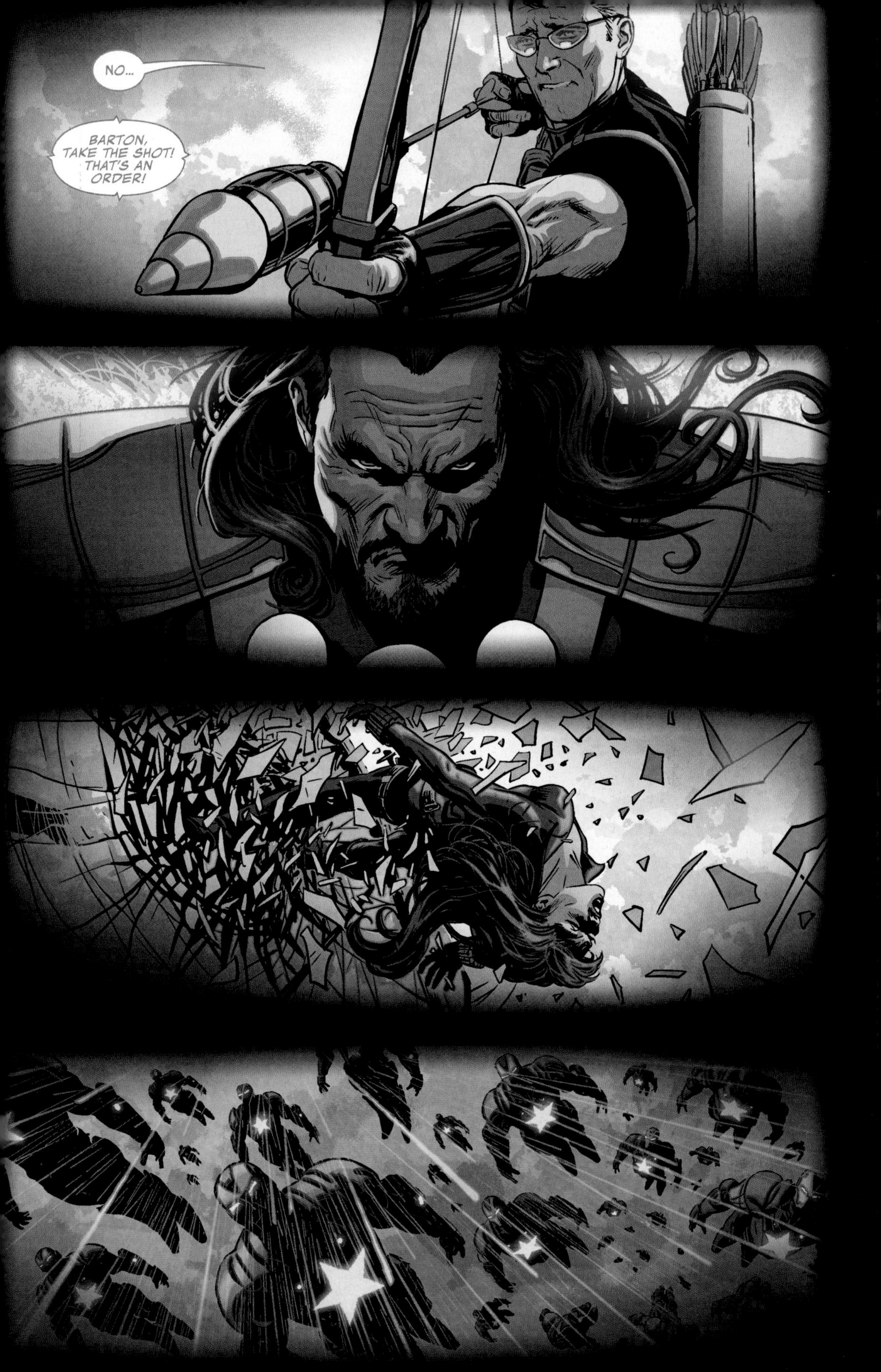
NO...
BARTON, TAKE THE SHOT! THAT'S AN ORDER!

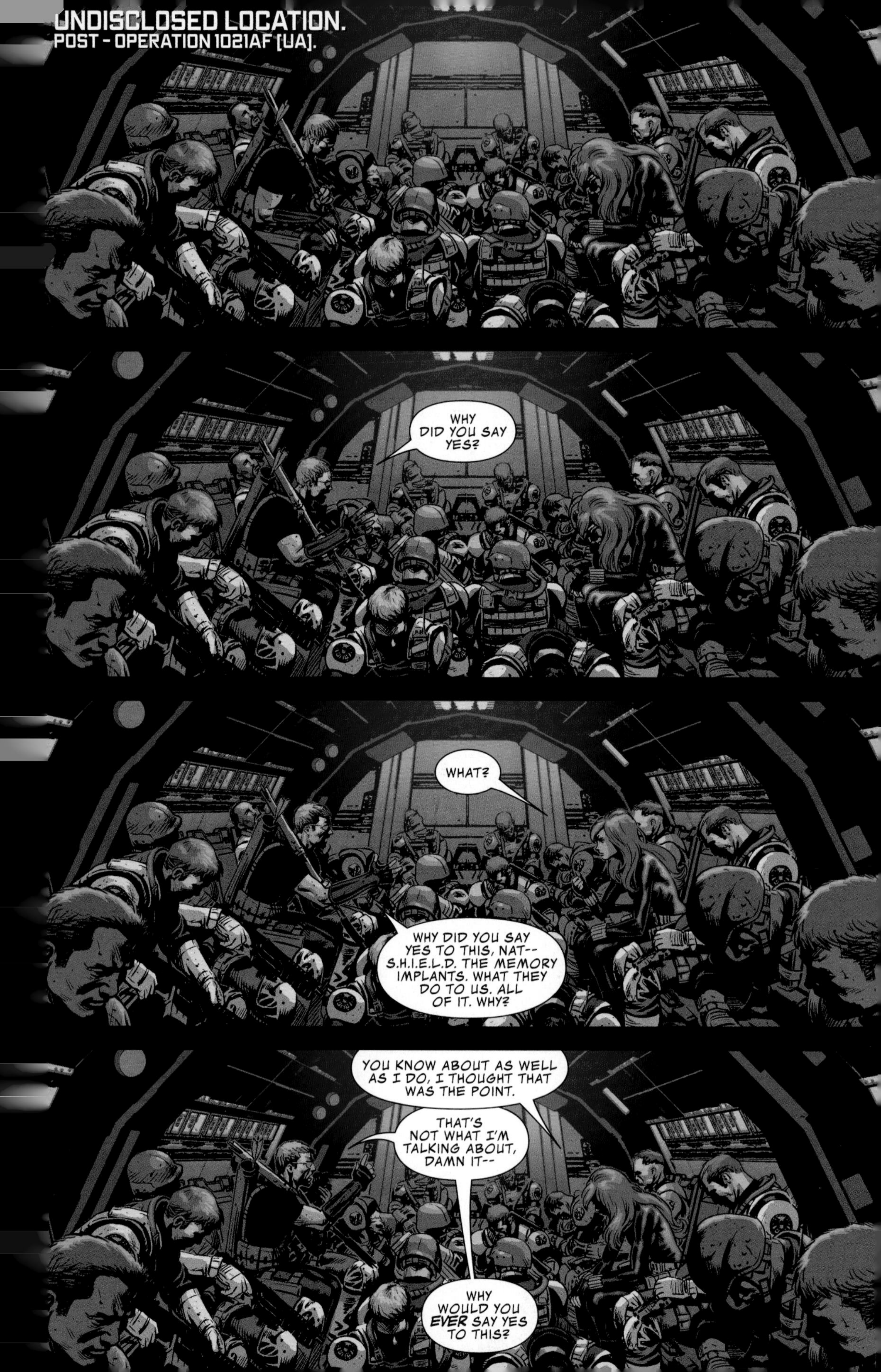
UNDISCLOSED LOCATION.
POST - OPERATION 1021AF [UA].
WHY DID YOU SAY YES?
WHAT?
WHY DID YOU SAY YES TO THIS, NAT-- S.H.I.E.L.D. THE MEMORY IMPLANTS. WHAT THEY DO TO US. ALL OF IT. WHY?
YOU KNOW ABOUT AS WELL AS I DO, I THOUGHT THAT WAS THE POINT.
THAT'S NOT WHAT I'M TALKING ABOUT, DAMN IT--
WHY WOULD YOU EVER SAY YES TO THIS?

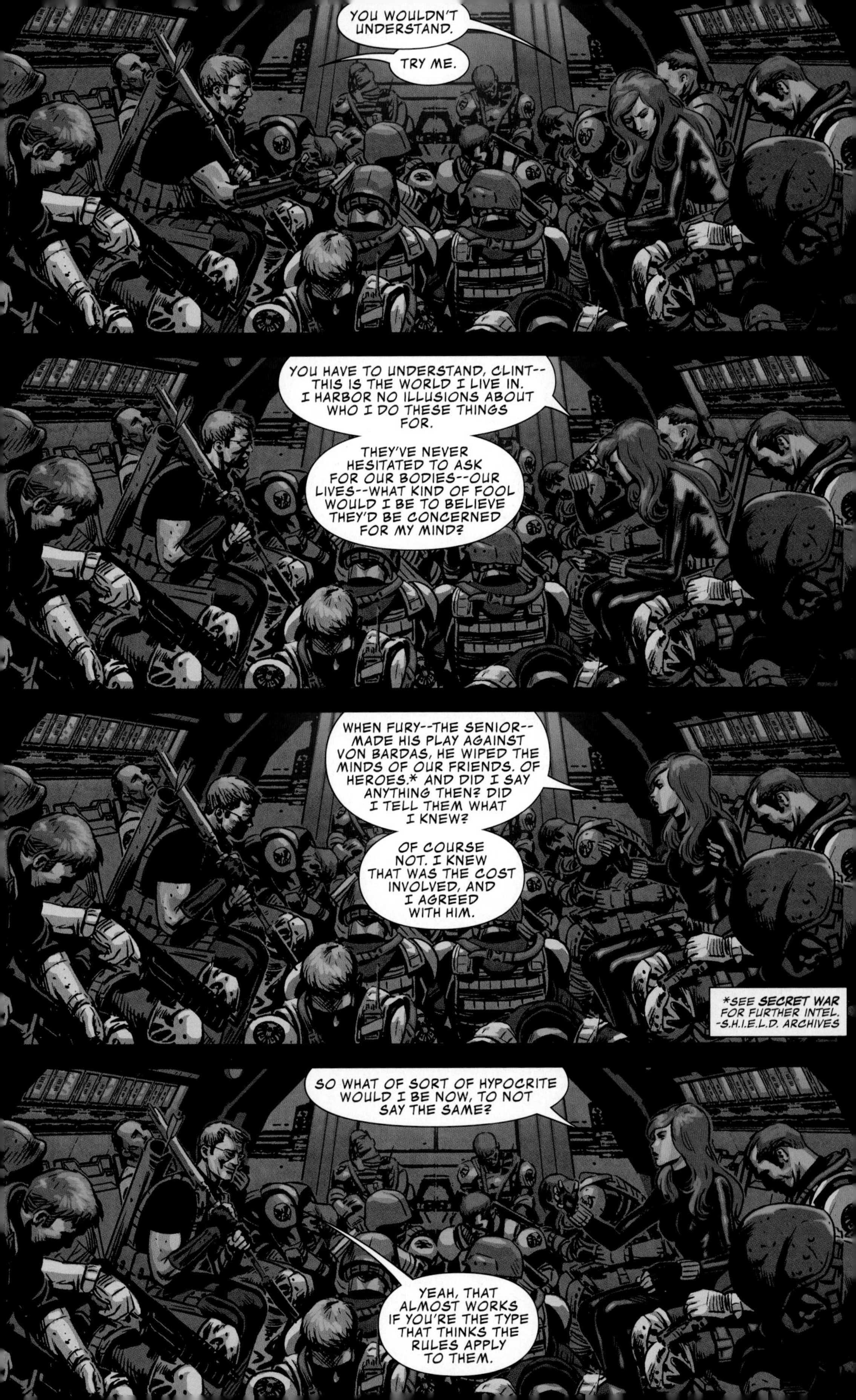
YOU WOULDN'T UNDERSTAND.
TRY ME.
YOU HAVE TO UNDERSTAND, CLINT-- THIS IS THE WORLD I LIVE IN. I HARBOR NO ILLUSIONS ABOUT WHO I DO THESE THINGS FOR.
THEY'VE NEVER HESITATED TO ASK FOR OUR BODIES--OUR LIVES--WHAT KIND OF FOOL WOULD I BE TO BELIEVE THEY'D BE CONCERNED FOR MY MIND?
WHEN FURY--THE SENIOR-- MADE HIS PLAY AGAINST VON BARDAS, HE WIPED THE MINDS OF OUR FRIENDS. OF HEROES.* AND DID I SAY ANYTHING THEN? DID I TELL THEM WHAT I KNEW?
OF COURSE NOT. I KNEW THAT WAS THE COST INVOLVED, AND I AGREED WITH HIM.
*SEE SECRET WAR FOR FURTHER INTEL. -S.H.I.E.L.D. ARCHIVES
SO WHAT OF SORT OF HYPOCRITE WOULD I BE NOW, TO NOT SAY THE SAME?
YEAH, THAT ALMOST WORKS IF YOU'RE THE TYPE THAT THINKS THE RULES APPLY TO THEM.

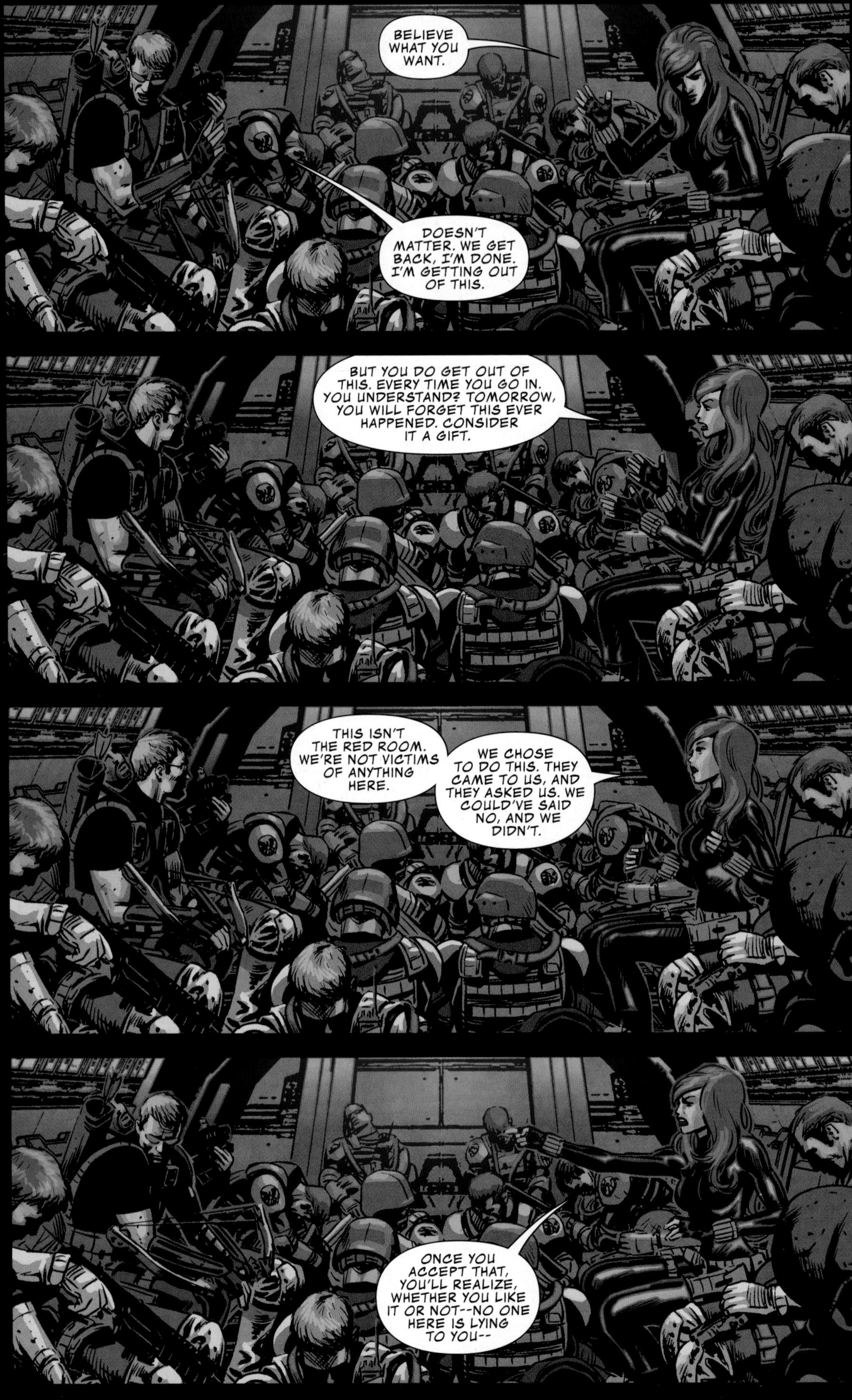
BELIEVE WHAT YOU WANT.
DOESN'T MATTER. WE GET BACK, I'M DONE. I'M GETTING OUT OF THIS.
BUT YOU DO GET OUT OF THIS. EVERY TIME YOU GO IN. YOU UNDERSTAND? TOMORROW, YOU WILL FORGET THIS EVER HAPPENED. CONSIDER IT A GIFT.
THIS ISN'T THE RED ROOM. WE'RE NOT VICTIMS OF ANYTHING HERE.
WE CHOSE TO DO THIS. THEY CAME TO US, AND THEY ASKED US. WE COULD'VE SAID NO, AND WE DIDN'T.
ONCE YOU ACCEPT THAT, YOU'LL REALIZE, WHETHER YOU LIKE IT OR NOT--NO ONE HERE IS LYING TO YOU--

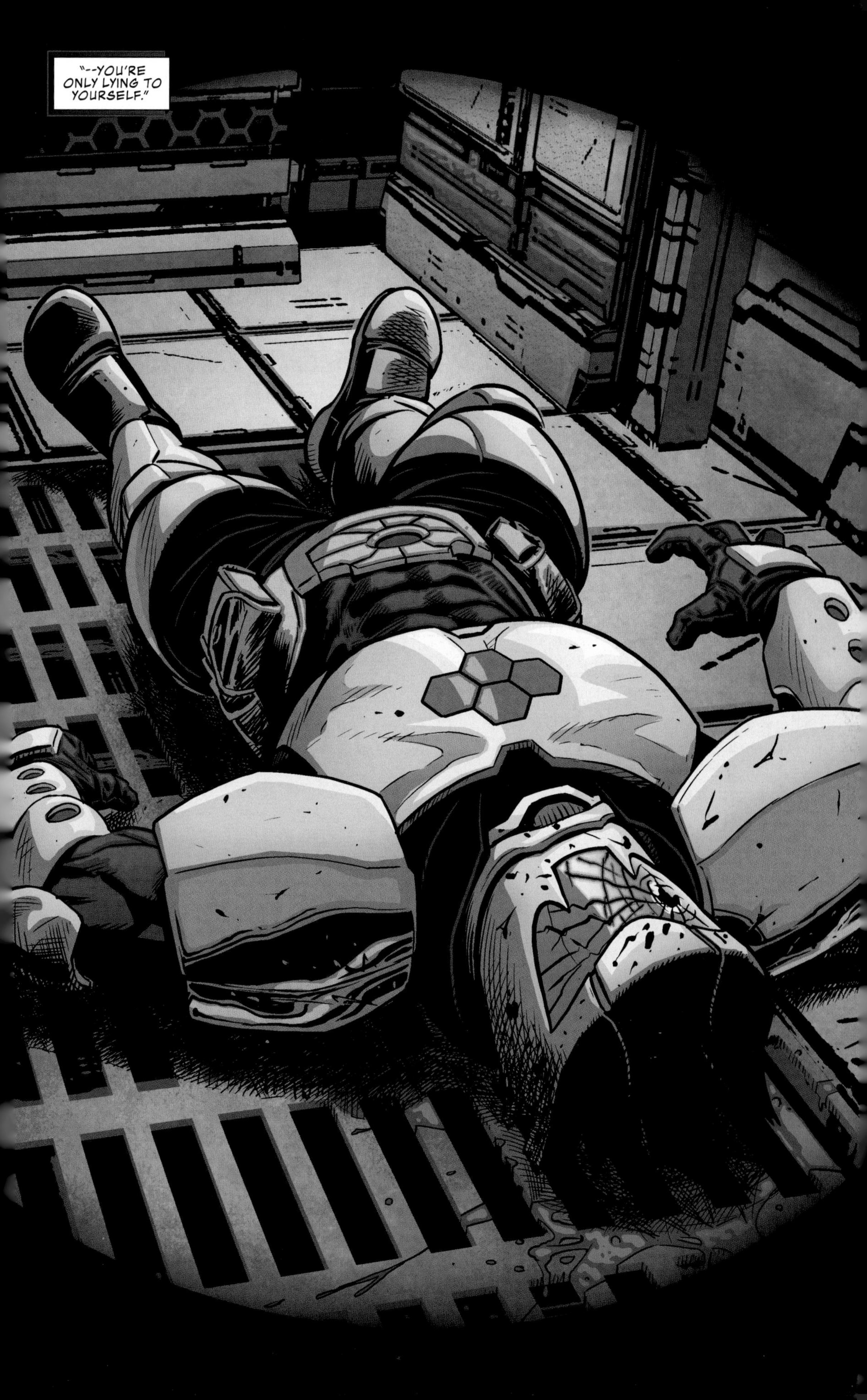
"--YOU'RE ONLY LYING TO YOURSELF."

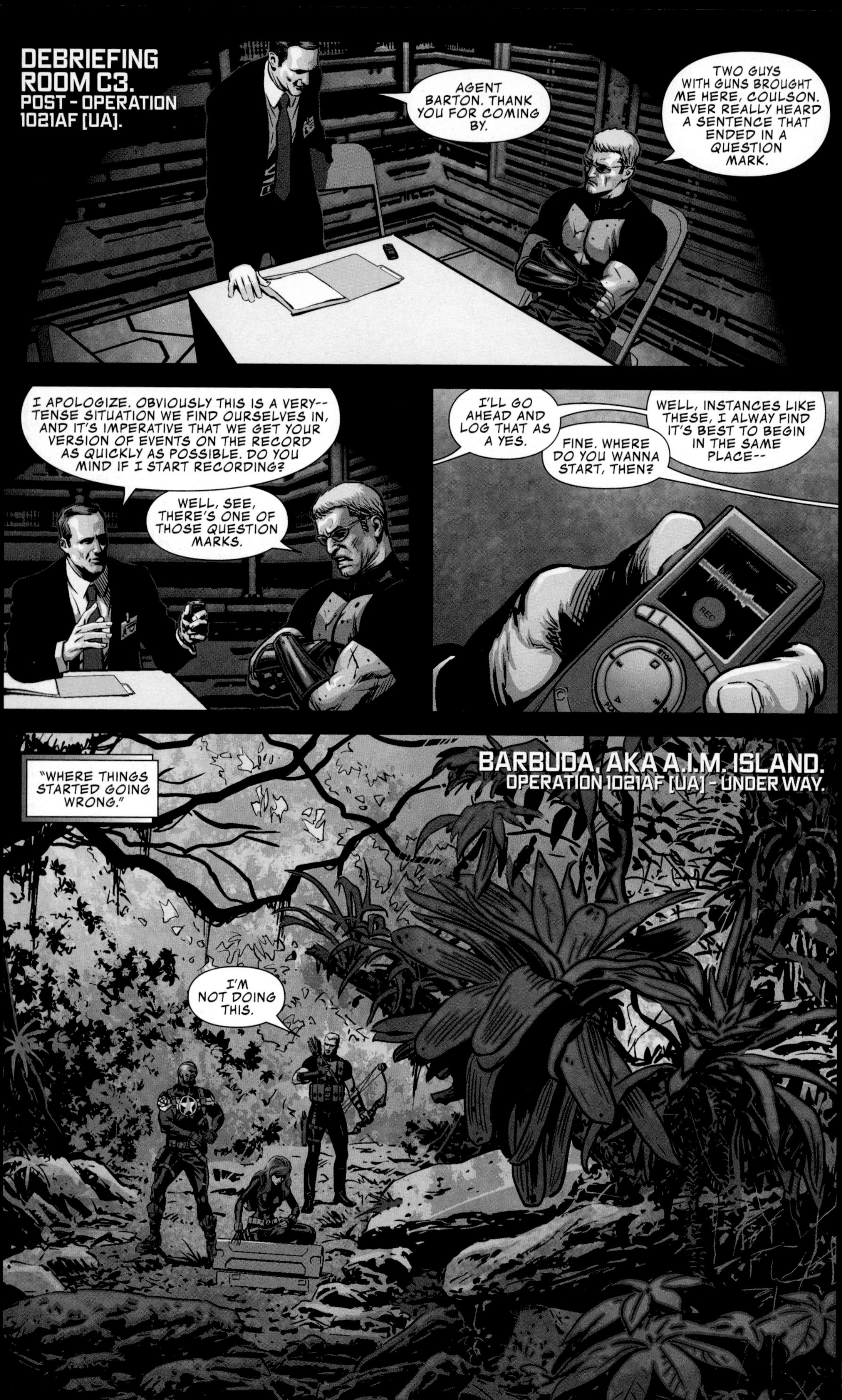
DEBRIEFING ROOM C3.
POST - OPERATION 1021AF [UA].
AGENT BARTON. THANK YOU FOR COMING BY.
TWO GUYS WITH GUNS BROUGHT ME HERE, COULSON. NEVER REALLY HEARD A SENTENCE THAT ENDED IN A QUESTION MARK.
I APOLOGIZE. OBVIOUSLY THIS IS A VERY--TENSE SITUATION WE FIND OURSELVES IN, AND IT'S IMPERATIVE THAT WE GET YOUR VERSION OF EVENTS ON THE RECORD AS QUICKLY AS POSSIBLE. DO YOU MIND IF I START RECORDING?
WELL, SEE, THERE'S ONE OF THOSE QUESTION MARKS.
I'LL GO AHEAD AND LOG THAT AS A YES.
FINE. WHERE DO YOU WANNA START, THEN?
WELL, INSTANCES LIKE THESE, I ALWAY FIND IT'S BEST TO BEGIN IN THE SAME PLACE--
REC
STOP
"WHERE THINGS STARTED GOING WRONG."
BARBUDA, AKA A.I.M. ISLAND.
OPERATION 1021AF [UA] - UNDER WAY.
I'M NOT DOING THIS.

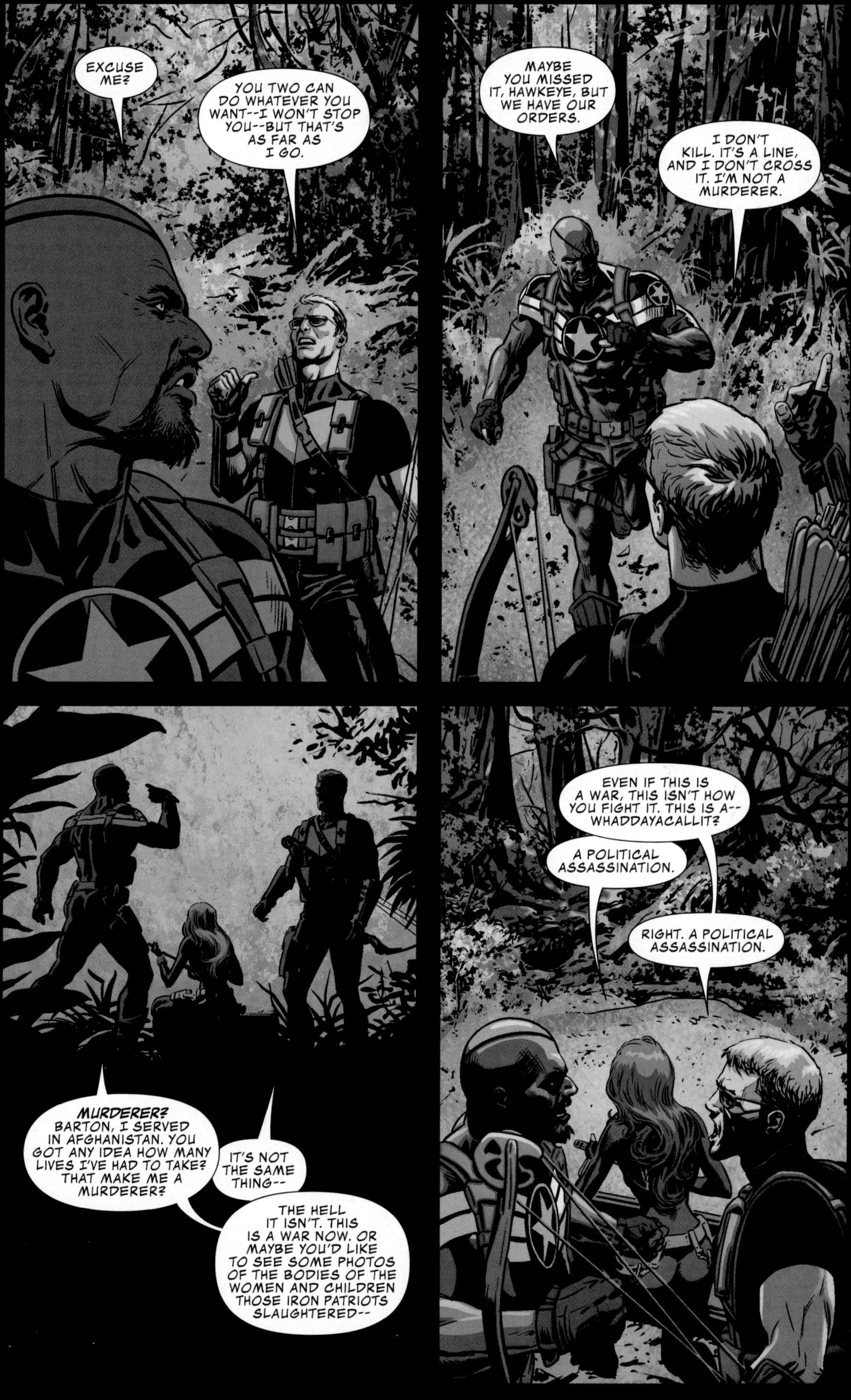
EXCUSE ME?
YOU TWO CAN DO WHATEVER YOU WANT--I WON'T STOP YOU--BUT THAT'S AS FAR AS I GO.
MAYBE YOU MISSED IT, HAWKEYE, BUT WE HAVE OUR ORDERS.
I DON'T KILL. IT'S A LINE, AND I DON'T CROSS IT. I'M NOT A MURDERER.
MURDERER? BARTON, I SERVED IN AFGHANISTAN. YOU GOT ANY IDEA HOW MANY LIVES I'VE HAD TO TAKE? THAT MAKE ME A MURDERER?
IT'S NOT THE SAME THING--
THE HELL IT ISN'T. THIS IS A WAR NOW. OR MAYBE YOU'D LIKE TO SEE SOME PHOTOS OF THE BODIES OF THE WOMEN AND CHILDREN THOSE IRON PATRIOTS SLAUGHTERED--
EVEN IF THIS IS A WAR, THIS ISN'T HOW YOU FIGHT IT. THIS IS A--WHADDAYACALLIT?
A POLITICAL ASSASSINATION.
RIGHT. A POLITICAL ASSASSINATION.

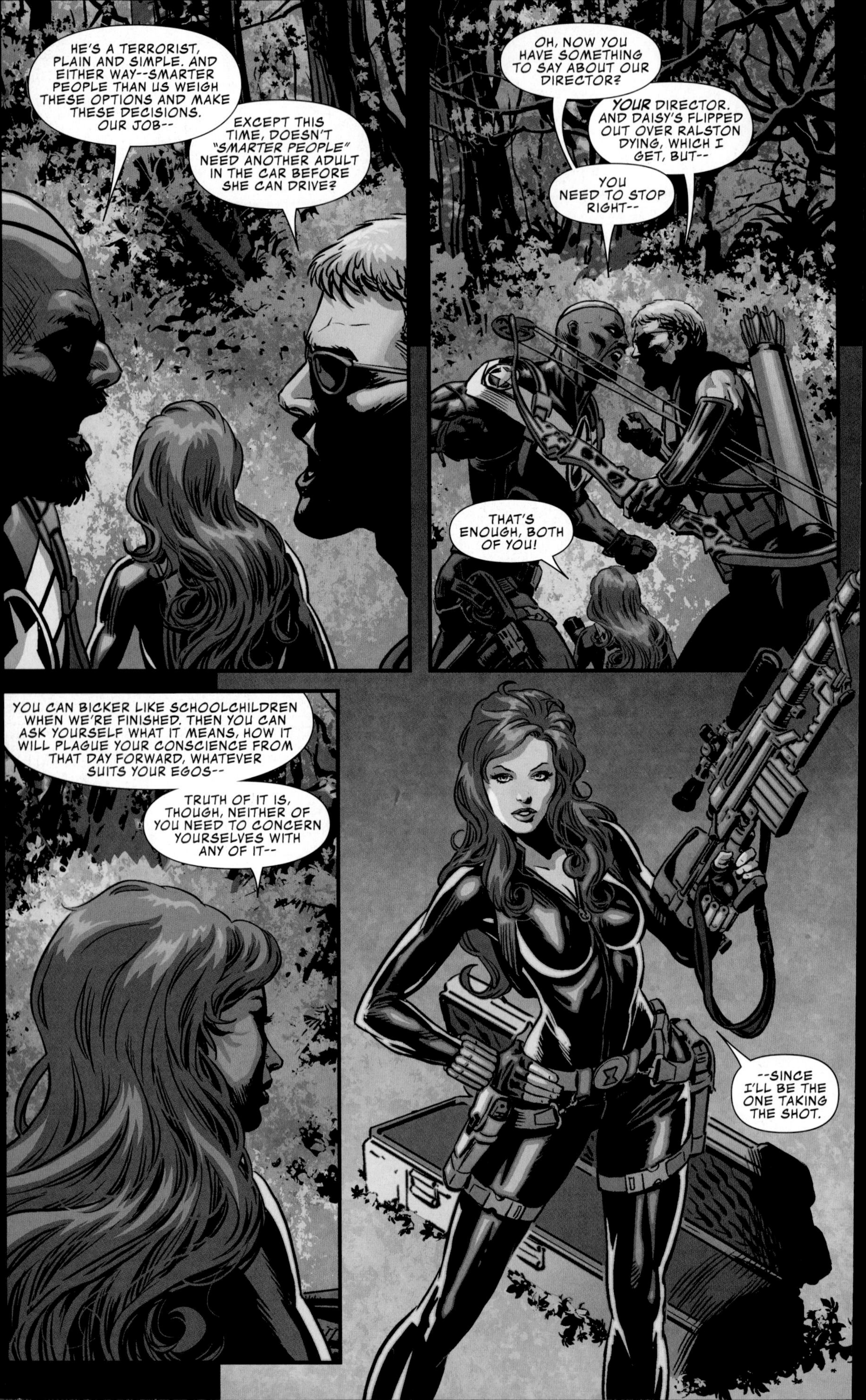
HE'S A TERRORIST, PLAIN AND SIMPLE. AND EITHER WAY--SMARTER PEOPLE THAN US WEIGH THESE OPTIONS AND MAKE THESE DECISIONS. OUR JOB--
EXCEPT THIS TIME, DOESN'T "SMARTER PEOPLE" NEED ANOTHER ADULT IN THE CAR BEFORE SHE CAN DRIVE?
OH, NOW YOU HAVE SOMETHING TO SAY ABOUT OUR DIRECTOR?
YOUR DIRECTOR. AND DAISY'S FLIPPED OUT OVER RALSTON DYING, WHICH I GET, BUT--
YOU NEED TO STOP RIGHT--
THAT'S ENOUGH, BOTH OF YOU!
YOU CAN BICKER LIKE SCHOOLCHILDREN WHEN WE'RE FINISHED. THEN YOU CAN ASK YOURSELF WHAT IT MEANS, HOW IT WILL PLAGUE YOUR CONSCIENCE FROM THAT DAY FORWARD, WHATEVER SUITS YOUR EGOS--
TRUTH OF IT IS, THOUGH, NEITHER OF YOU NEED TO CONCERN YOURSELVES WITH ANY OF IT--
--SINCE I'LL BE THE ONE TAKING THE SHOT.

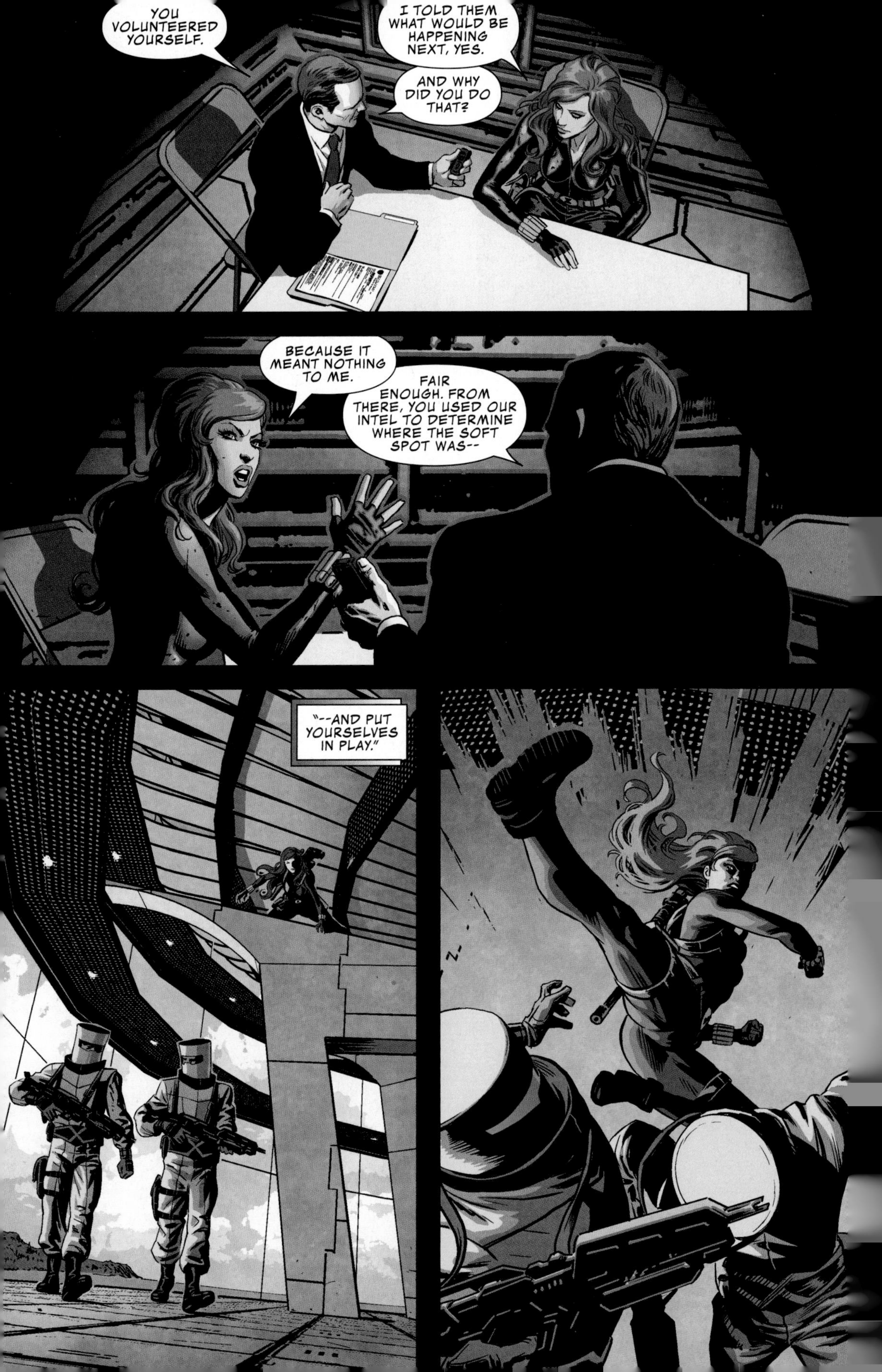
YOU VOLUNTEERED YOURSELF.
I TOLD THEM WHAT WOULD BE HAPPENING NEXT, YES.
AND WHY DID YOU DO THAT?
BECAUSE IT MEANT NOTHING TO ME.
FAIR ENOUGH. FROM THERE, YOU USED OUR INTEL TO DETERMINE WHERE THE SOFT SPOT WAS--
"--AND PUT YOURSELVES IN PLAY."

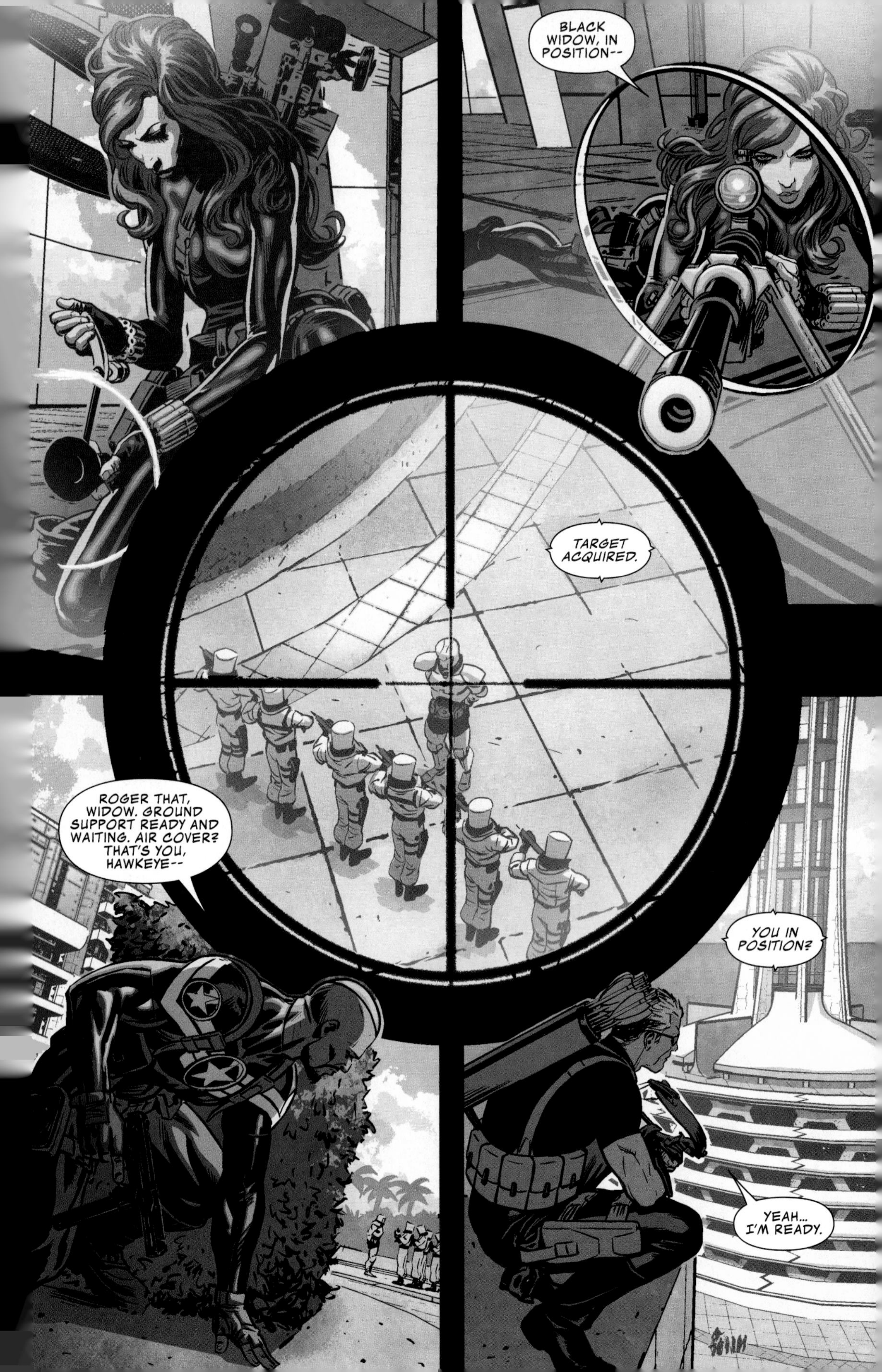
BLACK WIDOW, IN POSITION--
TARGET ACQUIRED.
ROGER THAT, WIDOW. GROUND SUPPORT READY AND WAITING. AIR COVER? THAT'S YOU, HAWKEYE--
YOU IN POSITION?
YEAH... I'M READY.

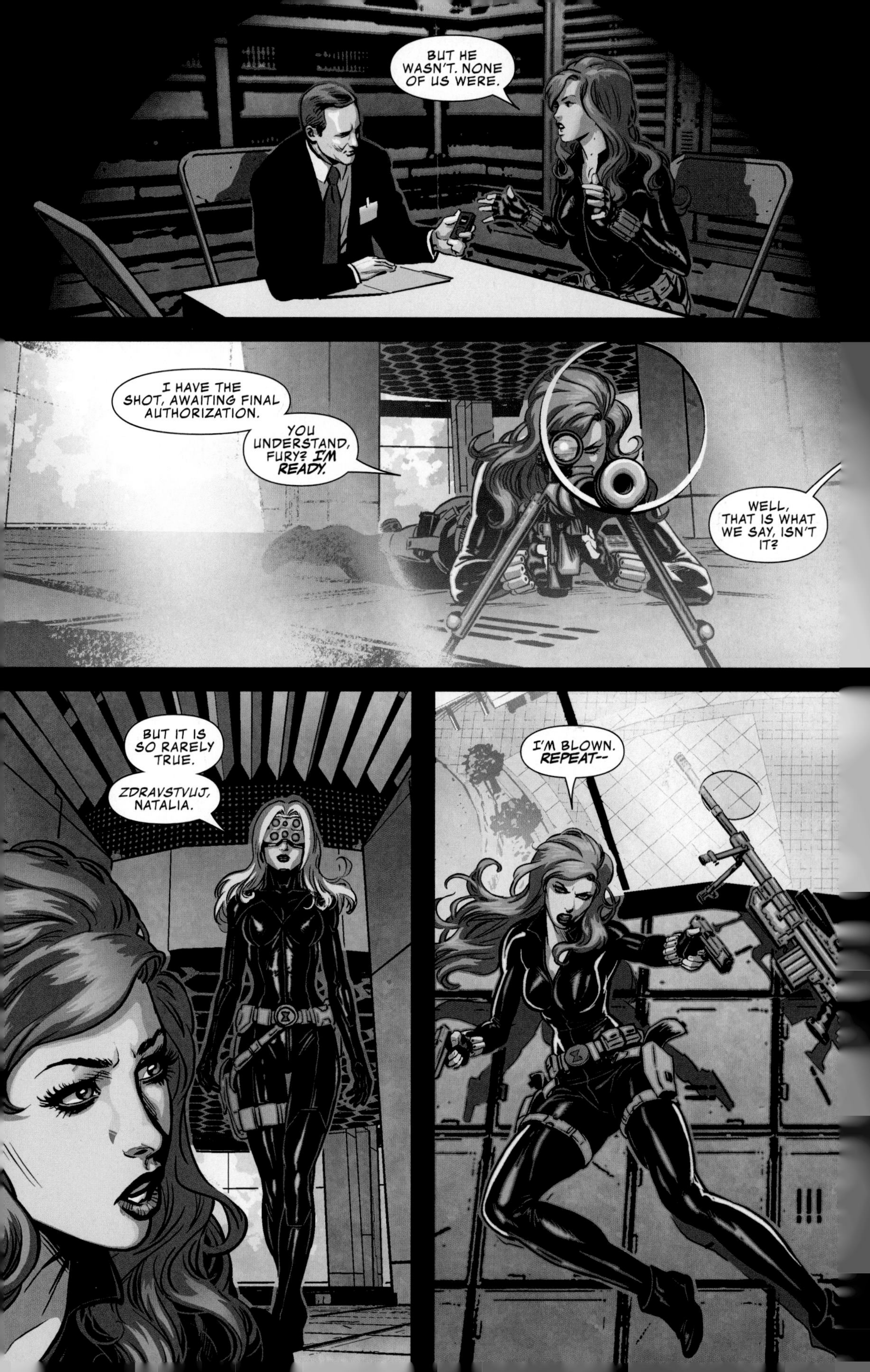
BUT HE WASN'T. NONE OF US WERE.
I HAVE THE SHOT, AWAITING FINAL AUTHORIZATION.
YOU UNDERSTAND, FURY? I'M READY.
WELL, THAT IS WHAT WE SAY, ISN'T IT?
BUT IT IS SO RARELY TRUE.
ZDRAVSTVUJ, NATALIA.
I'M BLOWN. REPEAT--
!!!

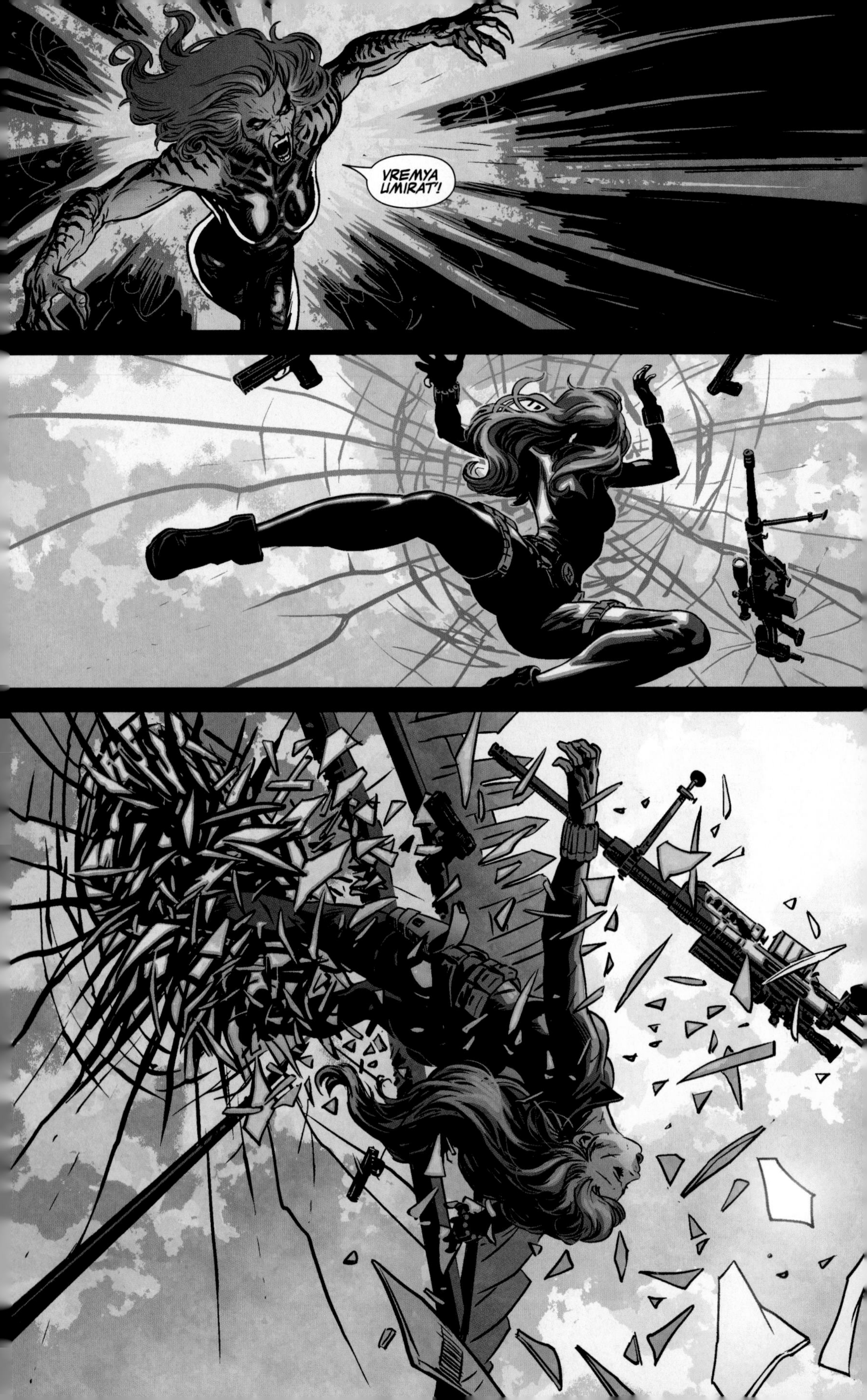
VREMYA UMIRAT'!

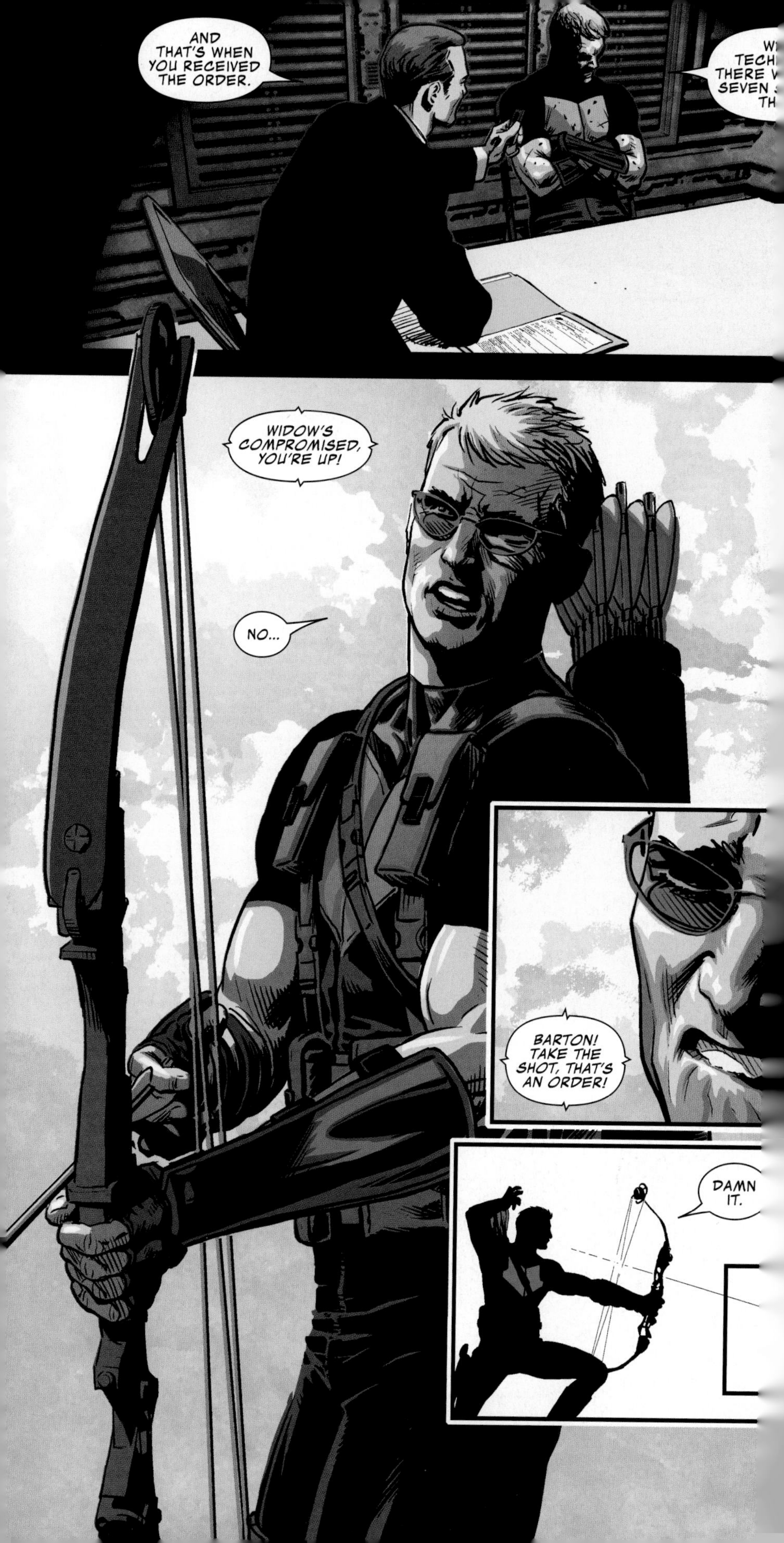
AND THAT'S WHEN YOU RECEIVED THE ORDER.
WIDOW'S COMPROMISED, YOU'RE UP!
NO...
BARTON! TAKE THE SHOT, THAT'S AN ORDER!
DAMN IT.

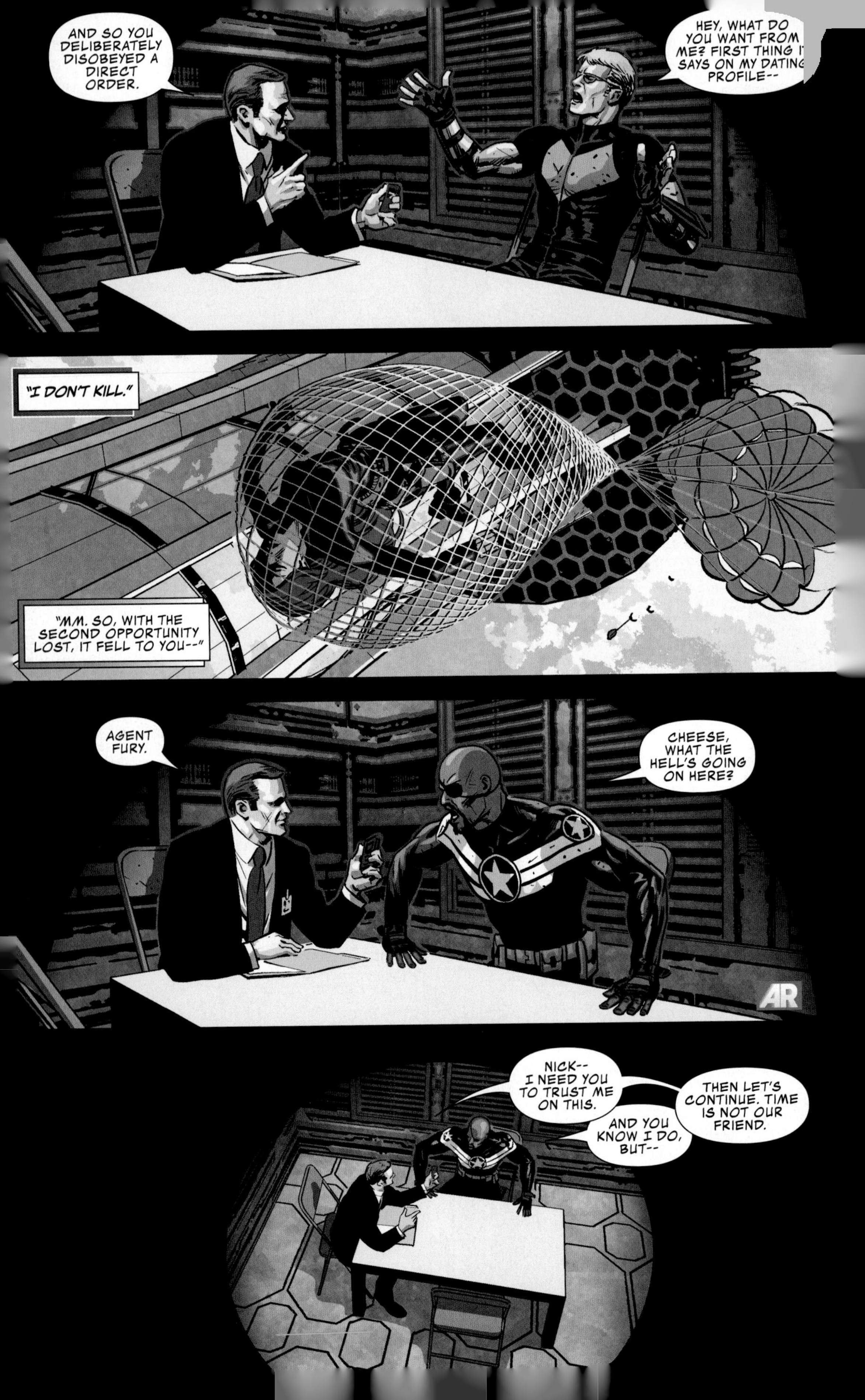
AND SO YOU DELIBERATELY DISOBEYED A DIRECT ORDER.
HEY, WHAT DO YOU WANT FROM ME? FIRST THING IT SAYS ON MY DATING PROFILE--
"I DON'T KILL."
"MM. SO, WITH THE SECOND OPPORTUNITY LOST, IT FELL TO YOU--"
AGENT FURY.
CHEESE, WHAT THE HELL'S GOING ON HERE?
NICK-- I NEED YOU TO TRUST ME ON THIS.
AND YOU KNOW I DO, BUT--
THEN LET'S CONTINUE. TIME IS NOT OUR FRIEND.

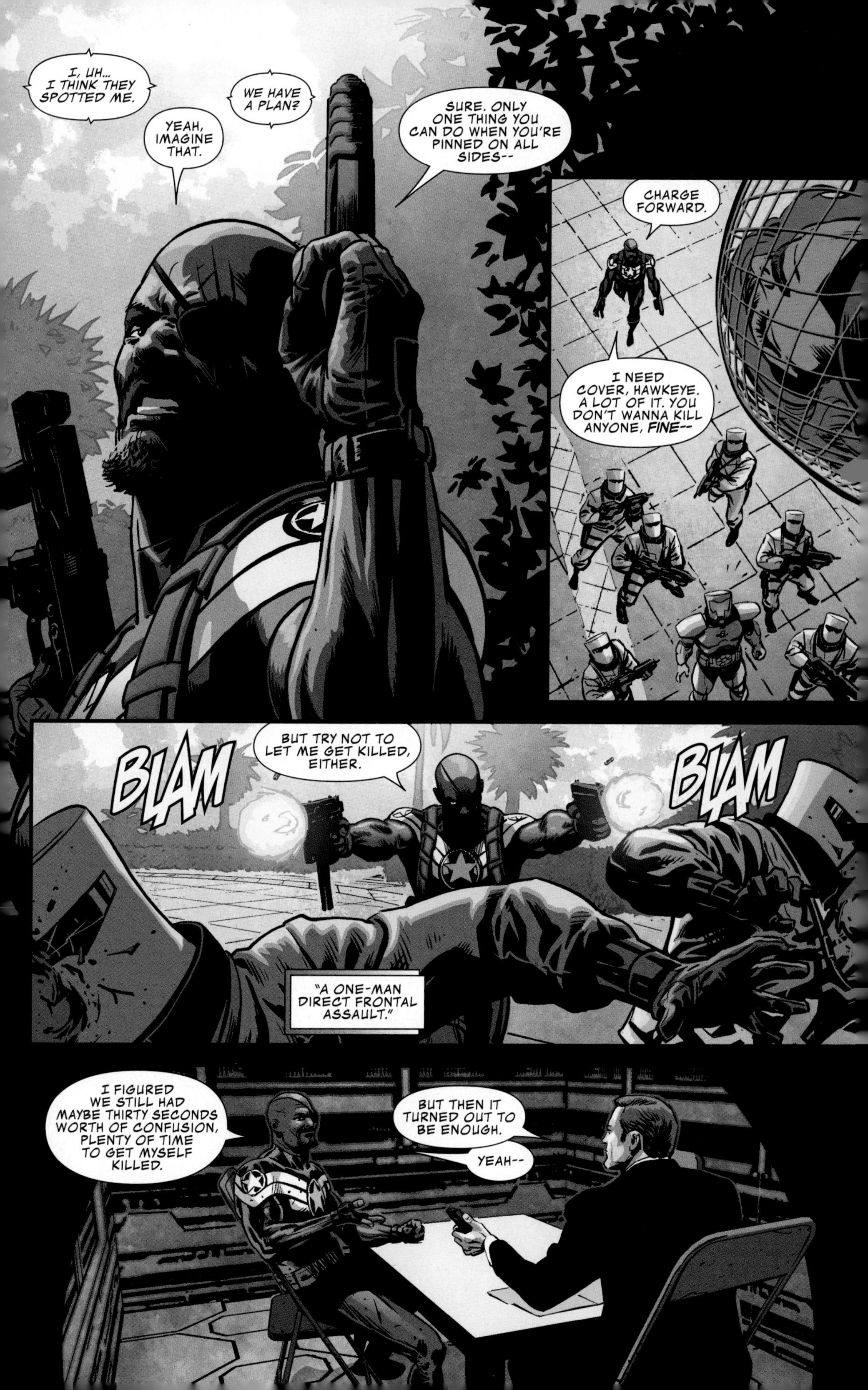
I, UH... I THINK THEY SPOTTED ME.
YEAH, IMAGINE THAT.
WE HAVE A PLAN?
SURE. ONLY ONE THING YOU CAN DO WHEN YOU'RE PINNED ON ALL SIDES--
CHARGE FORWARD.
I NEED COVER, HAWKEYE. A LOT OF IT. YOU DON'T WANNA KILL ANYONE, FINE--
BLAM
BUT TRY NOT TO LET ME GET KILLED, EITHER.
BLAM
"A ONE-MAN DIRECT FRONTAL ASSAULT."
I FIGURED WE STILL HAD MAYBE THIRTY SECONDS WORTH OF CONFUSION, PLENTY OF TIME TO GET MYSELF KILLED.
BUT THEN IT TURNED OUT TO BE ENOUGH.
YEAH--

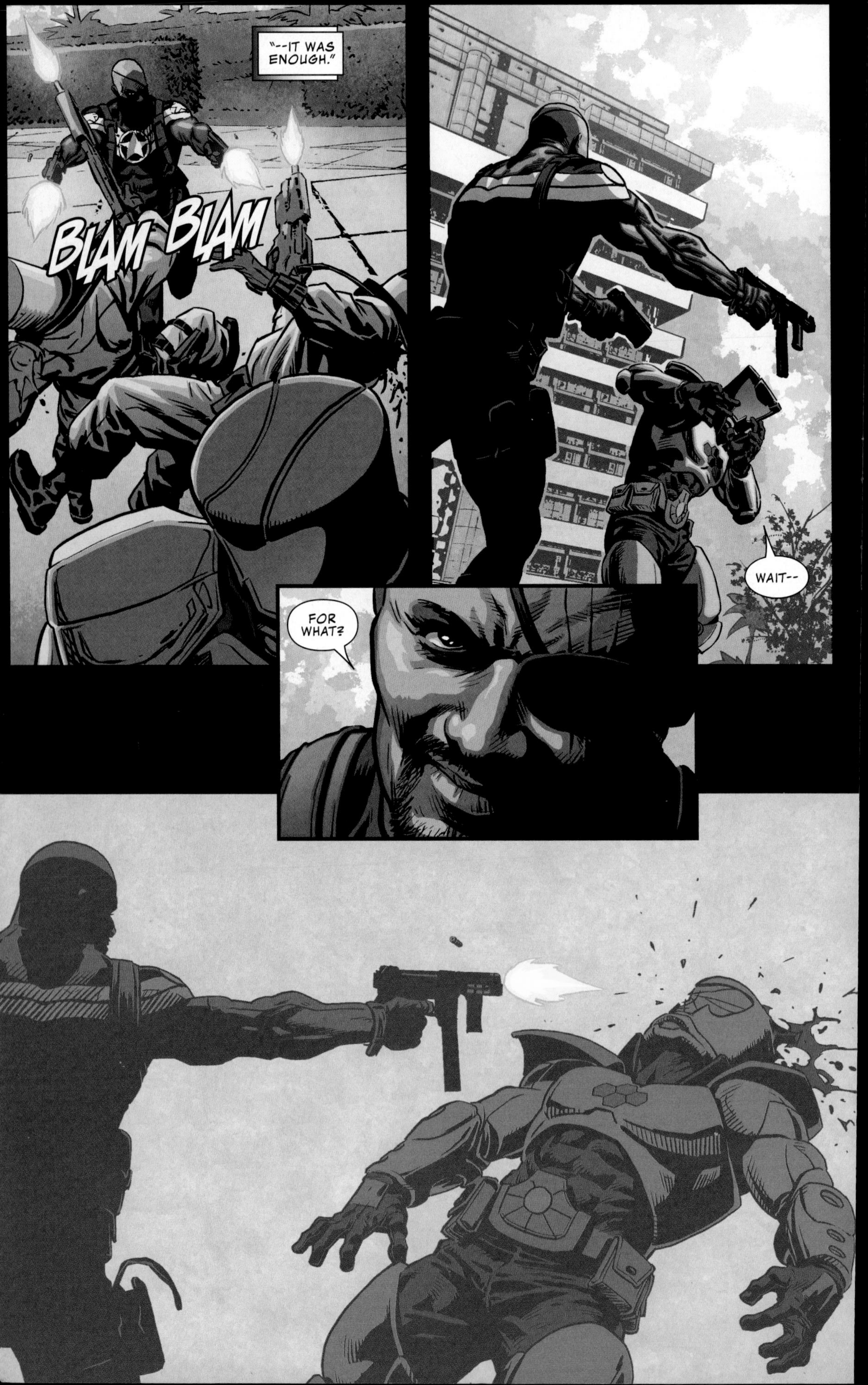
"--IT WAS ENOUGH."
BLAM BLAM
WAIT--
FOR WHAT?

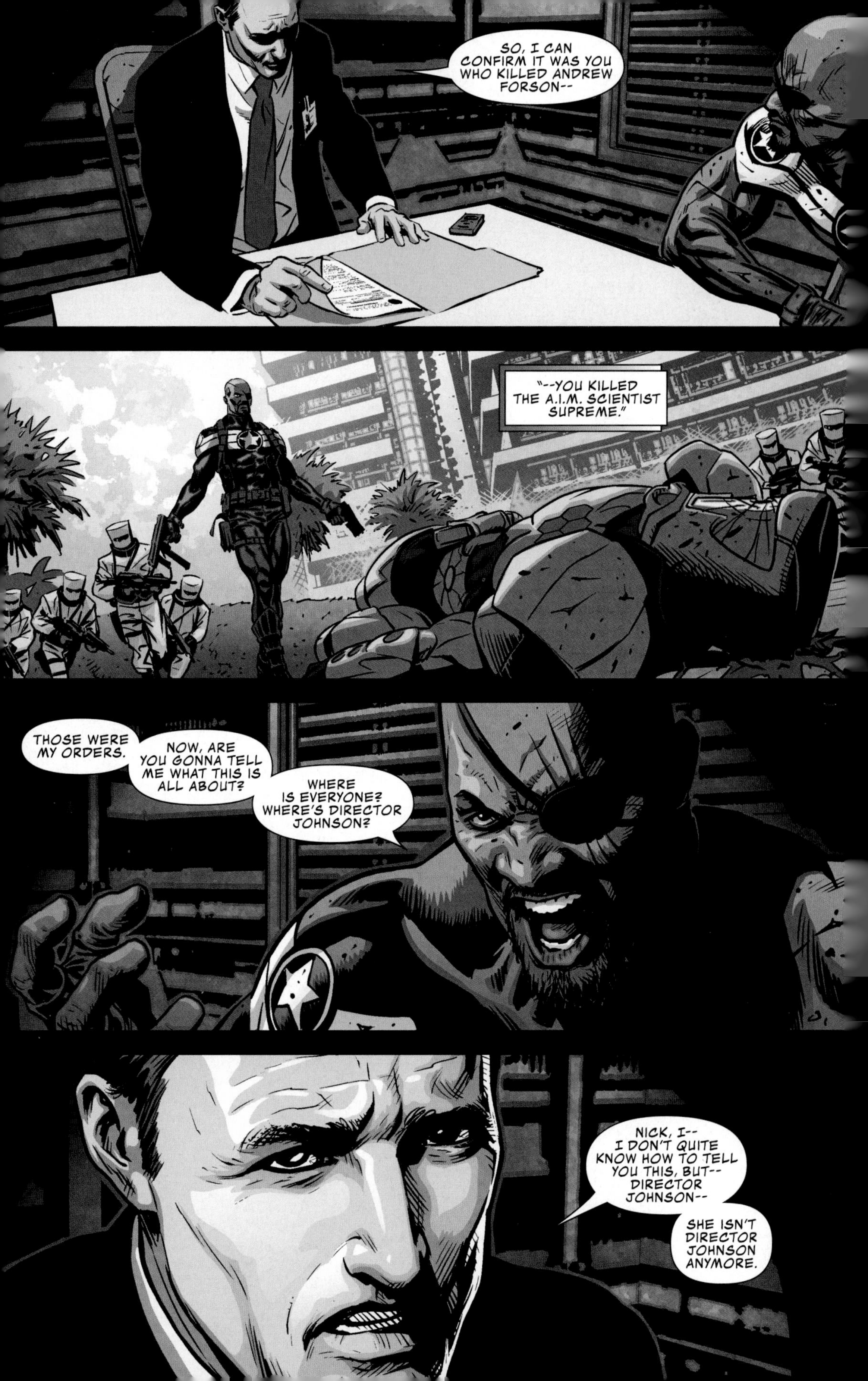
SO, I CAN CONFIRM IT WAS YOU WHO KILLED ANDREW FORSON--
"--YOU KILLED THE A.I.M. SCIENTIST SUPREME."
THOSE WERE MY ORDERS.
NOW, ARE YOU GONNA TELL ME WHAT THIS IS ALL ABOUT?
WHERE IS EVERYONE? WHERE'S DIRECTOR JOHNSON?
NICK, I-- I DON'T QUITE KNOW HOW TO TELL YOU THIS, BUT-- DIRECTOR JOHNSON--
SHE ISN'T DIRECTOR JOHNSON ANYMORE.

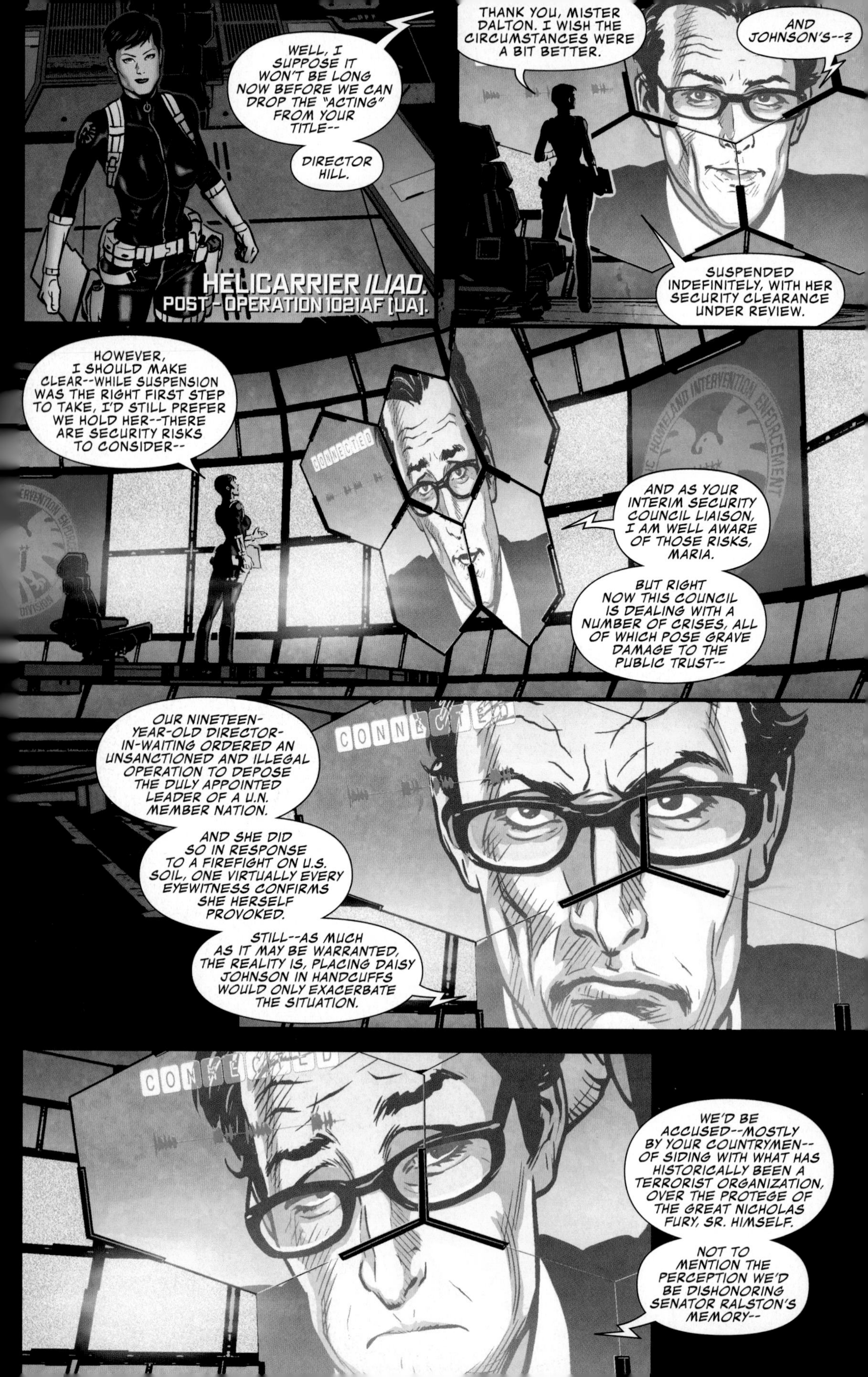
WELL, I SUPPOSE IT WON'T BE LONG NOW BEFORE WE CAN DROP THE "ACTING" FROM YOUR TITLE--
DIRECTOR HILL.
HELICARRIER ILIAD.
POST - OPERATION 1021AF [UA].
THANK YOU, MISTER DALTON. I WISH THE CIRCUMSTANCES WERE A BIT BETTER.
AND JOHNSON'S--?
SUSPENDED INDEFINITELY, WITH HER SECURITY CLEARANCE UNDER REVIEW.
HOWEVER, I SHOULD MAKE CLEAR--WHILE SUSPENSION WAS THE RIGHT FIRST STEP TO TAKE, I'D STILL PREFER WE HOLD HER--THERE ARE SECURITY RISKS TO CONSIDER--
CONNECTED
AND AS YOUR INTERIM SECURITY COUNCIL LIAISON, I AM WELL AWARE OF THOSE RISKS, MARIA.
BUT RIGHT NOW THIS COUNCIL IS DEALING WITH A NUMBER OF CRISES, ALL OF WHICH POSE GRAVE DAMAGE TO THE PUBLIC TRUST--
OUR NINETEEN-YEAR-OLD DIRECTOR-IN-WAITING ORDERED AN UNSANCTIONED AND ILLEGAL OPERATION TO DEPOSE THE DULY APPOINTED LEADER OF A U.N. MEMBER NATION.
AND SHE DID SO IN RESPONSE TO A FIREFIGHT ON U.S. SOIL, ONE VIRTUALLY EVERY EYEWITNESS CONFIRMS SHE HERSELF PROVOKED.
STILL--AS MUCH AS IT MAY BE WARRANTED, THE REALITY IS, PLACING DAISY JOHNSON IN HANDCUFFS WOULD ONLY EXACERBATE THE SITUATION.
WE'D BE ACCUSED--MOSTLY BY YOUR COUNTRYMEN--OF SIDING WITH WHAT HAS HISTORICALLY BEEN A TERRORIST ORGANIZATION, OVER THE PROTEGE OF THE GREAT NICHOLAS FURY, SR. HIMSELF.
NOT TO MENTION THE PERCEPTION WE'D BE DISHONORING SENATOR RALSTON'S MEMORY--

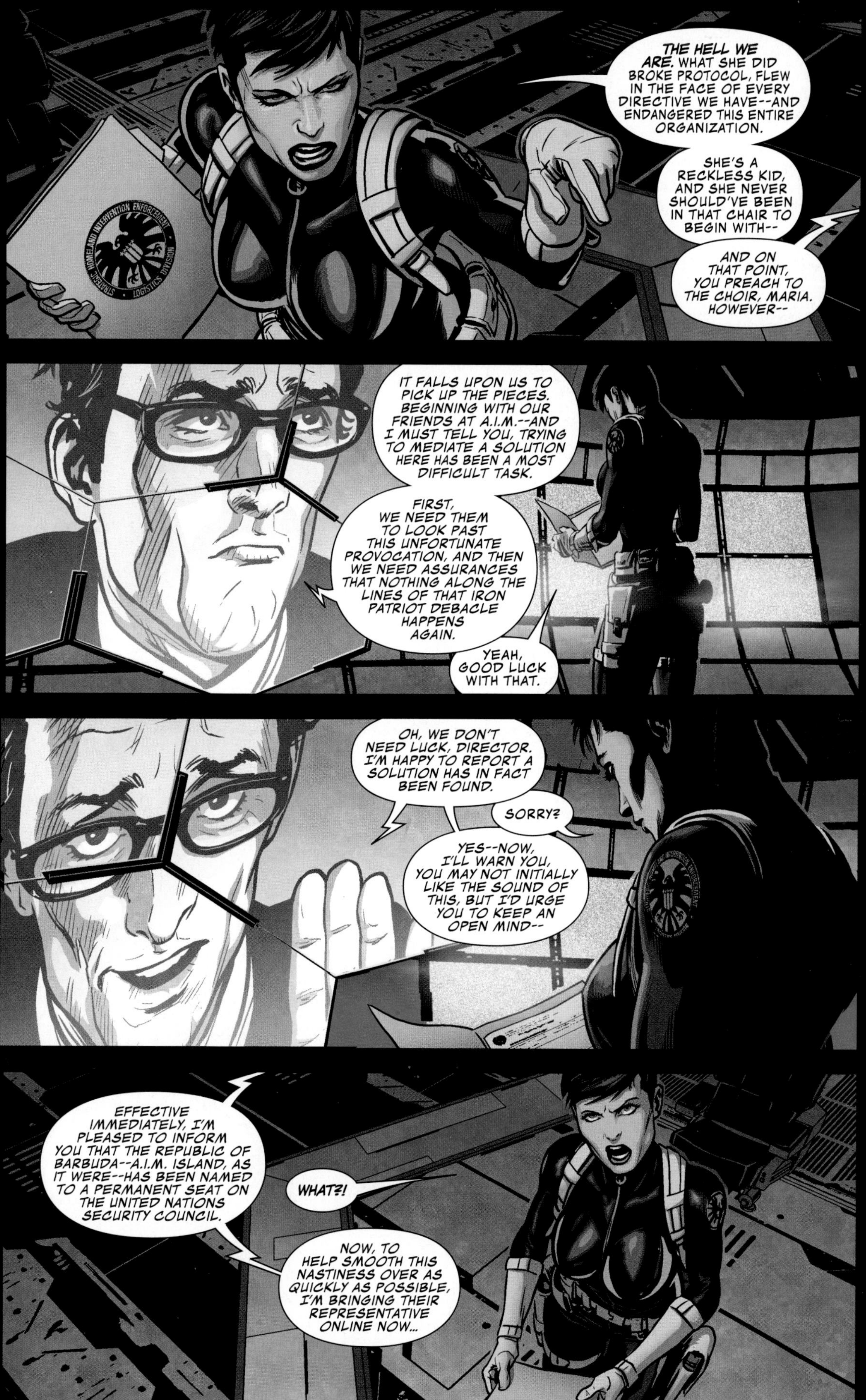

THE HELL WE ARE. WHAT SHE DID BROKE PROTOCOL, FLEW IN THE FACE OF EVERY DIRECTIVE WE HAVE--AND ENDANGERED THIS ENTIRE ORGANIZATION.
SHE'S A RECKLESS KID, AND SHE NEVER SHOULD'VE BEEN IN THAT CHAIR TO BEGIN WITH--
AND ON THAT POINT, YOU PREACH TO THE CHOIR, MARIA. HOWEVER--
STRATEGIC HOMELAND INTERVENTION ENFORCEMENT LOGISTICS DIVISION
IT FALLS UPON US TO PICK UP THE PIECES. BEGINNING WITH OUR FRIENDS AT A.I.M.--AND I MUST TELL YOU, TRYING TO MEDIATE A SOLUTION HERE HAS BEEN A MOST DIFFICULT TASK.
FIRST, WE NEED THEM TO LOOK PAST THIS UNFORTUNATE PROVOCATION, AND THEN WE NEED ASSURANCES THAT NOTHING ALONG THE LINES OF THAT IRON PATRIOT DEBACLE HAPPENS AGAIN.
YEAH, GOOD LUCK WITH THAT.
OH, WE DON'T NEED LUCK, DIRECTOR. I'M HAPPY TO REPORT A SOLUTION HAS IN FACT BEEN FOUND.
SORRY?
YES--NOW, I'LL WARN YOU, YOU MAY NOT INITIALLY LIKE THE SOUND OF THIS, BUT I'D URGE YOU TO KEEP AN OPEN MIND--
EFFECTIVE IMMEDIATELY, I'M PLEASED TO INFORM YOU THAT THE REPUBLIC OF BARBUDA--A.I.M. ISLAND, AS IT WERE--HAS BEEN NAMED TO A PERMANENT SEAT ON THE UNITED NATIONS SECURITY COUNCIL.
WHAT?!
NOW, TO HELP SMOOTH THIS NASTINESS OVER AS QUICKLY AS POSSIBLE, I'M BRINGING THEIR REPRESENTATIVE ONLINE NOW...

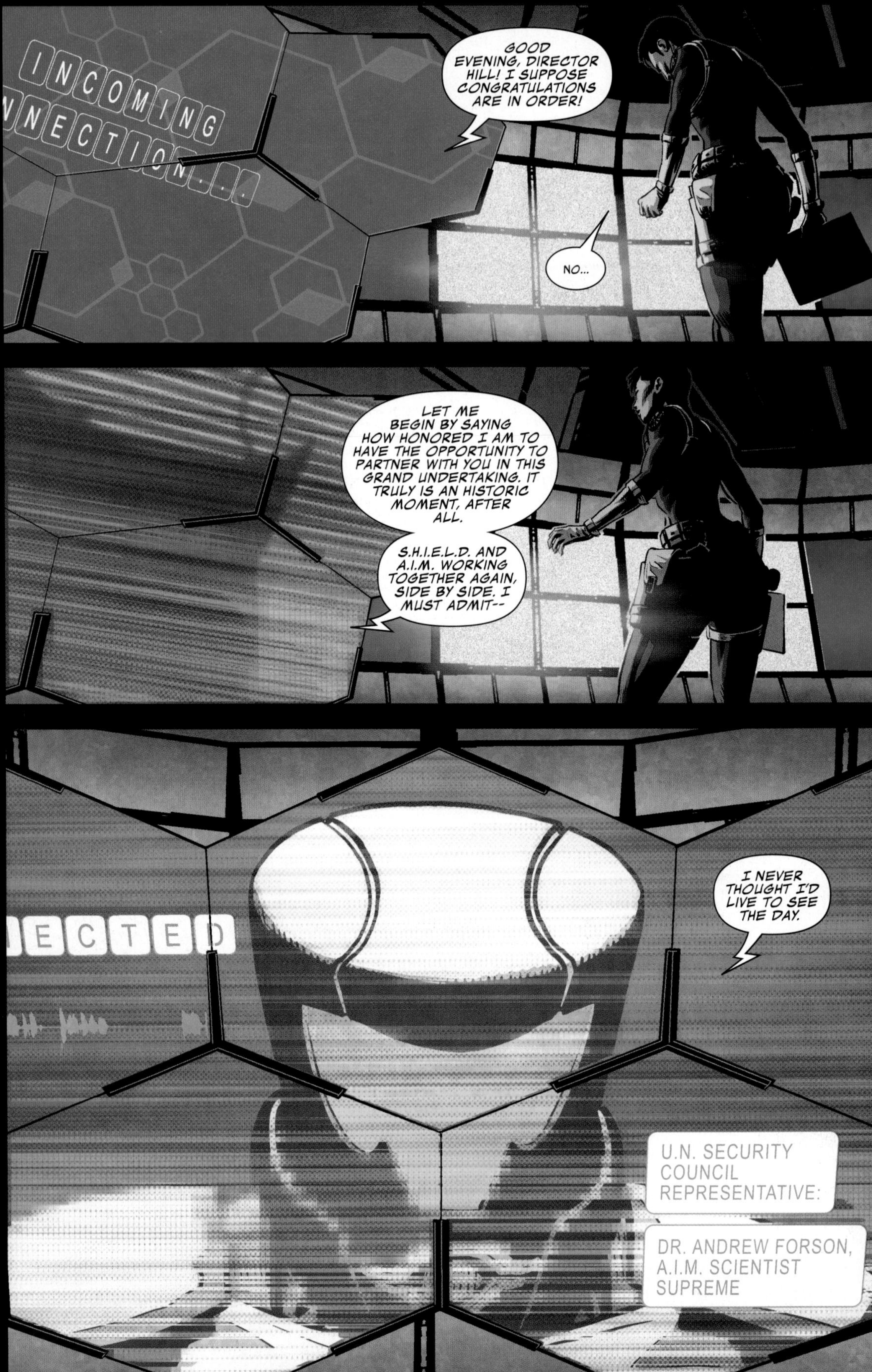
INCOMING
NECTION...
GOOD EVENING, DIRECTOR HILL! I SUPPOSE CONGRATULATIONS ARE IN ORDER!
NO...
LET ME BEGIN BY SAYING HOW HONORED I AM TO HAVE THE OPPORTUNITY TO PARTNER WITH YOU IN THIS GRAND UNDERTAKING. IT TRULY IS AN HISTORIC MOMENT, AFTER ALL.
S.H.I.E.L.D. AND A.I.M. WORKING TOGETHER AGAIN, SIDE BY SIDE. I MUST ADMIT--
ECTED
I NEVER THOUGHT I'D LIVE TO SEE THE DAY.
U.N. SECURITY COUNCIL REPRESENTATIVE:
DR. ANDREW FORSON, A.I.M. SCIENTIST SUPREME
NEXT: WHAT *REALLY* HAPPENED ON A.I.M. ISLAND!

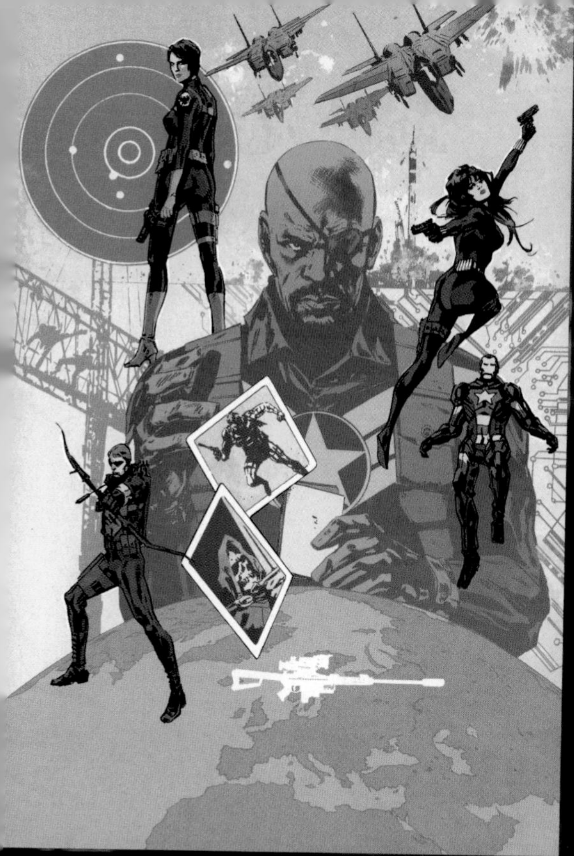

SECRET AVENGERS #1 HASTINGS VARIANT
BY BUTCH GUICE & JORDIE BELLAIRE

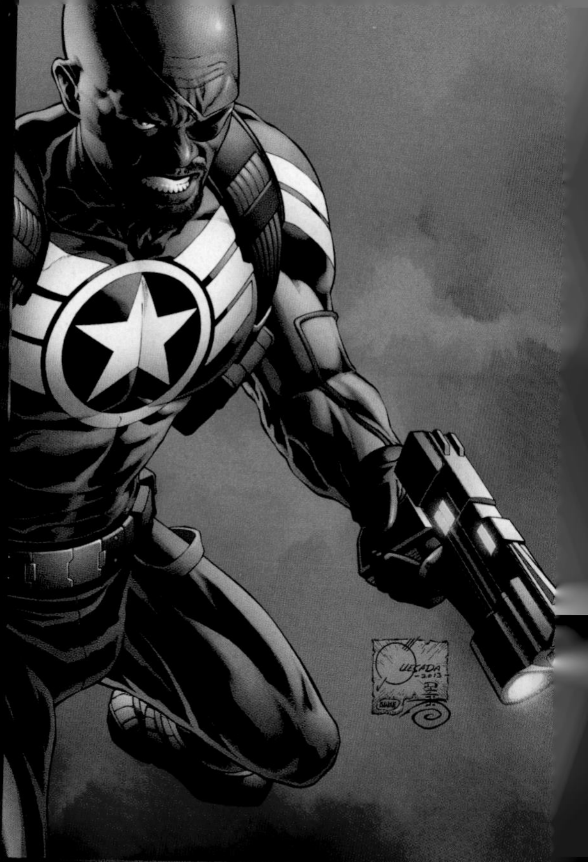

SECRET AVENGERS #1 VARIANT
BY JOE QUESADA, DANNY MIKI & RICHARD ISANOVE

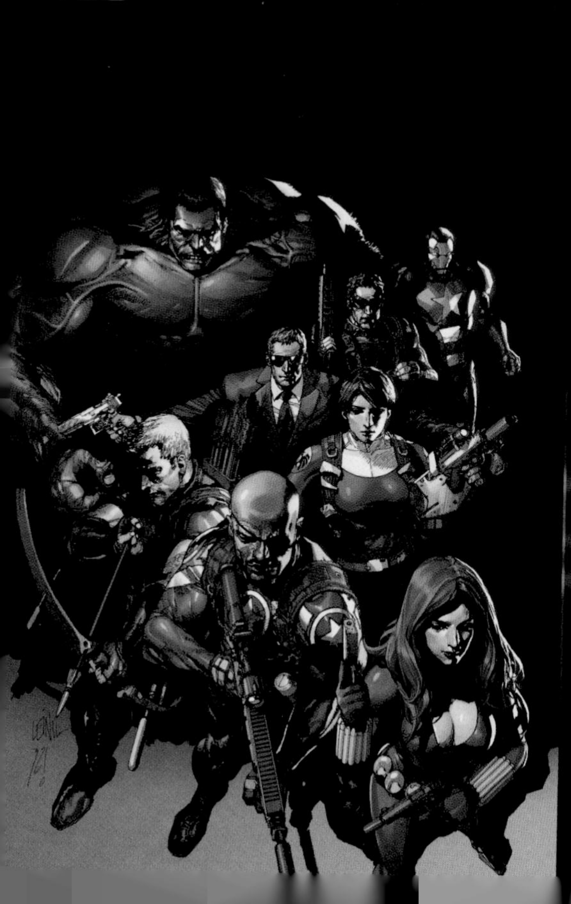

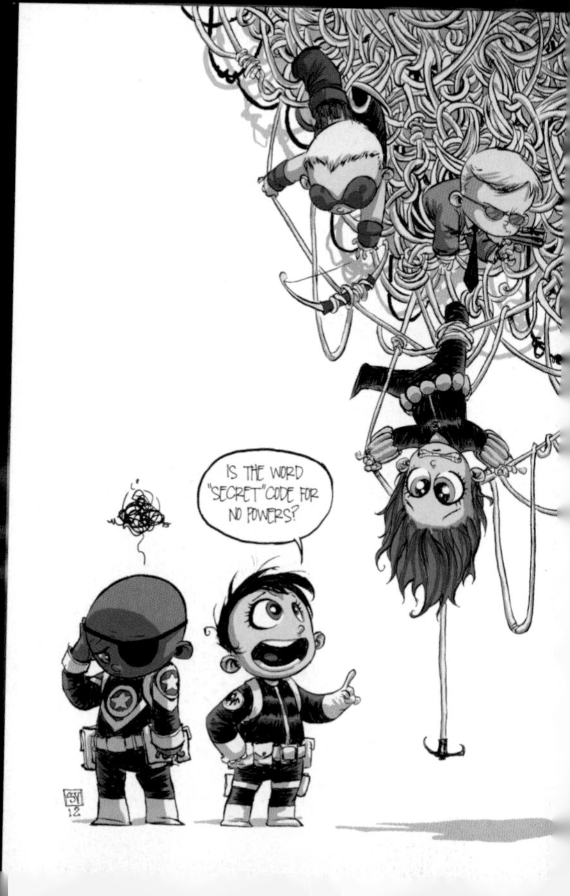
IS THE WORD "SECRET" CODE FOR NO POWERS?

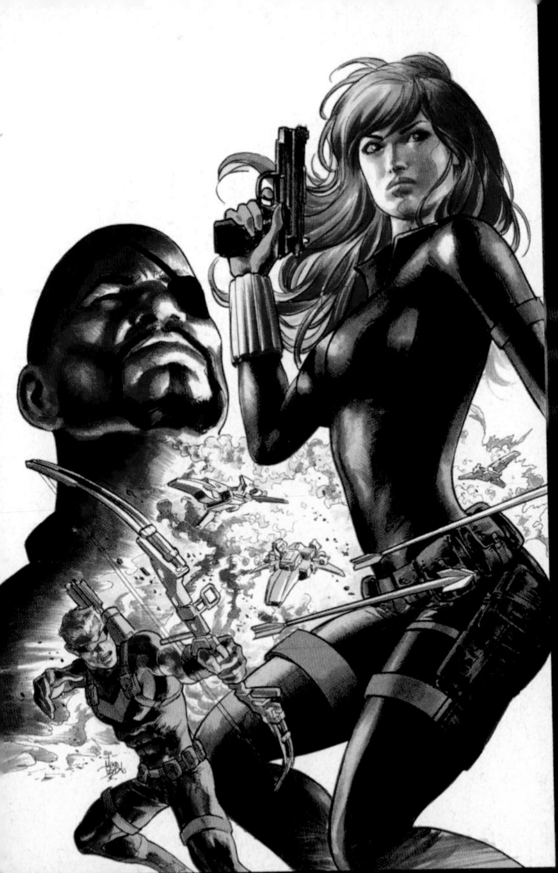

SECRET AVENGERS #2 VARIANT
BY MIKE DEODATO & RAIN BEREDO

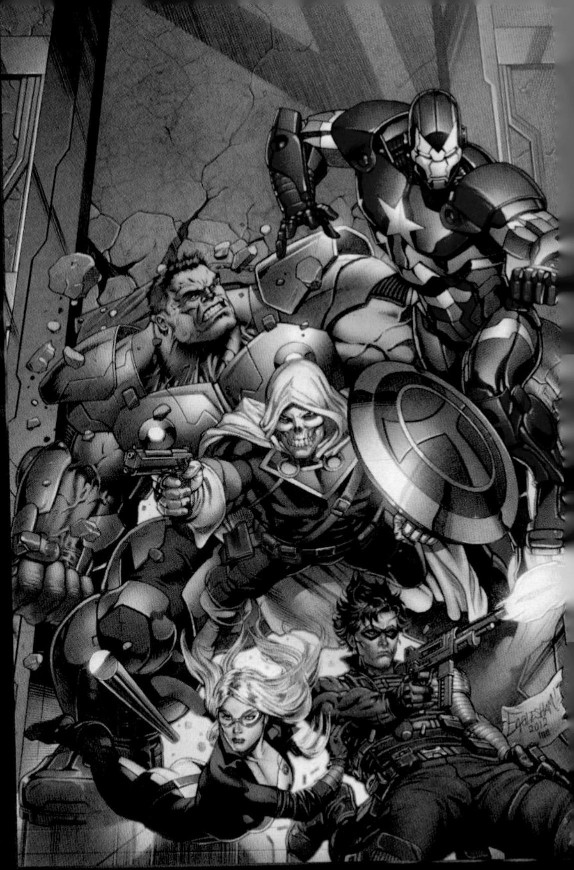

SECRET AVENGERS #3 VARIANT
BY DALE EAGLESHAM & FRANK D'ARMATA

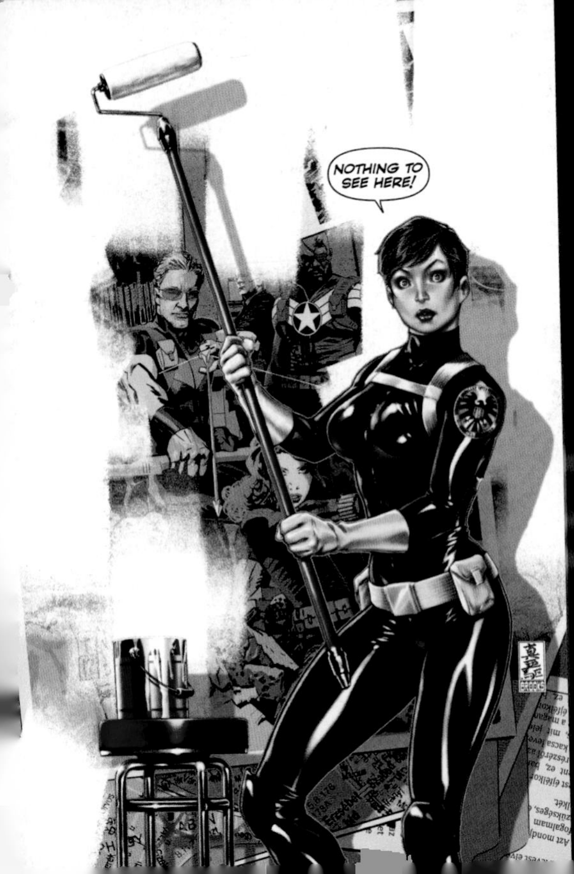
NOTHING TO SEE HERE!

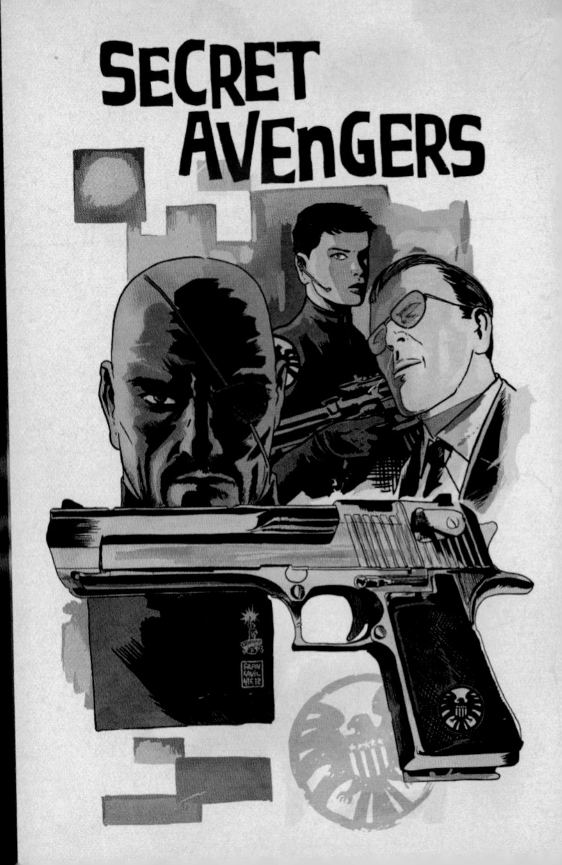
SECRET AVENGERS

TO ACCESS THE FREE *MARVEL AUGMENTED REALITY APP* THAT ENHANCES AND CHANGES THE WAY YOU EXPERIENCE COM

1. **Download the app for free via** marvel.com/ARapp
2. **Launch the app on your camera-enabled Apple iOS® or Android™ device***
3. **Hold your mobile device's camera** any cover or panel with the **AR** gr
4. **Sit back and see the future of comi** in action!

*Available on most camera-enabled Apple iOS® and Android™ devices. Content subject to change and availability.

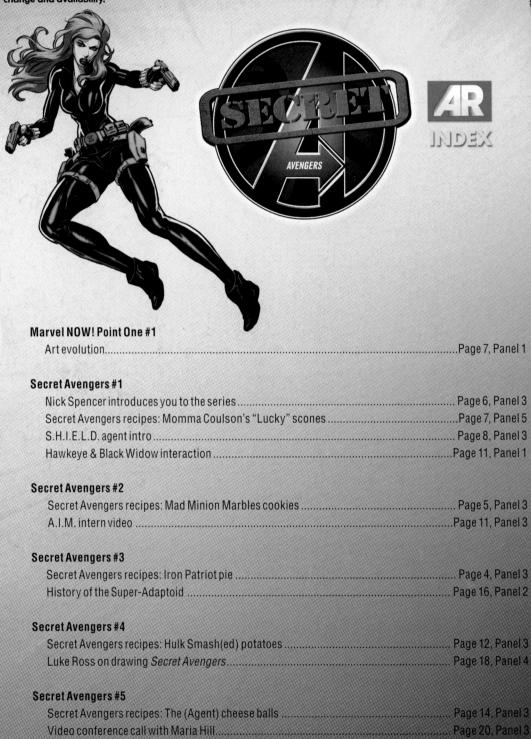

AR INDEX